LITERATURE, NATIONALISM, AND MEMORY IN EARLY MODERN ENGLAND AND WALES

The Tudor era has long been associated with the rise of nationalism in England, yet nationalist writing in this period often involved the denigration and outright denial of Englishness. Philip Schwyzer argues that the ancient, insular, and imperial nation imagined in the works of writers such as Shakespeare and Spenser was not England but Britain. Disclaiming their Anglo-Saxon ancestry, the English sought their origins in a nostalgic vision of British antiquity. Focusing on texts including *The Faerie Queene*, English and Welsh antiquarian works, *The Mirror for Magistrates*, *Henry V*, and *King Lear*, Schwyzer charts the genesis, development, and disintegration of British nationalism in the sixteenth and early seventeenth centuries. An important contribution to the expanding scholarship on early modern Britishness, this is the first study of its kind to give detailed attention to Welsh texts and traditions, arguing that Welsh sources crucially influenced the development of English literature and identity.

PHILIP SCHWYZER is Lecturer in Renaissance Literature and Culture at the University of Exeter. He is co-editor of *Archipelagic Identities: Literature and Identity in the Atlantic Archipelago, 1550–1800* (2004), and has published on early modern English and Welsh literature and identity in journals including *Representations*.

LITERATURE, NATIONALISM, AND MEMORY IN EARLY MODERN ENGLAND AND WALES

PHILIP SCHWYZER

CAMBRIDGE
UNIVERSITY PRESS

PUBLISHED BY THE PRESS SYNDICATE OF THE UNIVERSITY OF CAMBRIDGE
The Pitt Building, Trumpington Street, Cambridge CB2 1RP, United Kingdom

CAMBRIDGE UNIVERSITY PRESS
The Edinburgh Building, Cambridge, CB2 2RU, UK
40 West 20th Street, New York, NY 10011-4211, USA
477 Williamstown Road, Port Melbourne, VIC 3207, Australia
Ruiz de Alarcón 13, 28014 Madrid, Spain
Dock House, The Waterfront, Cape Town 8001, South Africa
http://www.cambridge.org

First published 2004

Printed in the United Kingdom at the University Press, Cambridge

Typeset in 11/12.5pt Adobe Garamond   [PND]

A catalogue record for this book is available from the British Library

ISBN 0 521 84303 0 hardback

For Naomi

Contents

Acknowledgments

These acknowledgments, like the book itself, deal with the rich splendors of the past. In this case, however, the splendors are in no way fictitious. They consist in the many people who have been so remarkably generous with their time, advice, and support over the last ten years. This book began as a dissertation written at the University of California, Berkeley, where I benefited from the warm and alert guidance of my director, Jeffrey Knapp. I am also deeply grateful to Jennifer Miller for her interest and faith in this project from the earliest stages, and to Ruth Tringham for providing the vital (if, in the following pages, somewhat buried) perspective of archaeology. A special and enduring debt of thanks is owed to Stephen Greenblatt, from whose advice and support I have benefited for many years. At Hertford College, Oxford, where I was Junior Research Fellow in the years 1999–2001, I received generous assistance and conversation from Emma Smith. Since then, I have found myself fortunate in my colleagues at the University of Exeter, and wish to thank in particular Karen Edwards, Regenia Gagnier, Colin MacCabe, Nick McDowell, and Andrew McRae.

This book has been written as a contribution and a response to the emerging interdisciplinary field of early modern British (or "Archipelagic") Studies. Whether because the approach is still relatively new, or because of the stress it lays on inclusivity, or simply by great good luck, I have found the scholars in this area unusually supportive and interested in the work of a junior colleague. I'm especially grateful to David Baker, Kate Chedgzoy, Andrew Hadfield, John Kerrigan, Willy Maley, and Swen Voekel for the help they offered as I ventured down the paths they were opening. Here I should also thank the two readers of the manuscript for Cambridge University Press for guidance of the best kind. I also wish to express thanks to Lesel Dawson, Matthew Fisher, Clare Harraway, Daniel Hedley, Jason Lawrence, Ruth McElroy, Simon Mealor, Julian Murphet, and Dominic Oliver. As my intellectual and academic role models and interlocutors (and for a great deal else), I am grateful to Alison, Hubert, and Hugo Schwyzer.

This book is dedicated to Naomi Howell, whose influence and ideas are felt on every page, and who, in our daily life together, proves some of its central arguments about beauty and nostalgia entirely wrong.

An earlier version of chapter 2 appeared as "The Beauties of the Land: Bale's Books, Aske's Abbeys, and the Aesthetics of Nationhood" in *Renaissance Quarterly* (2004). The first pages of chapter 3 rework sections of "British History and 'The British History': The Same Old Story?" in *British Identities and English Renaissance Literature*, ed. David Baker and Willy Maley (Cambridge: Cambridge University Press, 2002), pp. 11–23.

Note on the text

All quotations retain the spelling of the edition cited, but u/v and i/j have been regularized throughout. Punctuation and capitalization have been lightly modernized where appropriate.

All references to Shakespeare's works are to *The Norton Shakespeare*, ed. Stephen Greenblatt (New York: W. W. Norton, 1997). All references to Spenser's *Faerie Queene* are to Edmund Spenser, *The Faerie Queene*, ed. A. C. Hamilton (London: Longman, 1977).

INTRODUCTION
Remembering Britain

In November 2000, the Romanian poet Corneliu Vadim Tudor came a surprisingly strong second in his country's presidential elections. The leader of the far-right Greater Romania Party, Vadim Tudor had risen to national prominence with calls for the ethnic cleansing of Hungarians and gypsies. When questioned by a British journalist about his ultra-nationalist policies, the poet retorted: "Yes, I am a nationalist. Jonathan Swift was a nationalist. William Shakespeare was a nationalist. There is nothing wrong with being a nationalist. It means to love your country."[1] This response succinctly raises several of the questions central to this book. What does it mean to be a nationalist? Was Shakespeare a nationalist? Is there something about nationalism as a doctrine that makes it particularly attractive to poets? And does the phrase "Tudor nationalism" have any meaning, outside of Romania?

As Corneliu Vadim Tudor went on to explain, "what is wrong is to be an extremist, a chauvinist, a xenophobe." While it is difficult to see how all of these terms do not also apply to the Romanian poet, the distinction being drawn is important. Not all nationalists, in all times and places, have been xenophobes, nor are all xenophobes necessarily nationalists. The latter point is particularly pertinent to our understanding of sixteenth-century England, where the evidence of strong ethnic loyalties and the hatred of "strangers" is incontrovertible. From the anti-alien riots of Ill May Day (1517) to the boisterous chauvinism of William Haughton's *Englishmen for My Money* (1598), there is no question that Tudor England was a thoroughly and unapologetically xenophobic society. Yet to acknowledge this is quite different from accepting that England in this era was a nation or that

---

[1] Nick Thorpe, "Romanians Gamble with their Future," BBC News: *From Our Own Correspondent*, Sunday December 3, 2000; http://news.bbc.co.uk/hi/english/world/from_our_own_correspondent/ newsid_1052000/1052551.stm. Following his initial strong showing, Vadim Tudor was soundly beaten in a run-off election on December 10, 2000.

its inhabitants tended to be English nationalists. Indeed, the development of national consciousness arguably requires individuals to rise above the very same xenophobic impulses to which Tudor subjects were so notoriously prone.

One of the distinctive features of national communities, even the most apparently exclusive or xenophobic, is their boundless inclusiveness when it comes to two sorts of "strangers": the dead, and the unborn. As Benedict Anderson has put it, while "nation-states are widely conceded to be 'new' and 'historical,' the nations to which they give political expression always loom out of an immemorial past, and . . . glide into a limitless future."[2] Coming to national consciousness is not simply a matter of accepting that the people over the hill, whom one has never met, are part of the same community – the people under the hill must be acknowledged too. For many nationalists, the affective and political claims of the dead easily outweigh those of the living. W. B. Yeats was hardly alone in his tendency to embrace the dead and unborn with an ardor he withheld from those presently alive:

> Scorn the sort now growing up
> All out of shape from toe to top . . .
> Sing the lords and ladies gay
> That were beaten into the clay
> Through seven heroic centuries;
> Cast your mind on other days
> That we in coming days may be
> Still the indomitable Irishry.[3]

As a way of living in and through history, nationalism involves a special understanding of the relationship between the present and the past, and a peculiarly intimate communion with the national dead. For the nation to live in the imagination of its members, they must come to recognize that those who lived in "other days," and whose customs, politics, and even language may at first glance appear dauntingly alien, were all along members of the same community – that "they" were in fact "us." This book is a study of why and how English and Welsh writers of the Tudor era were capable of taking this remarkable imaginative leap. The leap was a particularly extraordinary one for the English, I shall argue, for the ancients

---

[2] Benedict Anderson, *Imagined Communities: Reflections on the Origin and Spread of Nationalism*, revised edition (London: Verso, 1991), pp. 11–12.

[3] W. B. Yeats, "Under Ben Bulben," in *The Collected Works of W. B. Yeats*, ed. Richard J. Finneran (London: Macmillan, 1983), p. 327.

with whom they were required to imagine community were not their own ancestors. They were not even English.

The Tudor era was long associated by literary historians with the "discovery of England" – the process by which the English people became proudly conscious of their national language, geography, history, and destiny. A host of recent critical interventions, by Richard Helgerson, Andrew Hadfield, Claire McEachern, David Baker, Jodi Mikalachki, and Willy Maley among others, have challenged this comfortable narrative in a variety of ways.[4] They have demonstrated conclusively that England, like all nations, was not there to be "discovered," but had rather to be invented or constructed – even "written." Moreover, Englishness is not a self-generated but rather a relational identity, a matter of complex and often bitter negotiation among the nations of the Atlantic archipelago (England, Ireland, Scotland, and Wales). These arguments have won the day to the extent of largely ceasing to be controversial, at least in broad terms, and within academic circles. At the same time, however, one central assumption of the old "Discovery of England" narrative has persisted all but unchallenged. Scholars still tend to assume that the nation constructed, invented, or written by the English in the sixteenth century was, indeed, England.[5] By contrast, I intend to argue that national consciousness in Tudor England was largely "British" rather than narrowly "English" in its content and character.

Most studies of nationalism in early modern and modern Britain take it for granted that a sense of being Welsh, Scottish, or English is historically prior to and more fundamental than an awareness of being British. Linda Colley's remarkably influential book, *Britons: Forging the Nation, 1707–1837,*

---

[4] See Richard Helgerson, *Forms of Nationhood: The Elizabethan Writing of England* (Chicago: University of Chicago Press, 1992); Andrew Hadfield, *Literature, Politics and National Identity: Reformation to Renaissance* (Cambridge: Cambridge University Press, 1994), and *Shakespeare, Spenser, and the Matter of Britain* (Basingstoke: Palgrave, 2003); Claire McEachern, *The Poetics of English Nationhood, 1590–1612* (Cambridge: Cambridge University Press, 1996); David J. Baker, *Between Nations: Shakespeare, Spenser, Marvell, and the Question of Britain* (Stanford: Stanford University Press, 1997); Jodi Mikalachki, *The Legacy of Boadicea: Gender and Nation in Early Modern England* (London: Routledge, 1998); *British Identities and English Renaissance Literature*, ed. David Baker and Willy Maley (Cambridge: Cambridge University Press, 2002); Willy Maley, *Nation, State and Empire in English Renaissance Literature: Shakespeare to Milton* (Basingstoke: Palgrave Macmillan, 2003). John Kerrigan's forthcoming study of British themes and problems in the literature of the seventeenth century will mark an important contribution to this field.

[5] David J. Baker, in *Between Nations*, comes closest to challenging this assumption. However, he still tends to see Britishness in its various guises as confronting, complicating, or undermining a pre-existing English identity. The difference between Baker's position and my own may be to some extent a matter of emphasis.

has merely strengthened the traditional perception that only after the union of Scotland and England in 1707 did the peoples of these kingdoms (and of Wales) begin to regard themselves as Britons. In contemporary debates over the future of the United Kingdom, the relative belatedness of Britishness is a point on which all sides seem prepared to agree. To its defenders, Britishness presents a more advanced and "civic" stage of nationalism than that to which, say, Scottishness can aspire; demands for the devolution of sovereignty to Britain's constituent nations can thus be branded as atavistic, a dangerous descent into tribalism. For its opponents, on the other hand, Britishness is no more than the wool that England pulled over the eyes of Scotland and Wales in 1707; devolution and (potentially) independence for these nations can thus be heralded as the restoration of older and more authentic identities.

Those seeking to demonstrate that Scotland, Wales, and England were authentic nations before the idea of Britain came into being generally look to the late medieval and early modern periods. Scottishness is summed up in the Declaration of Arbroath (fourteenth century), Welshness in the revolt of Owain Glyndwr (fifteenth century), and Englishness – curiously tardy – in the triumph of the Reformation, the defeat of the Armada, and the history plays of William Shakespeare (sixteenth century). A number of historians are justly skeptical about the relevance of the former examples to modern ideas of Scottish and Welsh nationhood; for the moment, I will limit myself to considering the case of England. There is no doubt that the Reformation and subsequent conflicts with Catholic powers encouraged the development of national consciousness in England, at least among a vocal minority, and that we find this consciousness expressed in Shakespeare's plays. The question is whether this national consciousness was in fact *English*.

Let us begin by considering this question in relation to the most well-known celebration of "England" found in Elizabethan literature. "This England," so memorably extolled by Shakespeare's John of Gaunt in *Richard II*, turns out, rather remarkably, to be an island: "this scept'red isle . . . This precious stone set in the silver sea" (2.1.40, 46).[6] This topographical slippage is of course testimony to the notorious and still-witnessed tendency of the

---

[6] All references to the play are from *The Norton Shakespeare*, ed. Stephen Greenblatt (New York: W. W. Norton, 1997). On Gaunt's notorious slip, see Kate Chedgzoy, "This Pleasant and Sceptered Isle: Insular Fantasies of National Identity in Anne Dowriche's *The French Historie* and William Shakespeare's *Richard II*," in *Archipelagic Identities: Literature and Identity in the Early Modern Atlantic Archipelago*, ed. Philip Schwyzer and Simon Mealor (Aldershot: Ashgate, 2004).

English to forget the existence of their northern and western neighbors – but the long history of English arrogance should not prevent us from recognizing how much that arrogance may depend on ascribing to England qualities that are not in fact English. Insularity – *British* insularity – is not merely one agreeable attribute of John of Gaunt's England, it is its defining feature, referred to repeatedly from the beginning to the end of the panegyric. Grasping this, we are in a position to see how little of his speech in fact applies to the historical English nation. If the isle itself is to be considered "scept'red," a "royal throne of kings," the reference must be to the pre-Anglo-Saxon era, when Britain was indeed thought to have been ruled by a single monarch. If "England" has proved a "fortress . . . Against the envy of less happier lands" (2.1.43, 49), this can hardly apply to the defensive achievements of the English, who had barely consolidated their rule over one corner of Britain before succumbing to the invading Danes and Normans in rapid succession – for examples of foreign invaders effectively repelled we must turn to the eras of Cassivellaunus and King Arthur. Similarly, if England was ever "wont to conquer others," the reference is more probably to Arthur's fabled conquests in Europe and beyond than to the futile efforts of later English kings to defend their inherited territories in France. Finally, who are the "happy breed" who call this island theirs? Gaunt is not, in all probability, thinking of the racial stock of the Anglo-Saxons, who were held in remarkably low esteem in the Elizabethan era.

As this analysis of Gaunt's speech indicates, "England" in the Tudor era was a name to conjure with – but what it conjured was very often Britain. England itself, the state bounded by the Wye and Tweed with its roots in the old kingdom of Wessex, was woefully inadequate to the nationalism of the English. The tendency of the English to lay claim to the historical and geographical attributes of Britain had been witnessed for centuries, but this tendency was greatly intensified – indeed, it became an imperative – in the Tudor era, particularly in the wake of the Reformation. The very nature of the traumatic break entailed by the Reformation, cutting England off from most of the continent, encouraged the English to regard themselves as inhabiting a world apart – as *penitus toto divisos orbe*, in Virgil's well-known phrase. That phrase, of course, applied to the entire island of Britain, and it was in *insularity* that the English discerned the key to their unique and sacred national destiny.[7] Nor was simple geographical logic the only factor

---

[7] See Jeffrey Knapp, *An Empire Nowhere: England, America, and Literature from Utopia to The Tempest* (Berkeley: University of California Press, 1992).

in determining the cast of English national consciousness in the sixteenth century. Equally important, as I shall demonstrate in chapter 1, were the presence on the throne of a dynasty thought to be descended from the ancient (pre-Anglo-Saxon and pre-Roman) rulers of Britain, and the need, following the Reformation, to assert the existence of an ancient British Empire and British Church, uncorrupted by and older than their Roman competitors.[8]

Later English nationalism, as it developed from the seventeenth through the nineteenth centuries, would celebrate a trio of specifically English virtues: the English language, racial descent from the Anglo-Saxons, and parliamentary and legal traditions and privileges. By contrast, in the Tudor era all of these were objects of significant anxiety, if not of outright contempt. Of the three virtues which Tudor writers cherished most highly in their nation – insularity, antiquity, imperiality – not one was properly English.[9] For the sense of national belonging that found expression in Tudor England, there is no term readily available but *Britishness*. Of course, it was a version of Britishness that served English interests – but that, as Scottish and Welsh historians are fond of pointing out, is what the idea of Britain has almost always done, from the twelfth century onwards.

British nationalism, the nationalism of the English, had much in common with Welsh national consciousness in this period. Indeed, as I shall argue in several chapters, British nationalism took most of its facts, many of its tropes, and even much of its tone from Welsh sources. Both versions of nationalism were heavily dependent on an account of British antiquity derived from Geoffrey of Monmouth's *Historia Regum Britanniae* (c. 1136). Both looked to the Trojan Brutus as the nation's founding father, praised the same conquerors and peacemakers, lamented the Anglo-Saxon conquest, and interpreted the rise of the Tudors as the long-prophesied restoration of British rule. Yet the Welsh rarely if ever extended the category of Britishness to include the English, or saw themselves as participating with them in a national identity. Their methods of establishing a

---

[8] The importance of the idea of British empire for Tudor political thought has recently been underlined by David Armitage, *The Ideological Origins of the British Empire* (Cambridge: Cambridge University Press, 2000).

[9] The same point might be made about the common law, which was only beginning to emerge as a focus of patriotic enthusiasm in the Tudor era. Sixteenth-century legal theorists generally traced English institutions back to an ancient British "time immemorial," emphasizing the role of the pre-Christian law-giver Dunwallo Molmutius. See John E. Curran, Jr., *Roman Invasions: The British History, Protestant Anti-Romanism, and the Historical Imagination in England, 1530–1660* (Newark: University of Delaware Press, 2002), pp. 129–36; Colin Kidd, *British Identities Before Nationalism: Ethnicity and Nationhood in the Atlantic World, 1600–1800* (Cambridge: Cambridge University Press, 1999), pp. 83–84.

relation between the present and the ancient past were quite different, and, at least apparently, more straightforward. They were, as the English anxiously recognized, the descendants of those ancient people, still speaking the same language, practicing the same customs, and inhabiting the same land. Even for the Welsh, as I shall argue in chapter 3, the means for establishing a link with the ancient past were not as simple as might be supposed. But for the English, with no self-evident connection to the people of pre-Anglo-Saxon Britain, the task was a good deal more difficult.

All historically-based forms of nationalism rely to some extent on tropes – from Founding Fathers to Unknown Soldiers – to describe and ratify the connection between the living and the dead. In Tudor England, the need to forge a link between the present and an apparently alien (that is, non-English) past required the development of an unusually sophisticated figurative vocabulary. What might be termed the colonization of British antiquity was achieved by means of linguistic technology. Chapters 1, 2, and 4 explore some of the modes – genealogical, nostalgic, spectral – by which English readers and playgoers were induced to experience a sense of communion with the ancient Britons (and, as a crucial by-product, with one another). Chapter 5 surveys the deployment of these modes, forged in the crucible of British nationalism, in Shakespeare's "English" nationalist masterpiece, *Henry V*. The final chapter takes note of the fate of these figures in the early years of the seventeenth century, focusing on Shakespeare's *King Lear*.

The fact that nationalist discourse comes stuffed with the raw materials of literary creation explains why the most taciturn general or wooden politician is capable of waxing suddenly eloquent when speaking about the nation. It may also explain why nationalist causes seem in so many ages and places to have appealed especially to poets. (Here one might think of Hungary's Sándor Petőfi, Cuba's José Martí, Ireland's Patrick Pearse, and, of course, Corneliu Vadim Tudor.) In sixteenth-century England, where nationalism was unusually reliant upon figurative language, this general rule applied with special force. While the commitment of Tudor rulers and policy-makers to British nationalism was uneven and opportunistic, reaching a peak under Protector Somerset's regime (1548–51) and declining thereafter, the commitment of the poets was unflagging and genuine, increasing steadily from the mid-point of the century to its end.[10] In the

---

[10] On the English government's far from consistent approach to the question of Britain in the sixteenth century, see Hiram Morgan, "British Policies Before the British State," in *The British Problem, c. 1534–1707: State Formation in the Atlantic Archipelago*, ed. Brendan Bradshaw and John Morrill (London: Macmillan, 1996), pp. 66–88.

Elizabethan era, the poets drawn to the nation's flame included the likes of William Shakespeare, Edmund Spenser, Samuel Daniel, and Michael Drayton, among others. One could, of course, reverse the equation and suggest that it was because of the involvement of writers such as these that Tudor nationalism was so richly figurative and literary. But this would ignore the fact that, as I shall demonstrate, all of the central tropes had already been developed in prior generations by writers of far less literary ambition and ability.

One other reason has traditionally been advanced to explain the involvement of these writers, especially Shakespeare, in nationalist discourse – namely that in the decade after the defeat of the Armada England was swept by a wave of fervent patriotism, which made plays like *Henry V* guaranteed crowd-pleasers. However, the basic premise of this argument is almost certainly mistaken. As Eric Hobsbawm has observed, although "it would be pedantic to refuse this label [patriotism] to Shakespeare's propagandist plays about English history . . . we are not entitled to assume that the groundlings read into them what we do."[11] In fact, the evidence that the late Elizabethan era witnessed a groundswell of nationalist sentiment is fairly meager, once we discount those same poems and plays which, it is asserted, were responding to the public mood. An argument for nationalist groundlings, in other words, cannot easily escape tautology.

For a number of years, the study of nationalism has witnessed a stand-off between those who hold that nations and nationalism are a product of the second half of the eighteenth century, and others who hold that nations and nationalists have existed much longer than that, if not forever.[12] At times the debate can seem merely semantic, hinging on whether various pre-modern cultural formations should be described as nations, or rather as ethnic, linguistic, or proto-national groups. A key question, however, is that of mass participation. Central to the modernist position is the view that nations as we know them only exist when it becomes possible as well as desirable for a large proportion of the population and a wide range of social

[11] Eric Hobsbawm, *Nations and Nationalism since 1780: Programme, Myth, Reality*, second edition (Cambridge: Cambridge University Press, 1992), p. 75.
[12] Leading "modernists" include Benedict Anderson (*Imagined Communities*), Eric Hobsbawm (*Nations and Nationalism since 1780*), and Ernest Gellner (*Nations and Nationalism* [Ithaca: Cornell University Press, 1983]). The opposing camp is often associated with Anthony D. Smith, though he has recently sought to stake out a third position, that of the "ethno-symbolists" (*Myths and Memories of the Nation* [Oxford: Oxford University Press, 1999]). Of course, not all studies of nationalism fit into one of these two categories. Liah Greenfeld, for instance, discovers the roots of all modern nationalisms in sixteenth-century England; see *Nationalism: Five Roads to Modernity* (Cambridge, MA: Harvard University Press, 1992).

classes to experience and act on nationalist sentiments. It is beyond dispute that the conditions for such mass participation did not pertain either in Europe or the New World prior to the era of the American and French Revolutions.

In the sixteenth century, there were many people of all ranks and stations willing to kill or die for their religion, for their traditional lord, for customary rights, or for pay – few if any were willing to make similar sacrifices for an imagined transhistorical community, be it nominated England, Wales, or Britain. Sentiments that could be termed "nationalist" seem to have been largely confined to a small, economically and politically dominant sector of society. One (modernist) scholar has termed this the era of "psychological formation," when national consciousness of a recognizably modern cast emerged among the leading classes of the most economically advanced societies (notably, England and the Netherlands).[13] Some two to three centuries separate "psychological formation" from "social diffusion," when this kind of consciousness became available to the mass of the population. To put it crudely, sixteenth-century nationalists talked the talk, but only after 1750 would whole nations walk the walk. What we discern in some early modern texts is not the nation *per se* so much as the nation *in potentia*. Strictly speaking, then, "Tudor nationalism" has only ever existed in Romania.

Recognition of this fact has not prevented me from using terms such as "Tudor nationalism" and "British nationalism" freely throughout this book. I use them in part as a kind of shorthand (for "emergent-national-consciousness-seeking-to-propagate-itself-more-widely"), and in part because, as Hobsbawm acknowledges, it would be "pedantic" to do otherwise. And I use them above all in recognition of the fact that some of the literary works I discuss – notably Shakespeare's plays – have been regarded by later generations as among the most profound expressions of the national ideal in the history of English literature. There is matter in a play like *Henry V* that has spoken to audiences in 1803 and 1945 in ways that it could not possibly have done to the original audience in 1599.[14] While it would be easy to dismiss such later responses as anachronistic misreadings, Shakespeare's power to stir so deeply the national sentiments of people living centuries after his death deserves to be reckoned with. If audiences living in very different times are able to believe that they belong to the same

---

[13] Neil Davidson, *The Origins of Scottish Nationhood* (London: Pluto Press, 2000), p. 28.
[14] On the stage history of *Henry V*, see Emma Smith, *King Henry V* (Shakespeare in Production) (Cambridge: Cambridge University Press, 2002).

nation as Shakespeare, this, I shall argue, is because Shakespeare understands the nation primarily as a means of communicating across vast gulfs of time.

British nationalism captured the sixteenth-century imagination not only because it served the needs of the Tudor state and church after the Reformation, and not only because it was rich in the stuff of literary craftsmanship, but because it answered to a very deep and probably time- less desire: the desire to believe that the past can be recaptured, that what is forever lost may yet be found, that the dead may in some sense live again. This is a yearning found in all historical epochs, and doubtless in all cultures; yet it is also a desire definitive of the Renaissance. We tend to think of the Renaissance in terms of a longing to recapture the glories of Greek and Roman antiquity. Yet those English and Welsh writers of the Tudor era who aimed at the restoration of British antiquity were, as I shall argue in chapter 2, self-consciously following in the footsteps of Petrarch. The animating spirit of British nationalism was the quintessential mood of the Renaissance, the sense of nostalgia. To put this slightly differently, one mode by which Tudor writers gave expression to their culture's increased susceptibility to nostalgia was British nationalism.

If the spirit was that of the Renaissance, the body it animated was a medieval corpus of beliefs about the past. No version of British nationalism could entirely escape dependence on Geoffrey of Monmouth, the twelfth-century chronicler and fabulist who conjured almost two millennia of ancient British history out of disjointed scraps of Welsh tradition and liberal doses of his own imagination. The fact that faith in Geoffrey's account was finally beginning to wane in the sixteenth century (though neither as swiftly nor as steadily as is sometimes supposed) might lead us to perceive champions of ancient Britain like John Leland, John Bale, and Edmund Spenser as intellectual holdovers from the medieval era.[15] Yet though they relied on the same sources and often retold the same stories, the aims and methods of these Tudor writers were fundamentally different from their medieval predecessors.

The middle ages are often associated with a lack of appreciation of historical difference – of the pastness of the past.[16] Yet medieval writers

---

[15] On the sixteenth-century debate over Geoffrey's veracity, see Curran, *Roman Invasions;* T. D. Kendrick, *British Antiquity* (London: Methuen, 1950); F. J. Levy, *Tudor Historical Thought* (San Marino, 1967); May McKisack, *Medieval History in the Tudor Age* (Oxford: Clarendon Press, 1971); James Carley, "Polydore Vergil and John Leland on King Arthur: The Battle of the Books," *Interpretations* 15 (1984), 86–100.

[16] But see Monika Otter, "'New Werke': *St. Erkenwald,* St. Albans, and the Medieval Sense of the Past," *Journal of Medieval and Renaissance Studies* 24 (1994), 387–414.

knew well enough what fate awaited those who set out to recapture times that were forever lost. The point is well illustrated by an event said to have occurred at the exhumation of the bones of King Arthur and his wife Guinevere at Glastonbury, near the end of the twelfth century. A primary purpose of the exhumation was to demonstrate to the troublesome Welsh that the past was past – that their prophesied deliverer Arthur was definitely dead and gone. While the bodies of the buried king and queen had long since decayed, Gerald of Wales records one remarkable, even miraculous, survival. "A tress of woman's hair, blond, and still fresh and bright in colour, was found in the coffin." Sadly, the tress did not survive to be displayed among the relics of Glastonbury. "One of the monks snatched it up and it immediately crumbled into dust."[17] The message – to the Welsh and to every reader – could not be more clear. However vivid and beautiful the vision of past glory that dances before the eyes, nothing awaits those who foolishly grasp at it but the bitterness of a second, still more absolute loss.

Contrast the fate of Guinevere's tress with another lock of female hair, described in the Tudor era by the Anglo-Welshman John Dee. Dee offered his queen a welcome justification for English expansionism in the New World, promoting it as a restoration of the ancient British Empire, a "British discovery and recovery enterprise."[18] The formula captures the paradoxical faith of Dee's era, that a nation may leap forward by reaching back into its past. All that was required of the modern Britons, Dee insisted, was to reach out and grasp the beautiful vision that hovered before their eyes:

there is a little locke of Lady Occasion, flickering in the air, by our handes to catch hold on, whereby we may yet once more (before all be utterly past, and for ever) discreetly and valiantly recover and enjoy, if not all our ancient and due appurtenances to this Imperial Brittish monarchie, yet at the least some such notable portion thereof, as . . . this may become the most peaceable, most rich, most puissant, & most florishing monarchie of all els (this day) in christendome.[19]

It would be difficult to find a more succinct summation of both the aims and spirit of sixteenth-century British nationalism.

---

[17] Gerald of Wales. *The Journey Through Wales/The Description of Wales*, trans. and ed. Lewis Thorpe (Harmondsworth: Penguin, 1978), p. 282.

[18] See William Sherman, *John Dee: The Politics of Reading and Writing in the English Renaissance* (Amherst: University of Massachusetts, 1995), p. 148.

[19] Dee's exhortation is included in Richard Hakluyt, *The Principal Navigations, Voiages and Discoveries of the English Nation* (London, 1589), p. 245.

Two locks of hair: two radically dissimilar visions of history. In this instance, it is salutary to note, the medieval perspective comes rather closer to our own common sense than does the early modern one. Gerald's warning about the fate of those who seek to recapture the lost past was indeed prescient. Sixteenth-century nationalists were doomed to fail in their aim of restoring the glories of British antiquity – such projects are inevitably doomed, even when the past they seek to recover is not entirely fictional. Yet those who reached out to catch the lock of Lady Occasion were left with a good deal more than dust. If, in the final analysis, the political consequences of Tudor British nationalism were fairly slight (the British Empire would have come about with or without Dee's assistance), it found its more lasting legacy in the works of Spenser and Shakespeare – writers who continue to shape our understanding of what it means to be "English."

CHAPTER I

Spenser's spark:
British blood and British nationalism in the Tudor era

In 1485, the heir to the ancient throne of Britain came home to claim his birthright. Commanding a predominantly "British" (Welsh and Breton) army, he defeated the English and, by some accounts, personally slew their vile king.[1] His Welsh soldiers knew this man as "Harri Tudur," and saw in him the prophesied redeemer who would free them from centuries of English imperial domination. The English would know him as Henry VII, or Henry Tudor; their historians, in times to come, would credit him with founding the dynasty under which a proud and imperial England came into its own. Incompatible as they seem, both versions of the battle of Bosworth and its consequences are in some ways true, and both must be kept in mind if we are to understand the development in the following century of the distinctively Tudor vision of nationhood which I term British nationalism. The aim of this chapter is to trace the evolution of that grand vision, and at the same time to follow the fortunes of a single emblematic image, that of a spark from the island of Anglesey bursting into flame. The complex itinerary of this image will transport us from the Welsh patriot-bards of the fifteenth century, fanatically opposed to English domination, to the Elizabethan patriot-poet Edmund Spenser, himself an agent of that domination in Ireland.

BLOOD AND SPARKS: THE WELSH PROPHETIC TRADITION

Long before the Tudur family of Anglesey had received any notice in English literary circles, their bloodline had become a central theme of

---

[1] Addressing his army in Shakespeare's play, Richard III refers to Henry's troops as "a scum of Britons" and "these bastard Britons" (*Richard III*, 5.6.47, 63). Though the ethnonym is frequently glossed as (or, as in *The Norton Shakespeare*, revised to read) "Bretons," it clearly encompasses both Henry's followers from Brittany and those who have joined him in Wales. Richard is implying that one is as good (or as bad) as the other; both are equally foreign, both equally inferior to his "gentlemen of England" (5.6.68).

Welsh prophetic poetry.[2] Over the course of the fifteenth century, this bloodline had matured in richness and complexity, receiving infusions from several strains of European royalty. Born in 1457, Harri Tudur inherited the blood of the Valois (through his grandmother, Katherine of France) and that of the Plantagenets (through his mother, Margaret Beaufort). The latter line of descent happened to give Harri a valid (if not very plausible) claim to the English throne. What captivated the interest of the Welsh bards, however, was the lineage of Harri's grandfather, Owain Tudur, who drew his blood from the native princes of Wales, and by way of them from Cadwaladr, the last king of the Britons. Kinship with Cadwaladr was the crucial prerequisite for the role of *mab darogan* (Son of Prophecy). Cadwaladr's blood marked a man out as one who might fulfill the long-foretold deliverance of the Welsh from the English yoke.

The association of Cadwaladr, a historical figure of the seventh century, with a future Welsh reconquest of the isle of Britain dates back at least to the early tenth century. The prophetic poem *Armes Prydein* (c. 930) calls on the Britons, Norse, and Scots to join forces under the leadership of Cynan and Cadwaladr and drive the hated Saxons back to their German home-land.[3] But the prophecy with which Cadwaladr became most powerfully associated stems from Geoffrey of Monmouth's *Historia Regum Britanniae* (c. 1136) in which the last king of the Britons is ordered by an angelic voice to desist from resisting the Saxons:

God did not wish the Britons to rule in Britain any more, until the moment should come which Merlin had prophesied to Arthur . . . as a reward for its faithfulness, the British people would occupy the island again at some time in the future, once the appointed moment should come. This, however, could not be before the relics which once belonged to the Britons had been taken over again and they had transported them from Rome to Britain.[4]

In response to this prophecy, Cadwaladr renounces his throne and travels to Rome to become a holy man, while the Britons settle in to await their promised deliverance.

---

[2] The Welsh name Tudur (pron. TI-deer) became anglicized as Tudor (pron. TOO-dur). I use the former spelling when referring to the family and bloodline of Owain Tudur down to 1485, and when referring to subsequent Welsh perceptions of Harri Tudur. I use the latter spelling when referring to English perceptions of Henry VII, his descendants, and the Tudor dynasty generally.

[3] A. O. H. Jarman, "The Later Cynfeirdd," in *A Guide to Welsh Literature, Vol. 1,* ed. A. O. H. Jarman and Gwilym Rees Hughes (Cardiff: University of Wales Press, 1992), pp. 115–17.

[4] Geoffrey of Monmouth, *The History of the Kings of Britain,* trans. Lewis Thorpe (Harmondsworth: Penguin, 1966), p. 283.

The angelic prophecy in its original form makes no mention of Cadwaladr's bodily descendants, nor of his blood. Yet in the three and a half centuries that followed, a strong link was established between the national aspirations of the Welsh and the remains and progeny of Cadwaladr's body. At least by the fifteenth century, it had been decided that the unspecified "relics" mentioned by the angel were in fact the bones of that saintly King of the Britons, who had died in Rome. More importantly, British hopes were pinned on the restoration of Cadwaladr's own blood (encased in the body of a descendant) to the British throne. This permutation of the prophecy is unsurprising in an era when the line between national and dynastic aspirations was hardly clear cut. What could British rule mean other than a restoration of the ancient line of kings of whom Cadwaladr was the last? Fortunately for the prophets, any member of native Welsh society with the resources and influence to become the focus of national aspirations was by definition – at least by poetic definition – a descendant of Cadwaladr. Although Welsh prophetic poetry often represents the blood of Cadwaladr as a scarce and infinitely precious commodity, it is not much of an exaggeration to say that late medieval Wales was awash in the substance.

The bards were traffickers in praise. Among the chief themes in the praise of any patron was his ancient and distinguished lineage. All the leaders of native Welsh society – the *uchelwyr*, or high men – were duly flattered with genealogies tracing their descent back through Cadwaladr to Brutus and even beyond. The fascination with genealogy found in the fifteenth-century *cywydd moliant* (praise poem) is found as well in the related genre of *cywydd brud* (prophetic poem).[5] Both kinds of poem extol the ancient and glorious descent of a powerful man, but in the latter sort this descent is explicitly linked to the man's role as the Son of Prophecy who will deliver the Welsh from bondage, be avenged upon the English, and restore the ancient British royal line.

During the Wars of the Roses, both the Lancastrian offspring of Owain Tudur and Welshmen allied with the house of York such as William Herbert were made the focus of prophetic poetry, before the bardic consensus settled overwhelmingly in the early 1480s on the young exile, Harri

---

[5] See R. Wallis Evans, "Prophetic Poetry," *A Guide to Welsh Literature, II: 1282–c.1550* ed. A. O. H. Jarman and Gwilym Rees Hughes, new edition, revised by Dafydd Johnston (Cardiff: University of Wales Press, 1997), pp. 256–74; Glanmor Williams, "Prophecy, Poetry and Politics in Medieval Wales," in *British Government and Administration*, ed. H. Hearder and H. R. Loyn (Cardiff: University of Wales Press, 1974), pp. 104–16.

Tudur.[6] Dafydd Llwyd of Mathafarn, the most prolific and fervent com-
poser of *cywyddau brud*, lauded the young Harri and his uncle Jasper
Tudur during their exile in Brittany as future deliverers of the Welsh
nation:

> Siasbar a fag in ddragwn,
> Gwaed Brutus hapus yw hwn.
> Gwers yr angel ni chelir,
> Hwyntau biau tyrau'r tir.
> Tarw o Fôn yn digoni, –
> Hwn yw gobaith ein iaith ni.
> Mawr yw'r gras eni Siasber,
> Hil Cadwaladr paladr pêr.[7]

> Jasper will rear our dragon [i.e. Harri Tudur],
> One of the blood of fortunate Brutus.
> The angel's lesson will not be kept hidden,
> And theirs will be the towers of the land.
> The Bull of Anglesey [i.e. Jasper] succeeding –
> This is the hope of our people [language].
> Great is the grace of Jasper's birth,
> Of Cadwaladr's lineage, the sweet beam.

These lines include a number of the images and themes common to
cywyddau brud. The use of animal names to denote the hero is a ubiquitous

---

[6] Gruffydd Aled Williams, "The Bardic Road to Bosworth: A Welsh View of Henry Tudor,"
Transactions Of The Honourable Society Of Cymmrodorion (1985), 7–31; David Rees, *The Son of
Prophecy: Henry Tudor's Road to Bosworth* (Ruthin: John Jones, 1997); H. T. Evans, *Wales and the
Wars of the Roses* (Stroud: Alan Sutton, 1995); W. Garmon Jones, "Welsh Nationalism and Henry
Tudor," *Transactions Of The Honourable Society Of Cymmrodorion* (1917–18), 1–59.

[7] *Gwaith Dafydd Llwyd o Fathafarn*, ed. W. Leslie Richards (Cardiff: University of Wales Press,
1964), p. 82. All translations from Welsh are my own, unless otherwise noted. What may strike
some readers as the obscure sense and syntax of these verses is due in part to the extensive use of
symbolism and sometimes sheer obfuscation involved in prophecy, but also to *cynghanedd*,
a complex system of internal consonance ("Pen aeth dan, peunoeth i tyn") and/or rhyme ("Siasbar a
fag in ddragwn"). The fifteenth-century Welsh bard Ieuan ab Hywel Swrdwal composed an English
hymn to the Virgin in *cynghanedd*; a brief extract in modernized English spelling will convey
something both of the sound of *cynghanedd* and its drastic impact on normal grammatical
structures:

> Mighty, he took (me ought to tell)
> Out, souls of hell to soils of height.
> We ask with book, we wish with bell,
> To heaven full well to have on flight
> All deeds well done . . .

(See Tony Conran, "Ieuan ap Hywel Swrwal's 'The Hymn to the Virgin,'" *Welsh Writing in English*
1 (1995), 5–22.)

device, often in place of explicitly naming him.[8] The angel's words to
Cadwaladr are remembered, and the Tudurs' descent from the ancient
British line is described both in terms of blood and of Cadwaladr's "sweet
beam." Lineage here is figured as a ray of light or a spear (*paladr*, like beam,
admits both senses) piercing down through the centuries, uniting antiquity
to the present.

The image of lineage as light is also central to a poem by Dafydd
Nanmor addressed to the two sons of Owain Tudur in the 1450s. Here
lineage is imagined as a fire kept alight over the ages, if only in a single
spark.

> Pen aeth dan, peunoeth i tyn,
> Oll o aylwyd Llywelyn,
> O Fôn i cad gwreichionen,
> O Ffraink, ag o'r Berffro wen.
> Owain a'i blant yn un blaid
> Yw tywynion Brytaniaid.
> Iesu o'i gadu yn gadr
> I gadw aylwyd Gydwaladr.[9]

> When, in the mean night, the fire went
> Entirely from the hearth of Llywelyn,
> A spark was had from Anglesey,
> From France, and from white Aberffraw.
> Owain and his sons in one party
> Are the illumination of the Britons.
> In Jesus keeping, boldly
> To defend the hearth of Cadwaladr.

These lines convey a subtle and complex conception of lineage. As the
repetition of *cadw* (to keep, guard, or preserve), chiming with *cad* (was had)
emphasizes, the Tudurs are at once what has been preserved (as sparks from
the extinguished fire), and the preservers (of the hearth of Cadwaladr). The
fire that stands for the unbroken royal bloodline is the same fire that warms
the national hearth. The word *aelwyd*, meaning both hearth and home,
carries to this day a strong nationalist resonance.[10] If the hearth of Llywelyn
the Last was extinguished by Edward I, the hearth of Cadwaladr represents
the lost world of independence, comfort, and security to which the Welsh,

[8] See Evans, "Prophetic Poetry."
[9] *The Poetical Works of Dafydd Nanmor*, ed. Thomas Roberts and Ifor Williams, (Cardiff: University of Wales Press, 1923), pp. 35–6.
[10] The meeting places of the Urdd Gobaith Cymru (The Welsh League of Youth), a nationalist organization founded in the 1920s, are known as *aelwydydd*.

under the leadership of the Tudurs, will at last come home. The images of fire, spark, and hearth are conjoined as a complex figure for the ways in which the present is at once preserved from the past, and is the past's preserver.

These few examples are indicative both of the importance the bards attributed to lineage and of the wealth of metaphors they developed to describe it. Few other themes in late medieval Welsh poetry inspired such figural plenitude. For Lewys Glyn Cothi, writing in praise of Henry VII after the victory at Bosworth, the new king who comes "of the blood of Silvius" (*o waed Silius*) and the men of Troy is the "long prop of Brutus" (*ateg hir o Frutus*) – an architectural metaphor which, counter-intuitively, situates Brutus at the pinnacle of the lineage structure and makes Harri his bulwark.[11] Other images applied to ancestors include that of a well-spring giving rise to a genealogical river, and a host of botanical metaphors which are, if anything, more ubiquitous than references to blood.[12] The sheer range of available terms should counsel us against the assumption that blood, in any literal sense, is what is really at stake. The rivers, fires, beams, props, and stems are not simply figures for the passing on of blood; it would be more true to say that blood is a figure like these others for a privileged relationship to the past. Harri Tudur is no more literally the vessel of Cadwaladr's blood than he is, as one bard described him, "blessed Cadwaladr's tear" (*deigr Cadwaladr fendigaid*).[13] Rather, blood, like the unextinguished spark, stands metaphorically for an unbroken link between the present and British antiquity.

If the blood that features in these prophetic poems is not the sort that flows in veins and from wounds, still less is it the common inheritance of the Welsh nation in either a figural or a biological sense. What the bards term "British blood" or "Trojan blood" is the exclusive preserve of the *uchelwyr*. This is not because they alone were deemed by the bards to be of

---

[11] *Gwaith Lewys Glyn Cothi*, ed. Dafydd Johnston, (Cardiff: University of Wales Press, 1995), p. 44.

[12] *Bonedd*, signifying both gentility and good descent, is derived from *bôn*, meaning "trunk" or "stem," and terms such as "stock," "seed," and "branch," are, as in English, so ingrained in genealogical discourse as hardly to qualify as figurative language. See Williams, "The Bardic Road to Bosworth," 19; Glanmor Williams, *Renewal and Reformation: Wales, c. 1415–1642* (Oxford: Oxford University Press, 1993), p. 97.

[13] Cited in Elissa R. Henken, *National Redeemer: Owain Glyndwr in Welsh Tradition* (Cardiff: University of Wales Press, 1996), p. 54. Figures for lineage in bardic poetry may be roughly divided into four categories: botanical, architectural, luminous, and fluvial. Blood belongs to the last of these categories, along with springs, rivers, and tears. For a marvelous array of sixteenth-century bardic figures for lineage, in which the botanical overwhelmingly predominates, see J. Gwynfor Jones, *Concepts of Order and Gentility in Wales, 1540–1640* (Llandysul: Gomer, 1992), pp. 45–99.

Trojan stock, but because the maintenance of an unbroken relation to the past, for which blood was one figure, required more than the mere passing down of genetic material. Above all, it required a record of unbroken landed prosperity. As the Elizabethan Sir John Wynn noted in his *History of the Gwydir Family*, there were many families who in the centuries after the conquest had been "brought to the estate of mean freeholders and so, having forgotten their descents and pedigree, are become as if they had never been."[14] Celebrating the continued prosperity of his own line "under the same storm of oppression," Wynn praised God for having "left us a seed," and, employing another familiar image, likened God to "a man striking fire into a tinder-box for, by the beating of the flint upon steel, there are a number of sparkles of fire raised. Whereof but one or two takes fire the rest vanishing away."[15] The vanishing of the spark does not signify the literal dying out of the bloodline, but rather slippage below the social level at which one could lay claim to "blood." Where the Tudurs and Wynns had succeeded in keeping the spark of their ancestry alive, many others had not.[16]

What bound the Welsh together and defined them as a people in this era was not blood, but rather language. The most prevalent term for the national community was *iaith*, which literally means "language" (see the verses of Dafydd Llwyd, above).[17] Only in a later era would *iaith* be supplanted by *cenedl*, a word which initially meant "kindred," and which (like "nation") connotes common descent. Nevertheless, while the blood celebrated in prophetic poetry is not shared by all the Welsh, it is indispensably associated with the identity and aspirations of the *iaith*. The blood-link to the glorious past which is the preserve of such families as the Tudurs is not only a mark of status but a kind of service to the nation. The flame of their lineage is the illumination of the Britons, and it is the nation as a whole that will be warmed at the *aelwyd* (hearth/home) of Cadwaladr. Though the bloodless "mean freeholders" and laborers of

---

[14] Sir John Wynn, *History of the Gwydir Family and Memoirs* (Llandysul: Gomer Press, 1990), p. 15.

[15] Wynn, *History of the Gwydir Family*, pp. 16, 32.

[16] Comparisons can be drawn with English thought about lineage in a slightly later period. As the seventeenth-century Worcestershire gentleman William Higford advised his grandson, "every acre of land you sell you lose so much gentile blood." From a perspective such as Higford's, "the individual is seen as standing at the apex of a double helix intertwining land and blood." Felicity Heal and Clive Holmes, *The Gentry in England and Wales, 1500–1700* (London: Macmillan, 1994), p. 22.

[17] See Peter Roberts, "Tudor Wales, National Identity and the British Inheritance," in *British Consciousness and Identity: the Making of Britain, 1533–1707*, ed. Brendon Bradshaw and Peter Roberts (Cambridge: Cambridge University Press, 1998), p. 13.

Wales have no direct link or access to the British past, the bards proffer forth the blood of the *uchelwyr* as a sign to these classes that the past remains present in Wales. In their prophetic poetry the bards promise that the lost era of British ascendancy will, through the advent of the *mab darogan*, be recovered for the Welsh people as a whole.

I have suggested that blood in the *cywyddau brud* is not the sort that flows in and out of bodies, but there is in fact an important exception to this rule. The blood of the English in this poetry is undoubtedly visceral stuff, often described as filling the rivers when the Britons regain the land (an image drawn from Merlin's prophecies). Gory images of this kind are especially prominent in the works of the fanatically anti-English Dafydd Llwyd. The Thames will overflow "with the blood of the tribe of the children of Alice" (*O waed teulu plant Alis*). The false Saxons will wade "in their blood up to their fetlocks" (*A'u gwaed hyd eu hegwydydd*) "Inferior blood" (*adwaed*) will run over the feet in Charing Cross.[18]

The English whose blood will be flowing so freely are often described as the children of Rowena or of Alice. (Dafydd Llwyd congratulated the Cambro-French Jasper Tudur that he was "without the blood of the men of Rowena" (*diwaed wyr Rhonwen*)[19]). However, this account of English lineage is not a genealogical boast of the sort encountered elsewhere in bardic poetry. The bard is not writing of the blood of an elite descent-group but of an entire people, and the blood they share is manifestly inferior and base. The need in spite of this to posit a noble ancestress at the root of the bloodline is evidence of how, in Wales as elsewhere, the notion of race was constructed by analogy with noble lineage.[20] At the same time, the ancestor ascribed to the English is one no member of the *uchelwyr* would desire for their family tree. Describing the English as children of the legendary Saxon temptress and poisoner, Rowena, contributes to the construction of English blood as a precise inversion of the blood of the *uchelwyr*. Where the latter is a figure for an elite and masculine bond with the past, the former is viscerally real, feminized, and common to all the English nation as a marker of race.[21]

---

[18] *Gwaith Dafydd Llwyd*, pp. 34, 27, 62.
[19] *Gwaith Dafydd Llwyd*, p. 102.
[20] Benedict Anderson's claim that "The dreams of racism actually have their origin in ideologies of class, rather than in those of nation," clearly pertains in this case; Anderson, *Imagined Communities*, p. 149.
[21] The claim that all English people are descendants of Rowena cannot be taken literally as Rowena, the Saxon princess in *Historia Regum Britanniae* who married the British king Vortigern and poisoned his son, had no recorded children of her own. I have been unable to trace the identity of "Alice," who may be another legendary figure, or simply an alternative name for Rowena. Matthew

"CADWALADER'S BLOOD": VERSIONS OF THE TUDOR
BLOODLINE, 1485–1535

There is no doubt that Harri Tudur was familiar with the anti-English content of Welsh prophetic poetry. He and his uncle had used the bards to build support for their cause in Wales before 1485. Harri stopped at Mathafarn, the home of Dafydd Llwyd, en route to Bosworth, and after his victory made him an Esquire of the Body.[22] If such gestures worried English observers who knew the content of Welsh prophecy, steps taken by the new king in the first year of his reign would have heightened their unease. Both at Bosworth and subsequently at St. Paul's, the new king presented the standard of the red dragon, with clear reference to the Merlinic prophecy that this dragon, symbolizing the Britons, would eventually succeed in driving out the white dragon of the Saxons.[23] The red dragon featured prominently in the royal arms and on the royal coinage. The king apparently appointed a commission which, in consultation with Welsh bard-genealogists, "drew his perfect genelogie from ancient kings of Brytaine and the Princes of Wales."[24] And most importantly, in 1486 he gave his firstborn son the name of Arthur, unmistakably invoking the famous prophecy that Arthur would return and lead the Britons to victory.[25]

Fisher suggests (personal communication) that the name may refer to Alice Perrers, the mistress of Edward III. If so, this would accord with a bardic tendency to associate the consorts of English kings with Rowena (as in Lewys Morgannwg's slander of Anne Boleyn, below).

[22] Rees, *The Son of Prophecy*, p. 125.

[23] Sydney Anglo, who seeks with some justice to minimize the importance of British symbolism in the early Tudor period, argues that the red dragon "must be regarded as an expression of Henry's British descent as opposed to his more particular Cadwalader or Welsh descents." (Sydney Anglo, "The British History in Early Tudor Propaganda," *Bulletin of the John Rylands Library* (1961), 39.) It is true that the Merlinic prophecy pertaining to the red dragon is distinct from the angel's prophecy to Cadwaladr, though they have a common theme. However, given that the red dragon stands specifically for the Britons in their conflict with the Saxons, the distinction between British and Welsh descent seems quite arbitrary. The same must be said for Anglo's claim that in the later Tudor period, while the red dragon "became one of the best known of all heraldic animals...it symbolized the Tudor dynasty rather than the Tudor descent" (Anglo, *Images of Tudor Kingship* (London: Seaby, 1992), p. 60); as Anglo himself has demonstrated so effectively in his study of Tudor genealogies, the image of a dynasty was inextricable from its descent.

[24] David Powel, *The Historie of Cambria* (London, 1584), p. 391. Cardiff MS 50, a copy of this genealogy dating from the 1540s, does not mention a royally appointed commission, leading Anglo to suspect Powel of "dressing up the evidence" ("The British History," 25).

[25] That the Welsh were awaiting Arthur's return was a fact that seems to have been more widely known among the English than among the Welsh. Although medieval English chroniclers regularly deride the "Briton Hope" that Arthur was alive or would return, Arthur in fact never had more than a small role in Welsh vaticination, as compared with the redeemer-hero Owain. The sixteenth-century Welsh chronicler Elis Gruffydd asserted that the English were more interested than the Welsh in Arthur, and even claimed that it was the English who believed he would rise again. See Ceridwen Lloyd-Morgan, "The Celtic Tradition," in *The Arthur of the English: The*

The significance of this sustained iconographic campaign was not lost on foreign observers at the English court. As a Venetian emissary reported to his masters, "the Welsh may be said to have recovered their former independence, the most wise and fortunate Henry VII is a Welshman."[26] Foreign-born poets such as Pietro Carmeliano, Giovanni de' Giglis, Bernard Andre, and the Scot Walter Ogilvie, gladly celebrated the royal descent from Cadwaladr and hailed the birth of Arthur as the long-foretold second coming of the ancient British king. By contrast, English poets remained stubbornly and almost universally silent on the naming of Arthur, and on the king's Welsh connections in general. This silence, eloquent in itself, was broken only by a few anxious and ambivalent English voices.

One of the earliest of these voices is heard in the pageant prepared for Henry VII at Worcester in May of 1486. Nine months after his victory at Bosworth, the new king was coming back to the west of England in an angry mood. An abortive rebellion had been raised by Humphrey Stafford in Worcestershire just weeks before, and Henry had commissioned a court to sit in Worcester to investigate treasonous activity. The city fathers made ready to welcome their new monarch, and to beg him to show mercy to the wayward city. By appealing to the king's blood – at once English and Welsh – the commissioners of the Worcester pageant hoped to dissuade him from shedding theirs.

First to welcome the king in this pageant is his near-relation, the martyred Henry VI, who greets him as "Next of my blood" and reminds him of the mercy that characterized his reign. The value of mercy is further emphasized by the Virgin Mary, who instructs the king to emulate his saintly uncle "As welle in worke as in sanguinitie."[27] Finally, Henry VII is welcomed to the city by the gatekeeper, Janitor, who, professing not to know who the visitor is, runs through a series of complimentary guesses at his identity. Having recognized the king as a type of Jacob, Jason, and

Arthurian Legend in Medieval English Life and Literature, ed. W. R. J. Barron (Cardiff: University of Wales Press, 1999), p. 9; O. J. Padel, "Some South-Western Sites with Arthurian Associations," in *The Arthur of the Welsh: The Arthurian Legend in Medieval Welsh Literature*, ed. Rachel Bromwich, A. O. H. Jarman, Brynley F. Roberts (Cardiff: University of Wales Press, 1991), p. 240. See also C. Dean, *Arthur of England: English Attitudes to King Arthur and the Knights of the Round Table in the Middle Ages and Renaissance* (Toronto: University of Toronto Press, 1987), pp. 26–27.

26 Williams, *Renewal and Reformation*, p. 237.
27 "First Provincial Progress of Henry VII," in *Herefordshire, Worcestershire*, ed. David N. Klausner, REED (Toronto: Toronto University Press, 1990), pp. 406, 409. The content and political context of the Worcester pageant is discussed in John C. Meagher, "The First Progress of Henry VII," *Renaissance Drama*, n.s. 1 (1968), 45–73.

Julius Caesar, among others, Janitor concludes with a set of identifications that are closer to home:

> Welcome Scipio the whiche toked Hanyball
> Welcome Arture the very Britan kyng
> Welcome defence to England as a walle
> Cadwaladers blodde lynyally descending
> Longe hath bee towlde of such a prince comyng
> Wherfor frendez if that I shalnot lye.
> This same is the fulfiller of the profecye.[28]

In his quest to identify conclusively the man who stands before him, Janitor runs swiftly through a range of interpretive modes – typology, metonymy, simile – designed to elucidate the relationship of the present to the past. Finally, with other options exhausted, he resorts to the methods of the *cywyddau brud*, recognizing the king as the vessel of Cadwaladr's blood and hence as "the fulfiller of the profecye." This climactic identification involves not only a new cultural perspective (that of the Welsh bards) but a new understanding of the shape of history. Whereas the earlier comparisons posit a relation between two discrete figures, one belonging to antiquity and the other to the present, the invocation of Cadwaladr's blood invites an understanding of history as involving a kind of slippage or flow. Flowing irresistibly out of the past into the present, and out of Cadwaladr into Henry VII, the blood exists simultaneously in both eras, and in both royal bodies. The relationship between the two men could be described as metonymic, but this is a peculiarly intimate kind of metonymy, for what links Henry with Cadwaladr is nothing less than their common substance. The past, it appears, really can live again – indeed, insofar as it is instantiated in blood, the stuff of life itself, the past has never died.

One can imagine English auditors listening to Janitor's speech of welcome with mounting unease, from the moment Henry is identified as King Arthur, the "Britan [Briton, or Britons'] kyng." For centuries, the English had been familiar with the prophecy that Arthur would one day return to lead the Britons to victory over their Saxon oppressors. And to the citizens of Worcester, situated on the river which traditionally marked the

---

[28] "First Provincial Progress," 410. Though Janitor is the last to speak in the text of the pageant, Meagher argues that his speech was meant to come first, based on his role as welcomer and the ordering of an earlier pageant at York. I am inclined to follow the order in the text, in which Janitor's delivery of the keys signals Henry's entry into the city, but the point is not crucial to my reading of the pageant.

border between England and Wales, the notion of such a Welsh *reconquista* was no laughing matter.[29] Owain Glyndwr had claimed the right to rule as far as Severnside, and brought a Welsh and French army to Worcester in 1405. In 1436, "The Libel of English Policy" had testified to continuing fears on the border: "Beware of Walys, Criste Jhesu mutt us kepe / That it make not oure childeis childe to wepe."[30] Fifty years later, those children's children found themselves welcoming to their city a new Arthur who had landed – like Glyndwr's French reinforcements – at Milford Haven and conquered England with a predominantly Welsh and French army. Janitor's third line, welcoming Henry as England's wall, offers some momentary reassurance, but this comfort is swiftly undone by the identification of Henry as the vessel of Cadwaladr's blood. As many in Worcester – including Henry himself – knew well, Cadwaladr was associated even more closely than Arthur with the day when the Welsh would rise up, and stain the rivers red with the blood of the English. "Longe hath bee towlde of such a prince comyng."

The point of Janitor's invocation of Cadwaladr is not, of course, to identify England's new king as the long-dreaded Welsh scourge, but to assist in making safe (for the English) the highly volatile material of Welsh prophecy. Yet this is not an easy and straightforward act of cultural co-optation. It is rather an anxious negotiation at an anxious moment in time, for the English in general and the people of Worcester in particular. Janitor's words can be read as a kind of invitation to Henry to clarify his position regarding the Cadwaladr prophecy and the associated British symbolism which have featured so prominently in the first year of his reign. Does he really conceive of himself as the terrifying ethnic chauvinist *mab darogan*? Or is he "the fulfiller of the profecye" in a broader, more transcendent and irenic sense, a bringer of peace and deliverance to all the peoples of Britain, not the Britons alone? The pageant implicitly poses the question, and leaves it up to the king to respond with a sign – a sign that will inevitably be read in the judgment he passes on the city. By provocatively reminding him of the matter of Cadwaladr, the pageant offers the king the opportunity to invest his hoped-for act of mercy with prophetic significance (or conversely, by withholding mercy, to identify himself as

---

[29] On the Severn's status as border, see Philip Schwyzer, "Purity and Danger of the West Bank of the Severn: The Cultural Geography of *A Masque Presented at Ludlow Castle, 1634*," *Representations 60* (1997), 22–48; and "A Map of Greater Cambria" in *Literature, Mapping, and the Politics of Space in Early Modern Britain*, ed. Andrew Gordon and Bernhard Klein (Cambridge: Cambridge University Press, 2001), pp. 35–44.

[30] Evans, *Wales and the Wars of the Roses*, p. 11.

a vengeful Welshman). As things turned out, the wisdom of this strategy was never tested, for the king chose not to hear the pageant that had been prepared for him. He did, however, show mercy to the city.

The circumstances behind the Worcester pageant were unique, and prompted a unique forthrightness on a subject which the English generally preferred not to mention. Nothing said or done elsewhere in England in the years after Bosworth offers a parallel to Janitor's explicit invocations of Cadwaladr's blood and the ancient prophecy. In his progress through other English cities in 1486, Henry found his subjects happy to participate in celebrating the ancient British past, but only in carefully delimited ways. Both York and Bristol hit upon the idea of greeting Henry with a speech by the city's legendary British founder (Ebrancus and Brennus, respectively). Ebrancus greeted Henry as a lineal descendant, while Brennus called him "cosyn."[31] Yet what is clearly at stake in these presentations is neither genealogy nor race, but the cities' claims to antiquity and to ancient privileges. When Brennus welcomes Henry to the city he "Whilom bildede with her wallez old," the slightly odd turn of phrase – for of course the walls were not old when Brennus built them – further emphasizes that what binds the present to the past in this place is not British blood but Bristol stone.[32]

Setting the Worcester pageant to one side (as Henry himself did), we will look in vain for any early English acknowledgment of what seemed so obvious to the Welsh and foreign observers alike. As Sydney Anglo demonstrated years ago, rumors of a "cult of the British History" in early Tudor England have been greatly exaggerated.[33] To the extent that such a cult briefly flourished, it did so largely without native English participation. In the first half-century of Tudor rule the response of the English people to the proclaimed restoration of the ancient British bloodline ranged no further than from grudging to guarded. If he wished to publicize his

[31] Anglo, "The British History," 27; Meagher, "The First Progress of Henry VII," 69.

[32] It is possible to imagine a very different pageant at Bristol, given that the city had at this time not only a prosperous Welsh community but a Welsh mayor, and that Brennus (a.k.a. Brân) figured prominently in the British History as the conqueror of Rome. In the same year, Lewys Glyn Cothi and Dafydd Llwyd both composed praise poems associating the Tudur bloodline with Brennus / Brân (*Gwaith Lewys Glyn Cothi*, p. 43; *Gwaith Dafydd Llwyd*, p. 27.) In light of this, the absence of ethnic references in the Bristol pageant is particularly telling.

[33] Anglo, "The British History." Anglo also points out that Henry's claim to descent from ancient British kings was not an innovation. Yorkist genealogies displayed Edward IV's descent through the Mortimer line from Gwladus Ddu, daughter of Llywelyn the Great, and so on back to Cadwaladr and Brutus. See in addition Alison Allen, "Yorkist Propaganda: Pedigree, Prophecy and the 'British History' in the Reign of Edward IV," in *Patronage, Pedigree and Power in Late Medieval England*, ed. Charles Ross (Gloucester: Alan Sutton, 1979), pp. 171–92.

British descent outside of the Welsh heartland, Harri Tudur would have to rely on the services of foreign-born historians.

The most prominent early celebration of the Tudor bloodline occurs in Bernard Andre's history of the reign of Henry VII. Andre begins his work with a declaration of the king's descent from Brutus, and proceeds to give a short account of Cadwaladr's departure from Britain. Andre then skips over almost a millennium of English domination with acid brevity: "Anglorum saevitia intercalatum est."[34] The barbaric English interim came to an end when, by divine and human justice, the cruel murderer Richard III was struck down, and Henry VII ascended the throne. This capsulized version of the Tudor myth conveniently conflates "English" with "Yorkist," and eight centuries of oppression with the two-year reign of Richard III. The real consequences for the Welsh of Henry VII's accession are left vague. While Andre declares that Cadwaladr retired to Rome "divina admonitione consultus," there is no mention of the angel's prophecy, and hence no clear sense that Henry's victory marks the promised restoration of British rule.[35] The basic structure of the *mab darogan* narrative is present in Andre's history, but he is far more concerned with Henry's personal legitimacy than with his ethnic identity, or with the implications of that ethnicity for his new subjects, English or Welsh.

A similar understanding of Cadwaldr's bloodline as a matter of exclusively dynastic interest emerges in the work of the other, better-known continental historian in the Tudors' service, Polydore Vergil. While Polydore's name would be forever blackened in the memory of later British nationalists, the *Anglica Historia* (finished 1513, published 1534) is in fact as notable for its relative deference to the prophecy of Cadwaladr as it is for its skepticism about Arthur and other ancient Britons. In the third book, Polydore records that Cadwaladr was dissuaded from waging war on the Saxons by "an image havinge somwhat more than earthlie shape," which foretold that "Thie contrie shall fall into the hands of thine enemies, which thie progenie longe hereafter shall recover." The author is clearly skeptical as to the nature of the unearthly image (which could well be diabolical), and considers it a "Marvayle . . . how mutch credit Cadwalladre gave to these woordes."[36] Yet Cadwaladr's trust turns out to have been justified, as noted in the 24th book.

[34] Bernard Andre, *Historia regis Henrici septimi*, ed. J. Gairdner (London: Rolls Series, 1858), p. 10.
[35] Andre, *Historia*, p. 10.
[36] *Polydore Vergil's English History, Vol. 1*, ed. Sir Henry Ellis, Camden Society 36 (London: Camden Society, 1846), p. 124.

Thus Henry acquired the kingdom, an event of which foreknowledge had been possible ... many centuries earlier ... For 797 years before, there came one night to Cadwallader, last king of the Britons ... some sort of an apparition with a heavenly appearance; this foretold how long afterwards it would come to pass that his descendants would recover the land. This prophecy, they say, came true in Henry, who traced his ancestry back to Cadwallader.[37]

Even with its diffidence and notable lack of enthusiasm, this passage constitutes the most complete statement of the *mab darogan* theme in any text originating in England before the Reformation. Polydore Vergil makes explicit what was implied in Andre's history. The restoration of Cadwaladr's personal bloodline, which had no place in Geoffrey of Monmouth's account of the prophecy, has now become the sole content of the prophecy. Indeed, given Polydore's dismissal of ancient British glory and his generally hostile attitude to the Britons (whom he describes, following Gildas, as neither valiant in war nor faithful in peace), the fulfillment of the angel's prophecy could have no more than this limited dynastic significance.

There is every indication that this revised and limited version of the prophecy was precisely what Henry VII and his son desired. Certainly there was no attempt before the Reformation to suggest that the prophecy had been fulfilled in any wider sense, nor to satisfy its original conditions by, for instance, bringing from Rome the relics of the Britons (generally taken to mean the bones of Cadwaladr himself), as the angel had required and as Dafydd Llwyd eagerly anticipated.[38] Nor was there any systematic attempt in the first fifty years of Tudor rule to alter the status of the Welsh as a subjugated and disenfranchised people. Although Henry VII late in his reign granted charters of privilege to some districts of Wales (in return for large fees), the hated statutes dating from Glyndwr's rebellion, restricting the rights of the native Welsh to acquire property or office, to congregate or to bear arms, remained on the books.[39] Upholding the prophecy to Cadwaladr while despising the Welsh, Polydore Vergil may not have been so far from early Tudor orthodoxy as later generations believed.

English historians in this era were free in expressing their contempt for the Welsh in general, and Welsh historical traditions in particular. John Rastell in his *The Pastyme of People* (1529) was inclined to side with those

[37] *The Anglica Historia of Polydore Vergil, A.D. 1485–1537*, ed. with translation by Denys Hay, Camden Series 3: 74 (London: Royal Historical Society, 1950), p. 5.
[38] *Gwaith Dafydd Llwyd*, pp. 40, 169.
[39] Williams, *Renewal and Reformation*, pp. 242–43.

who "take that story of Galfridus but for a feyned fable supposyng that because this Galfridus was a Welchman born that he should fayn that story himself for the only preys of his contremen."[40] Rastell includes Geoffrey's history in his chronicle for its moral exemplarity, but omits the prophecy to Cadwaladr. As for Robert Fabyan, his greater reliance on the British History did not prevent him from producing a chronicle unrivaled in its century for its Cambrophobia. In his *New Chronicles of England and France* (1516) Fabyan makes clear that the reign of the Britons has finished forever. His prefatory verses promise to tell "howe longe the Brytons ruled / And howe by Saxons they were lastly put oute"; although the Saxons were in turn conquered by the Danes and Normans, "the blode of the Saxons" was eventually restored. The events recorded by Geoffrey of Monmouth did take place in some fashion, but his is the biased account of a Welshman: "Gaufride, for he was a Bryton, he shewed the beste for the Brytons."[41] As for Arthur, about whom Fabyan has pronounced doubts, stories of his deeds are fit only to "gladde the Welshmen."[42] When he comes to the angel's prophecy, rather than following Vergil and others in endorsing a revised version, Fabyan stresses that the original prophecy has not been and will never be fulfilled.

And of the angelis monicion that to hym was geven, with also the prophecy of Merlyn, that the Brytons shuld not recover this lande, tyll the relykes of Cadwaladyr, with other of holy sayntes, were broughte hyther oute of Rome: I holde yt for no parte of my beleve, though many Welshemen it doo.[43]

In his dismissal of the angel's prophecy, Fabyan implies that the Welsh are still awaiting its fulfillment; that is, that they have not been satisfied by the accession of Henry Tudor. This seems to have been a common perception among the English. The medieval chroniclers' view of the Welsh as a people whose faith in prophecy made them a constant threat continued to find expression into the sixteenth century. When Henry VIII saw fit in 1531 to execute Rhys ap Gruffydd, the most powerful of the *uchelwyr*, it was rumored that the young man had been moved to treason by

---

[40] John Rastell, *The Pastyme of People & A New Boke of Purgatory*, ed. J. Geritz, The Renaissance Imagination 14 (New York: Garland, 1985), p. 206.

[41] Robert Fabyan, *The New Chronicles of England and France*, ed. Henry Ellis (London, 1811), p. 36.

[42] Fabyan, *The New Chronicles*, p. 81. This view would be echoed three centuries later by Coleridge, who remarked of Arthur that "you could not by any means make a poem on him national to Englishmen"; *Coleridge's Miscellaneous Criticism*, ed. Thomas M. Raysor (London: Constable, 1936), p. 429.

[43] Fabyan, *The New Chronicles*, p. 126. This passage was omitted in the post-Reformation editions of 1542 and 1559.

"too much trust in prophecies," and one charge against him rested in his having claimed a link with ancient British kings by adopting the surname FitzUrien.[44] The Welsh prophetic tradition was not tamed in English eyes. And in spite of the several upheavals of the 1530s, this perception survived the decade intact. Although Fabyan's dismissal of the angel's prophecy is omitted from the 1541 edition of his chronicle, the last event recorded in that volume is "a Welshe manne drawen, hanged, & quarterid, for prophesiying of the kyng his maiesties death."[45]

Yet when we turn to Wales in the first half century of Tudor rule, we find relatively little evidence to confirm the English perception that the Welsh remained addicted to seditious prophecies. The victory at Bosworth largely spelt the end of the *mab darogan* theme and of the prophetic genre of *cywyddau brud*. Vaticination undoubtedly continued, perhaps especially in the less refined and more popularly accessible free meter poetry, of which less survives from this period. On the whole, however, the Welsh bards welcomed the restoration of Cadwaladr's blood in the person of Harri Tudur, even if his subsequent deeds did not always live up to their expectations.

Immediately after the victory at Bosworth a number of bards produced poems of praise hailing Henry VII as the prophesied deliverer of his people. Echoing Dafydd Nanmor a generation before, Lewys Glyn Cothi rejoiced that the spark from the hearth of Anglesey had burst into flame.[46] Two of Dafydd Llwyd's poems from this period ring with the joyous couplet:

> Harri a fu, Harri a fo,
> Harri y sydd, hiroes iddo![47]

> Harry was, Harry will be,
> Harry is, long life to him!

Yet the bards did not for a moment accept the English proposition that the fulfillment of the prophecy began and ended with the restoration of Cadwaladr's personal bloodline. That restoration had not even been part of

[44] Williams, *Renewal and Reformation*, p. 256; John Davies, *A History of Wales* (Harmondsworth: Penguin, 1993), p. 223. Urien was a northern British king of the sixth century whose deeds were celebrated by Taliesin, the earliest Welsh bard whose work survives and the source of a considerable legend in himself. Rhys's adoption of this title may suggest an attempt to establish a link with a British past which could not be assimilated by the English as easily as Geoffrey of Monmouth's.

[45] Fabyan, *The New Chronicles*, p. 702.

[46] *Gwaith Lewys Glyn Cothi*, p. 46.

[47] *Gwaith Dafydd Llwyd*, pp. 61, 70.

the original prophecy, after all. For the Welsh bards, the advent of the *mab darogan* was not so much a fulfillment in itself as the sign and trigger of the fulfillment to follow (the opening, as it were, of the first seal). Hence some of Dafydd Llwyd's most bloodthirsty calls for vengeance on the English occur in poems written *after* Harri's victory. There would be weeping in Wales, he warned, if a single Englishman remained in Harri's council. "Drive to the devil – harsh destruction – the men that do not know a word of our language" (*gyr i ddiawl, garw ddilaith/Y gwyr na wyr gair o'n iaith*).[48]

In spite of the calls for a wholesale massacre of the English found in poems written both before and after Harri's coronation, it is difficult to believe that even Dafydd Llwyd took seriously the prospect of a restoration of Welsh rule in Britain, much less the expulsion of the Saxons from the island. Images which form part of the symbolic vocabulary of the *cywyddau brud* should not be taken as a mirror of real aspirations, which were generally limited to something like Welsh home-rule.[49] Power and office in Wales should rest in the hands of the *uchelwyr*, not arrogant children of Rowena.[50] Such goals, which along with the lifting of the penal statutes might just conceivably have been expected from a Tudur king, were the practical correlative of those apocalyptic images of vengeance and destruction found in the *cywyddau brud*.

In the absence of such basic reforms, hints of disillusionment crop up amid the general celebration of the Son of Prophecy, including Dafydd Llwyd's impatient calls for more substantive action, and Llywelyn ap Hywel's complaint that Jasper and Harri Tudur preferred men from the north of England to the Welsh.[51] Anti-English sentiment continues to occur in non-prophetic bardic poetry, and outbursts in the spirit of Dafydd Llwyd occur as late as the 1530s, when Lewys Morgannwg hailed the downfall of Anne Boleyn as that of a second Rowena, and called on Henry VIII to give high offices to Welshmen rather than low-bred Englishmen.[52] Yet the fundamental spirit of the *cywydd brud* made it

---

[48] *Gwaith Dafydd Llwyd*, pp. 61, 66.

[49] As Ceridwen Lloyd-Morgan notes, "sub-Galfridian prophecy and legendary history do not lend themselves to describing the contemporary political scene with much accuracy"; "Prophecy and Welsh Nationhood in the Fifteenth Century," *THSC* (1985), 25.

[50] The bard Guto'r Glyn had urged Sir William Herbert, the Yorkist earl of Pembroke, to unite Wales under his authority and exclude the children of Rowena from office. *Gwaith Guto'r Glyn*, ed. J. Llywelyn Williams and Ifor Williams (Cardiff: University of Wales Press, 1939), pp. 130–31. William Herbert's brother Richard was similarly counseled by Ieuan Delwyn to lock the English out of office; see Evans, *Wales and the War of the Roses*, p. 2.

[51] Williams, "The Bardic Road to Bosworth," 29.

[52] Roberts, "Tudor Wales," 17.

impossible to adapt as an instrument of continued nationalist protest after the heralded restoration of Cadwaladr's blood. Moreover, Welsh patriotism had ceased to be a useful or meaningful stance for most of the rapidly anglicizing *uchelwyr*, and they were, as always, the holders of the purse-strings. Half-heartedly, and perhaps with a touch of irony, the increasingly irrelevant bardic class carried on celebrating the return of Cadwaladr's blood to the throne.

In the first half century of Tudor rule, the response to the fulfillment of the angel's prophecy was generally one of guarded welcome. In Wales, the welcome was outwardly enthusiastic, but bore an undertone of disillusion-ment. In England (foreign-born historians aside), the response tended to be more muted and grudging, with an undertone of apprehension. From 1485 to 1530, the Tudor kings avoided doing very much either to reward Welsh expectations or exacerbate English fears. By 1530 it would have seemed safe to conclude (with a sigh of either disappointment or relief) that the prophesied "spark" had been bit of a damp squib. No one in either country was in a position to predict how central the Tudor bloodline would shortly become to new conceptions of the nation and its destiny.

BRITISH BLOOD AND BRITISH NATIONALISM, 1536–1603

Harri Tudur had found his descent from British kings politically useful, and perhaps psychologically rewarding, but he had never made it the basis of his claim to the throne, much less a model for his style of kingship. His son, who for most of his life evinced far less interest in the Galfridian tradition, would ultimately make far more use of the British History. In the 1530s and 1540s, the redemptive vision of history vaguely espoused under Henry VII took on an aggressive ideological form. Henry VIII's break with Rome was justified at every step by appeals to national history. [53] As the Act in Restraint of Appeals proclaimed in 1533, "by divers sundry old authentic histories and chronicles, it is manifestly declared and expressed, that this realm of England is an empire, and so hath been accepted in the world."[54] From the break with Rome to the union of England and Wales and the attempted conquest of Scotland, the great upheavals of the 1530s and 1540s were represented as a restoration of ancient (British) rights and privileges.

---

[53] Levy, *Tudor Historical Thought*, p. 79; see Edwin Jones, *The English Nation: The Great Myth* (Stroud: Sutton, 1998), pp. 33–40.

[54] Richard Koebner, "'The Imperial Crown of this Realm': Henry VIII, Constantine the Great, and Polydore Vergil," *Bulletin of the Institute of Historical Research* 26 (1953), 29.

These developments allowed the return of Cadwaladr's bloodline to the throne to be understood in a new light. At last, the *mab darogan* was fulfilling his destined role of restoring the ancient British empire.

In 1530, the Duke of Norfolk had an interview with the imperial ambassador Chapuys on the matter of the King's marital predicament. He informed the surprised emissary that Henry "had a right of Empire in his kingdom and recognized no superior. There had been an Englishman who had conquered Rome, to wit Brennus. Constantine had reigned here and the mother of Constantine was English."[55] As a further argument, Norfolk produced the evidence of King Arthur's seal at Westminster in which he was nominated "Brittanniae, Galliae, Germaniae, Daciae imperator." In this interview we find figures familiar from the pageants of 1486 pressed into a very different kind of service. Arthur, the "very Britan kyng," is now emperor of many lands; Brennus, father of Bristol, is conqueror of Rome.

Unfortunately, the interview revealed how unfit Arthur and Brennus were for service in the field of international politics. Chapuys declared he had never heard of Arthur and scathingly professed himself "sorry he was not also called emperor of Asia." Norfolk cannot have escaped the uncomfortable sense of being jeered at by a foreigner (a sense that would trouble British nationalists more and more as the century wore on, leading at times to explosions of vehement xenophobia). Recognition of Arthur's inherent weaknesses in the field of international relations may have encouraged Henry's advisers to play up the (slightly) more plausible claims derived from Constantine. In this, the court historian Polydore Vergil was called upon to assist. Already in the first version of his *Anglica Historia* (1513), Polydore Vergil had traced Britain's greatness to the British-born Constantine; the text revised for publication in 1534 was more explicit in stating that "the majestie of the emperie could not perish, sithe that even at this presente the kinges of England, according to the usage of their aunciters, doe weare the imperiall diadem as a gift exhibited of Constantinus to his successors."[56]

If Arthur and Constantine provided the basis for Henry's imperial claims, British antiquity also served the turn of contemporary Protestant reformers struggling to answer the vexing question: "Where was your church before Luther?"[57] Insisting that their aim was *restoration* rather

[55] See Koebner, "'Imperial Crown," 40.
[56] Ellis, ed., *Polydore Vergil's English History*, pp. 98–99.
[57] Levy, *Tudor Historical Thought*, p. 99. See Curran, *Roman Invasions*, pp. 37–86.

than innovation, the reformers sought evidence of an early if not apostolic church in Britain uncontaminated by the church of Rome. In this task, Geoffrey of Monmouth himself was of dubious assistance, as he recorded that King Lucius had received Christianity from Pope Eleutherius in the second century. But the reformers could draw upon Tertullian's reference to still earlier Christianity in Britain, upon the tradition that the British church had been founded by Joseph of Arimathea, and upon the writings of the sixth-century British monk Gildas.[58] For William Tyndale, Gildas was a prophet sent by God to warn his countrymen to repent in time before the punishment of the Saxon conquest.[59]

In every account of the early British church, the Saxons were doomed to play an ignominious role, having beyond dispute been converted by the papal emissary Augustine. The reformers made much of Geoffrey of Monmouth's story that twelve hundred British monks had been massacred at Chester by the Saxons, urged on by that proud and ruthless Roman. Future generations would learn from Foxe how "religion remained in Britain uncorrupt, and the word of Christ truly preached, till, about the coming of Augustine and of his companions from Rome, many of the same Britain-preachers were slain by the Saxons."[60] The Church of England, according to this account, was the restoration of the church destroyed long ago by the English.

Gildas's *De Excidio Britanniae* had been published for the first time in 1525 by Polydore Vergil, who would go on to uphold the Cadwaladr and Constantine traditions in his *Anglica Historia*. Few historians had done more valuable service for both the Tudor dynasty and the cause of Protestant reform. Yet within a few years Polydore would be excoriated by British nationalists as "that most rascall, dogge knave in the worlde," an Italian double-agent who set out to defame the glory of the ancient Britons to please his Roman masters.[61] The reason for this outpouring of abuse was Polydore's deep skepticism about the veracity of Geoffrey of Monmouth, the very existence of King Arthur, and the valor of the ancient Britons. It was hardly an unprecedented stance. Indeed, Polydore was writing within

---

[58] All arguments employed by John Foxe, *Acts and Monuments*, ed. S. R. Cattley and G. Townsend (1837–41), 1:306. Foxe further notes that even if Eleutherius was responsible for the conversion of the Britons, he lived before the era of papal supremacy and corruption.
[59] See Glanmor Williams, "Some Protestant Views of Early Church History" in *Welsh Reformation Essays* (Cardiff: University of Wales Press), p. 210.
[60] Foxe, *Acts and Monuments*, 1:516.
[61] The phrase is from a denunciation scribbled in the margin of a copy of John Bale's *Scriptores*. Quoted in Denys Hay, *Polydore Vergil: Renaissance Historian and Man of Letters* (Oxford: Clarendon Press, 1952), p. 159.

an established native tradition, stretching back to William of Newburgh in the twelfth century. More recently, Fabyan had accused Geoffrey of telling lies to favor the Britons. Rastell, himself a fervent reformer, had been inclined to reject the whole of the British History as recently as 1529. But much had changed in five short years – and Polydore was an Italian priest. He was, in short, the perfect target for patriotic Protestant rage. Attacks on Polydore were unremitting throughout the sixteenth century, from John Leland's *Assertio inclytissimi Arturii Regis Britanniae* (1544) to Sir John Prise's *Historiae Brytanicae Defensio* (1573) to Richard Harvey's *Philadelphus, or a Defence of Brutes, and the Brutans History* (1593). All in all, whatever harm Polydore did to Geoffrey's reputation was ultimately far outweighed by his serviceability in providing a pretext for the proliferation of British nationalist discourse.

If Polydore's skepticism about the British past was unacceptable in 1534, it became even more so two years later, when the government took another step toward reviving Arthur's empire. The Act which laid the basis for the union of England and Wales was imbued with the new imperial ideology, asserting in its preamble that Wales "ever hath been incorporated, annexed, united, and subject to and under the Imperial Crown of this Realm."[62] Henceforth there would be no "distinction and diversity" between the two peoples. In hindsight, historians have seen the proclaimed abolition of diversity as a scarcely veiled program for the abolition of Welshness, as embodied in language, custom and law. Nevertheless, the new dispensation was enthusiastically embraced by the *uchelwyr* whose traditional authority in their communities was now unchallenged and sanctioned by English law. George Owen of Pembrokeshire, writing at the end of the century, would look back upon the Acts of Union as "a joyfull metamorphosis" in which the Welsh at last received "magistrates of theyr owne nation."[63] There was cause for rejoicing among the English as well – for if they and the Welsh were now one and the same, they too were entitled to call themselves Britons.

Under Elizabeth and James, the successful union with Wales would be held up as a model for England's relations with Ireland.[64] But its impact on English imperial thought became apparent much sooner than that, in the

---

[62] Hugh Thomas, ed., *Cyfnod y Tuduriaid* (Cardiff: University of Wales Press, 1973), 29.

[63] George Owen, "The Dialogue of the Government of Wales," in *The Description of Pembrokeshire*, ed. Henry Owen (London, 1902–36), 3: 57, 55.

[64] See Ciaran Brady, "Comparable Histories?: Tudor Reform in Wales and Ireland," in *Conquest and Union: Fashioning a British State, 1485–1725*, ed. Steven G. Ellis and Sarah Barber (London: Longman, 1995), pp. 64–86.

"Rough Wooing" of Scotland under Protector Somerset in the late 1540s. The attempt to impose a union between the crowns of England and Scotland was presented by Somerset and his supporters as a "British" policy. In the propaganda campaign that accompanied England's military assault, England was no longer portrayed as Scotland's feudal superior, but rather as "the onely supreme seat of th'empire of Great Briteigne."[65] Somerset was hailed as the descendant of the British earl who had slain the Saxon Hengist, restoring "the whole Empire & name of greate Briteigne" – the Protector was called upon to emulate his ancestor in performing "the like restitucion of the name and Empire of great Briteigne" (249). Somerset himself, in his *Epistle or Exhortacion to Unitie and Peace* (1548), urged the Scots to accept unification and, like the English, "take the indifferent old name of Britaynes again."[66]

The imperial and British vision propounded by Somerset and his propagandists was essentially without precedent.[67] Never before, neither in the middle ages nor the early Tudor era, had it been possible for an English writer to identify himself unreservedly as a Briton. It is true that there had been attempts throughout the later middle ages to co-opt and Anglicize the British History, with talk of "the Bretouns that beth Inglisse no[w]."[68] But the success of such attempts was always limited by the knowledge that there were some Britons who were still Britons, with their own historical agenda. With remarkable audacity, the mid-Tudor ideologues of British nationalism simply reversed the medieval formula, speaking in the name of "the English that are Britons now." And they did so even as the Tudor state was seeking, at least in theory, to cleanse Wales of the language, laws, and culture of the ancient Britons.

---

[65] Nicholas Bodrugan, alias Adams, *An Epitome of the Title that the Kynges Majestie hath to the Sovereigntie of Scotlande*, in *The Complaynt of Scotland*, ed. J. A. H. Murray (EETS, 1872), p. 250.

[66] [Protector Somerset], *Epistle or Exhortacion to Unitie and Peace*, in *The Complaynt of Scotland*, ed. Murray, p. 241.

[67] "The empire of Great Britain was … the invention of the unionist pamphleteers who wrote on behalf of Henry VIII and Protector Somerset"; Armitage, *Ideological Origins of the British Empire*, p. 42. Even this formulation slightly understates the radical innovation in Somerset's approach to union. Henry VIII had relied largely on the traditional feudal claim – devised by Edward I – that the first English king, Locrinus, was overlord to Scotland's Albanactus, giving English kings suzerainty over their Scottish counterparts; it was under Somerset that the idea of a unified British state inhabited by British subjects was mooted for the first time. See Roger A. Mason, "The Scottish Reformation and the Origins of Anglo-British Imperialism," in *Scots and Britons: Scottish Political Thought and the Union of 1603* (Cambridge: Cambridge University Press, 1994), pp. 161–86.

[68] From the fourteenth-century poem *Of Arthour and Merlin*, quoted in Turville-Petre, *England the Nation*, p. 126.

Such sweeping acts of cultural appropriation only work if they are made to look easy. They rarely if ever are. In fact, the transformation in the meaning of "Briton" in the propaganda accompanying the Scottish campaign raised acute problems of blood and identity, not least for the English. A term that previously referred exclusively to the Welsh and the Bretons was now being used to designate an identity shared by – or at least available to – all inhabitants of the isle of Britain. According to England's propagandists, the Scots were being offered a golden opportunity to recover their true identity as Britons, just as the English had done. But how exactly had the English managed to transform themselves so rapidly into Britons? Could a king's bloodline change the ethnic identity of his people? Did the fact that Edward VI was "a right Briton both bred and borne" mean that all his subjects were as well?[69]

The argument that the rise of the Tudors with their much-vaunted bloodline somehow amounted to a general restoration of ancient British liberties did not much impress Scotland's defenders. As one retorted, "quhou beit that the kyng of Ingland nou present be discendet of the blude of Valis [Wales], yit noch the les the pepil of Valis ar in sic subjectione that thai dar never ryde bot iiii to giddir."[70] By the same token, uniting the Scottish and English royal lines would not necessarily produce a breed of rulers sympathetic to Scotland; lineage offered no guarantee of ethnic affinity. What then could form the basis of an identity subsuming Scots and English on an equal basis? Ironically, it was a Scot, the Edinburgh merchant James Henrisoun, who came up with the most radical argument for common Britishness. For Henrisoun, British identity was rooted in blood – not the blood of royal pedigrees, but the blood of the masses. Appealing to both peoples to abandon "those hatefull termes of Scottes & Englishemen" in favor of "the onely title and name of Britons," he proclaimed: "I doubt not to saie, and am able to prove, that the great parte of both realmes, is come of the old Britayns. And thoughe we have been mixed with foreyn nacions, whereby the Britayne tongue is changed & out of use, yet doth the bloud and generacion remain."[71]

[69] William Patten, *The Expedicion into Scotlande* (London, 1548), sig. b6ᵛ.
[70] *The Complaynt of Scotland*, p. 95.
[71] James Henrisoun, *Exhortacion to the Scottes to Conforme themselves to the Honourable, Expedient & Godly Union Betweene the Realmes of England and Scotland*, in *The Complaynt of Scotland*, pp. 230, 216.

Henrisoun had proposed an elegant and wonderfully convenient solution to the problem of Britain's ethnic diversity. Moreover, he was probably right.[72] Yet the notion that the Welsh, the English, and the Scots were racially homogenous found almost no supporters at the time.[73] English proponents of British unification were thus left in the awkward position of having to claim a common identity with the ancient inhabitants of Britain, without being related to them in either a linguistic or a biological sense. This difficulty did not forestall the further development of Anglo-British nationalism in the later Tudor period. It did, however, require its supporters to imagine their relationship to the past – and to the Welsh – in complexly figurative ways. Even before Britain became an important theme in early modern English literature, literary modes of thought (metaphor, metonymy, *figurae*) had become indispensable to the project of imagining Britain. In part for this very reason, literary interest in British nationalism would remain consistently strong in the later Tudor era, even when political commitment to the British project was on the wane.[74]

The literary history of British nationalism in the later Tudor period begins – rather inauspiciously, it must be said – with Arthur Kelton of Shrewsbury. In his two published books of verse, *A Commendacion of Welshmen* (1546) and *A Chronycle with a Genealogie Declaryng that the Brittons and Welshemen are Lineallye Dyscended from Brute* (1547), Kelton propounds a new national vision, discovering in the upheavals of the last few years the fulfillment of the angel's prophecy to Cadwaladr. With marvelous ingenuity and a bit of fuzzy logic, Kelton interprets the English Reformation as the accomplishment of the long-awaited return

[72] Although the archaeological and genetic evidence remains difficult to interpret, the old belief that Anglo-Saxon invaders settled in southern Britain in large numbers, displacing or exterminating the native British population, looks increasingly shaky. It has even been tentatively suggested that there may have been no invasions as such, merely a choice by some inhabitants of Britain to opt for a newly prestigious Germanic identity in place of an outmoded Romano-British one. See Catherine Hills, *Origins of the English* (London: Duckworth, 2003).

[73] In an era still much closer to the middle ages than the modern era in its understanding of ethnicity, legal and linguistic diversity was generally taken as proof in itself of racial diversity, just as common customs and law indicated common descent. Susan Reynolds, "What Do We Mean by 'Anglo-Saxon' and 'Anglo-Saxons'?," *Journal of British Studies* 24 (1985), 395–414.

[74] Although William Cecil, who had been heavily involved in Somerset's propaganda campaign, did attempt to craft a coherent British policy for Elizabeth I, the queen herself was never convinced, and her government would adopt a comparatively conservative approach to British affairs after 1565. See Jane E. A. Dawson, "William Cecil and the British Dimension of Early Elizabethan Foreign Policy," *History* 74 (1989), 196–216; Hiram Morgan, "British Policies Before the British State."

home of Cadwaladr's bones. Henry VIII is Cadwaladr's descendant, his bones are thus Cadwaladr's bones, and in freeing himself from servitude to Rome he has brought himself home to Britain:

> For this is he
> Ye maye well se
> Whose bones are translated
> By sentence devyne
> From rome this tyme
> Newly seperated.[75]

On this basis, Kelton is able to meld Galfridian and Protestant anti-Romanism, and to align the accession of Henry Tudor, the Reformation, and the union of England and Wales within the grand prophetic pattern. British history becomes a string of glorious victories over an eternally envious Rome, ranging from the ancient conquests of Brennus and Arthur to Henry VIII's break with the Pope, and to Kelton's own trouncing of Polydore Vergil, who is made the hapless representative of ancient and modern Italy. Britain owes its triumphant rebirth to the preservation of the original British blood in the Tudor dynasty and the Welsh people (both described, quite unselfconsciously, as "Brutes"). While for the Tudors this blood-descent functions as a legitimating lineage – they alone among the world's monarchs are "of the first bloud and lyne" – the Welsh can claim *as a race* to be "Of the blood imperiall," and still unmixed "With any strange parentage."[76] The only ones apparently left out of the celebration are the English, who (unless they are somehow included in the phrase "*Brittans and Welshmen*"), seem relegated to the status of appreciative observers in the ongoing clash of British and Roman titans.

Yet Kelton himself was, by most definitions, English. A native of Shrewsbury with an English surname, he referred to the English language as "Oure vulger tong."[77] His work suggests little acquaintance with Welsh literature, and none of the concern shown by contemporary Welsh humanists such as William Salesbury and Sir John Prise for the preservation of the

---

[75] A. H. Dodd, "'A Commendacion of Welshmen'," *Bulletin of the Board of Celtic Studies* 19 (1961), 243.

[76] *A Chronycle with a Genealogie Declaryng that the Brittons and Welshemen are Lineallye Dyscended from Brute* (1547), sig. e4ᵛ; "Commendacion," 235, 237.

[77] "Commendacion," 244. There was a significant Welsh community in Shrewsbury, brought there by the cloth and cattle trades, whose members no doubt served as Kelton's informants. There is no indication that he himself had visited Wales, or that he spoke to his informants in any language but English.

language. Nothing in his first published poem, in which the Welsh are always "they," would prevent English readers from regarding him as anything other than a Cambrophilic Englishman. In the *Chronycle with a Genealogie*, however, the Welsh have become "we." Possibly Kelton had remembered a Welsh ancestor and was claiming Welsh identity on that basis. Possibly the fact that Shrewsbury fell within the jurisdiction of the Council in the Marches of Wales was enough for Kelton to nominate himself an honorary Welshman. Neither of these arguments would have made much sense within native Welsh society (where linguistic and ethnic identity remained fused in the word *iaith*). Yet more than a few later Tudor Englishmen would lay claim to Welshness on these or even flimsier grounds.[78]

One of the most remarkable features of Tudor national consciousness, especially in its later phase, is the extent to which it ignored or sidelined the English and their history. Robert Fabyan, it is true, had considered "the blode or dissent of the Saxons to be farre above the Brytons," but his was near to being a lone voice, especially as the century wore on.[79] The general silence on the subject of the Saxons in this period and the low esteem in which they were held stands in remarkable contrast to the Teutonomania of later centuries.[80] The difference in the reputations of the ancient Britons and Saxons is highlighted in Richard Harvey's *Philadelphus, or a Defence of Brutes, and the Brutans History* (1593). Whilst Harvey's praise of "the genealogies of Camber . . . kinsmen of true auncient Brutans" is infinite, the Saxons are consigned to the dustbin of history: "let their owne men commend them if they wil, I owe them no service by writing or speaking."[81] Who "their owne men" might be, if not the English, is left unspecified. Perhaps Harvey meant the likes of Thomas Stapleton, the Catholic translator of Bede. In the heyday of British nationalism, Anglo-Saxon history

---

[78] The scholar–magician John Dee made much of his Welsh parentage when it suited him, while Thomas Churchyard deemed his Shrewsbury origins sufficient to grant him an insider's view of *The Worthines of Wales* (London, 1587). Richard Harvey (see below) seems to have had no real basis whatsoever for his identification as a "Brutan." On the important ideological role played by such pseudo-Welshmen, see Philip Schwyzer, "British History and 'The British History': The Same Old Story?," in *British Identities and English Renaissance Literature*, ed. Baker and Maley, pp. 11–23.

[79] Fabyan, *The New Chronicles*, p. 127.

[80] It was "almost with a shock" that T. D. Kendrick realized that the question of Saxon ancestry in the Tudor period was "by general consent left alone"; *British Antiquity* (London: Methuen, 1950), p. 116.

[81] Richard Harvey, *Philadelphus, or a Defence of Brutes, and the Brutans History* (London, 1593), pp. 83, 97.

seems to have appealed primarily to Catholic dissidents – "dissent of the Saxons," indeed.[82]

Long before, Bernard Andre had dismissed English history between the abdication of Cadwaladr and the accession of Henry VII as nothing more than "barbarity." If any history mattered during those benighted eight centuries, it must be the history of Wales, where the spark of Cadwaladr's blood had been kept alive. That history was finally made available to English readers in David Powel's *Historie of Cambria* (1584), covering the years from Cadwaladr, the last King of Britain, to Llywelyn ap Gruffudd, the last independent prince of Wales. Powel was completing the work of the antiquarian Humphrey Llwyd, who had begun the project of translating the Welsh chronicle *Brut y Tywysogion* because "I wolde not have the inhabitantes of this Ile ignorant of the histories and cronicles of the same."[83] In other words, the *Historie of Cambria* was the history of the whole island; Welsh history and British history were one and the same. Powel's use of the woodcuts from the first edition of Holinshed's *Chronicles* underwrote the work's claim to the status of national history. Six years later, Edmund Spenser would proclaim that this was indeed the true history of Britain.

The entire history of Britain, from the arrival of the Trojans down to Elizabeth's intervention in the Netherlands in the 1580s, is enclosed within the pages of Spenser's *Faerie Queene*.[84] The first part of the history, from

---

[82] Thomas Stapleton, *The History of the Church of England, compiled by Venerable Bede, Englishman* (Antwerp, 1565). In his dedication and preface, Stapleton reminds his readers of "oure dere forefathers of almost these thousand yeres" (p. *3*ᵛ) and that Bede was "a countreman of oures" (p. 2ᵛ). The appeal of Anglo-Saxon history to English Catholics was based on the fact that the Saxons, unlike the Britons, were converted directly from Rome. Besides Stapleton, the great Catholic exponent of Saxonism was Richard Verstegan, whose *Restitution of Decayed Intelligence in Antiquities* (Antwerp, 1605) finally succeeded in sparking a more general interest among the English in their Teutonic ancestors. Protestant enthusiasm for the Saxons in the Tudor era was largely confined to the circle of Archbishop Matthew Parker. On Catholic responses to the British question, see Christopher Highley, "'The Lost British Lamb': English Catholic Exiles and the Problem of Britain," in *British Identities and English Renaissance Literature*, ed. Baker and Maley, pp. 37–50.

[83] Humphrey Llwyd, *Cronica Walliae*, ed. Ieuan M. Williams (Cardiff: University of Wales Press, 2002), p. 82. Being the work of Welsh patriots, *The Historie of Cambria* does not conform in every way to the agenda of the British project. While Powel notes Henry Tudor's Welsh ancestry and links it to the emancipation of the Welsh, he considers Llywelyn to have been "the last Prince of the Welsh blood" (p. 10), and eschews the prophetic theme, calling the angel's promise to Cadwaladr "a fable confirmed with blind prophesies" (p. 3). For a reading of the *Historie* as "a dissident account of English state-building on the margins of the nation," see Christopher Highley, *Shakespeare, Spenser, and the Crisis in Ireland* (Cambridge: Cambridge University Press, 1997), pp. 71–76.

[84] On the background to Spenser's vision of British history, one of the best studies remains Edwin Greenlaw, *Studies in Spenser's Historical Allegory* (Baltimore: Johns Hopkins University Press, 1932). See also Charles Bowie Millican, *Spenser and the Table Round* (London: Frank Cass and Co., 1967).

Brutus to Uther Pendragon, is met with in the chronicle entitled "Briton moniments," which Arthur (Uther's son) reads in the chamber of Eumnestes (Book II, canto x). The second installment, running from the Arthurian era (though Arthur himself is not mentioned) to the Elizabethan present is revealed prophetically to Britomart by Merlin in Book III, canto iii. The setting is Merlin's enchanted cave under Maridunum (Carmarthen), in "*Deheubarth* that now South-wales is hight" (III.ii.18). With its earnest attention to Welsh topography and the shape of sixth-century society, this is the section of the poem in which Spenser's anti-quarian imagination is most powerfully at work. The landscape in which Britomart encounters Merlin is paradoxically more alien to the English reader than that of Fairyland itself.[85] The sense of alienation is set to deepen as the prophecy unfolds.

The larger part of Merlin's prophecy deals with the slow grinding down of the Britons in the face of the Saxon onslaught of the sixth and seventh centuries, truly a tale of "sorrowes, and huge hills / Of dying people" (III.iii.41) Although Merlin is not above acknowledging the virtue of an individual Saxon such as "the good king Oswald" (III.iii.38), he reserves his emphasis and his sympathy for the Britons, whose many valiant victories never quite succeed in turning back the Saxon tide. The 41st stanza foretells the abdication of Cadwaladr, "by vision staid from his intent." At this point the pace of Merlin's prophecy accelerates drastically, so that only six stanzas are devoted to the period separating Cadwaladr from Henry Tudor. Of these stanzas, four are devoted to the sufferings of the "antique *Troian* blood" (III.iii.42) and the fame of such historical rulers as Rhodoricke (Rhodri) the Great, Howell Dda, and Griffyth Conan, whose names and deeds Spenser undoubtedly derived from Powel. Only two stanzas serve to tell of the Saxons, Danes, and Normans, none of whose leaders are men-tioned by name, but are instead denoted by the beast imagery (Danish ravens, Norman lions) proper to Merlinic prophecies and the *cywyddau brud*. History, to the extent that there has been such a thing in the 800-year interregnum through which the prophet passes so swiftly, has been the history of the dispossessed Britons.

In recounting the long-awaited restoration of the British bloodline in the person of Henry Tudor, Merlin employs an image which, as we have seen, was already current in Welsh poetry well before 1485.

---

[85] As Bart van Es suggests, "If the past is a foreign country, that country is Deheubarth"; *Spenser's Forms of History* (Oxford: Oxford University Press, 2002), p. 54.

Tho when the terme is full accomplishid
There shall a spark of fire, which hath long-while
Bene in his ashes raked up, and hid,
Be freshly kindled in the fruitfull Ile
Of *Mona*, where it lurked in exile;
Which shall breake forth into bright burning flame,
And reach into the house, that beares the stile
Of royall maiesty and soveraigne name;
So shall the Briton bloud their crowne againe reclame.   (III.iii.48)

The direct source of this image was almost certainly neither Dafydd Nanmor nor Lewys Glyn Cothi, nor any text in the Welsh language, of which Spenser probably knew only a few words. The image of the rekindled spark probably reached him instead by way of a Latin text, Sir John Prise's *Historiae Britannicae Defensio* (1573), a learned and patriotic Welsh riposte to Polydore Vergil (discussed at greater length in chapter 3.) As Prise recalls, "I remember certain of our native poets have sung, for a long time now and not inelegantly, that when the fire of the hearth of King Cadwaladr is lulled, a spark will arise from the island of Mona which, as Virgil has it, stirs up the sleeping fire."[86]

Whereas Prise retains and even heightens Dafydd Nanmor's emphasis on the hearth (*lares/aelwyd*), with its rich significance in terms of Welsh nationhood, Spenser omits the hearth entirely. In doing so, he appears to make the restoration of the British bloodline a matter of purely dynastic significance, just as Polydore Vergil had done.[87] It is sufficient that "The royall seed, the antique *Troian* blood" (III.iii.42) has returned to the throne. No broader national restoration is necessarily implied; no community is seen warming itself around this "bright burning" yet (from the bardic point of view) strangely chilly flame. Spenser may take his imagery

---

[86] "Unde quendam nostratum Poetarum carmine non ineleganter iam olim cecinisse memini, in hanc videlicet sententiam, quod ex quo focus e laribus Regis Cadwaladeri sopitus est, orta fuerit scintilla ex Insula Mona, quae ut Vergilius habet, sopitos suscitat ignes"; Sir John Prise, *Historiae Britannicae Defensio* (London, 1573), sig. xxx2ᵛ. Prise's reference is to *Aeneid* 5.743. As far as I know, this source has not been noted previously. Claims have been made for Spenser's Welsh (e.g. Donald Williams Bruce, "Spenser's Welsh," *Notes and Queries* 230 (1985), 465–467), but there is in fact no need to seek any source for Spenser's knowledge of Welsh history and literature beyond *The Historie of Cambria* and *Historiae Britannicae Defensio*, nor to assume that his knowledge of the Welsh language extended far beyond the phrases "Scuith guiridh" and "y Scuith gogh"; *Faerie Queene* (II.x.24).

[87] But on the haziness of the division between royal and racial genealogies for Spenser and his contemporaries, see Christopher Ivic, "Spenser and the Bounds of Race," *Genre* 32 (1999), 141–73.

from a Welsh source, but his attitude to the fulfillment of the prophecy to Cadwaladr seems quintessentially English.

Yet what is most striking in this passage is Merlin's sudden evasiveness when he comes to speak of the English throne. His reticent reference to a "house, that bears the stile" of a name never specifies the wording of that style (not yet "King of Great Britain" in Spenser's era, but "King of England"). The house into which the Briton blood has at last reached seems in the interim to have been only a house of words, and the words themselves are unspoken. This is far from the version of history that proclaims "This realm of England is an empire." Indeed, the names of England and the English are absent not only from this passage but from the entire prophecy. Merlin's account of events east of the Severn has been so rapid and cursory that we cannot tell if the present inhabitants are Saxons, Danes, Normans, or, for that matter, ravens or lions. Only in the next stanza is a nation other than the Britons mentioned (but still not named), and then only to be instantly effaced: "Thenceforth eternall union shall be made / Betweene the nations different afore" (III.iii.49). The ending of difference between the nations echoes the abolition of "distinction and diversity" proclaimed in the first Act of Union. Whereas the force of that Act was to replace Welsh law with English, here it is apparently the English who must relinquish their old identity and go by the name of Britons – the name proper to union, and the only name available in Merlin's vocabulary.[88]

The nature of this "eternall union" must depend, of course, on how "different" the two nations actually were "afore." The historical conflict between Britons and Saxons is indeed represented in the poem as bloody and relentless. As Britomart's nurse tells her after the encounter with Merlin, "now all *Britanie* doth burne in armes bright" (III.iii.52). Britomart, Artegall, Arthur, and George (otherwise known as the Redcrosse Knight) are all born into one or the other ethnic camp in a world on a permanent war footing. Yet aspects of the poem suggest a truth deeper than even Merlin may suspect: that the Britons and the English

[88] Harry Berger, Jr. reads the prophecy to suggest that "the Britons as a nation have had their day in history," while allowing for "the implication that the native virtue of the Welsh would provide the redeeming element in the English character"; "The Structure of Merlin's Chronicle in *The Faerie Queene* III.iii," in *Revisionary Play: Studies in the Spenserian Dynamics* (Berkeley: University of California Press, 1988), pp. 127–8. I differ from this view chiefly in noting that the *English* are nowhere mentioned in the prophecy. If they do come out on top in the new dispensation, it is only by relinquishing their own savage past and embracing an inclusive British identity. See also Andrew Fichter, *Poets Historical: Dynastic Epic in the Renaissance* (New Haven: Yale University Press, 1982), pp. 175–81; Hadfield, *Shakespeare, Spenser, and the Matter of Britain*, pp. 116–20.

have all along been a single people, concealed from one another and themselves by the masks and illusions that bedevil every sojourner in Faerieland.

Spenser's British and English heroes and heroines are prone to doubling and prey to disguise. At first glance, the Saxon Redcrosse and the Briton Artegall, representing the highest ideals of their respective nations (as St. George and Arthur's equal), seem as irreconcilable as an unstoppable force and an immovable object. Redcrosse springs "from ancient race / Of *Saxon* kings" who have "High reard their royall throne in *Britane* land, / And vanquisht them, unable to withstand" (I.x.65); Artegall's destiny is precisely "Strongly to aide his countrey, to withstand / The powre of forrein Paynims, which invade thy land" (III.iii.27). However, the neat mirroring of these two couplets is itself an indication that these characters may be more closely connected than first appears, as is the fact that both heroes were stolen in infancy by Fairies and brought up in ignorance of their true ethnicity. Similarly, the very names of Britomart and Angela encourage us to view them as feminine embodiments of their respective nations. Nevertheless, Britomart resolves to take Angela as her "ensample" (III.iii.56) and disguises herself as a male warrior by donning Angela's captured armor.

In each of these cases, the disguise or deception seems to mask the "truth" of ethnic difference. Yet concealment and mistaking in *The Faerie Queene* are themselves educative and revelatory experiences.[89] George and Artegall are mistaken in believing themselves Fairies, but their mistake gives them a real experience of a common identity. Angela and Britomart use armor as a disguise, but the effect is to give them not only a shared appearance but a common external border or boundary – "England" and "Britain" turn out to be coextensive and coterminous. By way of such errors and disguises, the British and English characters embark upon a learning process leading towards a final recognition of commonality. Their apparently opposed ethnic identities are themselves masks concealing their deeper *identity*. Spenser's apparent solution in *The Faerie Queene* to the problem of ethnic difference within Britain is reminiscent of James Henrisoun's: we have all been Britons all along, prevented from recognizing ourselves by the historical accidents of language and law.

---

[89] See the chapter "Error as a Means of Empire," in Jeffrey Knapp, *An Empire Nowhere: England, America, and Literature from Utopia to The Tempest* (Berkeley: University of California Press, 1992), pp. 106–133.

We are all Britons – but some of us may not know it yet. The idea that some people, even some peoples, need to be led to a knowledge of their own Britishness reappears as a central point in Spenser's *View of the Present State of Ireland* (c. 1596). In spite of Spenser's apparent disillusionment with Geoffrey of Monmouth (he now considers it "impossible to proove, that there was ever any such Brutus of Albion or England"), the *View* is a profound expression of British nationalism, unique in its time in offering "a vision of a unified British monarchy within the Three Kingdoms, on ethnological as much as political grounds."[90] Like *The Faerie Queene*, the *View* veers between emphasizing ethnic distinctions – the Irish, famously, are identified with Scythians, Africans, Gauls, and others – and erasing them with sudden gestures toward a more inclusive identity: "Scotlande and Irelande are all one and the same"; "The Gaulish speech is the very British"; "Ireland is by Diodorus Siculus, and by Strabo, called Britannia, and a part of Great Brittaine."[91] The Irish, then, are not an alien and inferior race, as some of Spenser's contemporaries would argue, but British kin, suffering under the same delusion from which the English themselves have so recently been awakened by the kindling of a spark. In considering how the Irish may be brought to see the same light, Spenser seems to recall for a last time the image bequeathed to him by Dafydd Nanmor. The answer to Irish intransigence is not, as has been the policy of English governors in the past, to "smother and keepe downe the flame of the mischiefe, so as it may not breake out . . ."[92] Better, Spenser will argue, to let the spark kindle and, in the words of the poem, "breake forth into bright burning flame." Thus, the Irish rebel "flying from the fire shall fall into the water."[93] Spenser's British solution to Ireland, in short, is the fire next time.

THE PRIZE AND THE PRICE

The image of the spark from Anglesey had come a long way, as far as the once-obscure Tudurs themselves. Flaring up in the mid-fifteenth-century

---

[90] Edmund Spenser, *A View of the State of Ireland*, ed. Andrew Hadfield and Willy Maley (Oxford: Blackwell, 1997), p. 44; Armitage, *Ideological Origins*, p. 52.
[91] Spenser, *View*, pp. 45, 51, 52. As Willy Maley argues, "Spenser's chief strategy in the *View* is to efface rather than deface the Irish"; *Nation, State and Empire in English Renaissance Literature*, p. 74. See also Andrew Hadfield, "Briton and Scythian: Tudor Representations of Irish Origins," *Irish Historical Studies* 28 (1993), 390–408.
[92] Spenser, *View*, p. 90.
[93] Spenser, *View*, p. 98.

verses of Dafydd Nanmor, it had initially signified Welsh resistance to the English, and resonated with prophetic and historical traditions peculiar to the Britons. One hundred and forty years and two languages later, the wandering spark settled in the verses of Edmund Spenser, where it was associated with a unified Britishness, embracing the English no less than the Welsh (and arguably serving the interests of the English rather more than the Welsh). If it is right to speak of this trajectory in terms of a prize won, it is also right to speak of it in terms of a price paid. The prize, of course, was the neutralization and subsequently the appropriation by the English of those powerful prophetic traditions which underlie British nationalism. But the price was the emptying out of what had long been understood and experienced as Englishness, an identity for which British nationalism seemed to allow no possibility of continuance. At worst, as in Bernard Andre or Richard Harvey, Englishness was a form of barbarism to be rejected with abhorrence; at best, as in Spenser, it was a mask which could now be gratefully set by.

Nowhere do we receive a more vivid sense of both the prize and the price associated with British nationalism than in Shakespeare's history plays. I am thinking in particular of a pair of scenes from the second tetralogy. In the first of these, Act 3 scene 1 of *1 Henry IV*, there is an ethnically-charged clash between a Welshman and an Englishman. The Welshman is the rebel Owain Glyndwr. Puffed up with pride in his birth, obsessed with prophecies, signs, and portents, Glyndwr is a type of the Welshman familiar from Fabyan (who mocks such "brutisshe blastis") and from many an earlier English chronicle.[94] He is also a British nationalist in the traditional sense, which is to say a Welsh nationalist seeking to restore the ancient liberty of the Britons. His English antagonist in this scene has nothing but contempt for "the dreamer Merlin and his prophecies," and is quick to identify Glyndwr's way of reading the signs of history as an ethnic characteristic: "I think there's no man speaks better Welsh" (3.1.48).[95] Although Hotspur

---

[94] Fabyan, *The New Chronicles*, p. 127. As is said of the Welsh in the *Vita Edwardi Secundi*, "from the sayings of the prophet Merlin they still hope to recover England. Hence it is that the Welsh frequently rebel, hoping to give effect to the prophecy; but because they do not know the appointed time, they are often deceived and their labour is in vain"; *Vita Edwardi Secundi / The Life of Edward the Second*, trans. and ed. N. Denholm-Young (London: Thomas Nelson and Sons, 1957), p. 69. Shakespeare's Glyndwr is a complex personality, certainly not a crude ethnic stereotype. But what strike us as the individual touches to his character are largely extrapolations rather than divergences from the basic stereotype.

[95] Shakespeare has made a pointed alteration to his sources to heighten the ethnic contrast between the Englishman and the Welshman. The rebellious Percys had in fact made willing use of the prophecies of "the moldwarp and the ant" which Hotspur dismisses as so much Welsh nonsense.

and Glyndwr bury their differences for the sake of political expediency, their acrimonious encounter suggests no easy possibility of *rapprochement* between English and Welsh ways of understanding truth, nation, and history.

In Act 5 scene 1 of *Henry V*, there is again an ethnically charged clash between a Welshman and an Englishman. Standing in for Glyndwr is Captain Fluellen, who shares the rebel's love of historical lore and prophetic portents, but who places his interpretive capacities squarely at the service of the English king. His English opponent, Pistol, is a drastically debased version of Hotspur, partaking of his coarseness and taste for hyperbole, but lacking any shred of nobility or honor. Pistol's mockery of the Welsh and the British History – "Not for Cadwallader and all his goats" (5.1.25); "Base Trojan, thou shalt die" (5.1.28) – is expressive only of little English bigotry.[96] With his empty boasts, scurrilous insults, and garbled quotations from Marlowe, Pistol conforms remarkably closely to Richard Harvey's derogatory description of the Anglo-Saxon: "a deformed mocker with hys distorted mouthes, a venimous hisser with his noysom breath, a rayling stageplayer with his trifling actions." Having dared to "mock at an ancient tradition," the Englishman is himself made the butt of mockery, cudgeled by Fluellen and forced to swallow the emblem of his Welshness, the leek.

If Fluellen's fanatical loyalty to the English king signifies the prize achieved in the appropriation of British nationalism, the debasement of Hotspur into Pistol and the humiliation of Pistol by Fluellen suggest the price. In *Henry V*, an Englishness which holds itself apart from Britishness is revealed as nothing more than a leering mask, covering up sheer emptiness. As Captain Gower tells the vanquished Englishman, "Go, go, you are a counterfeit cowardly knave." A moment later, Gower suggests that the cause of Englishness is not entirely lost, advising Pistol to "let a Welsh correction teach you a good English condition." Fluellen's victory can thus as be read both as a vindication of Britishness against a false and empty Englishness, and as the means by which British authority is co-opted for the service of a deeper English identity.[97] There is no contradiction here.

---

[96] Taunting Fluellen as a "mountain-squire" (5.1.32), Pistol seeks by this reminder of the notorious poverty of the Welsh gentry to establish his class as well as ethnic superiority to the Welshman. In *The Merry Wives of Windsor* he shows the same bigoted contempt for Parson Hugh Evans, calling him "thou mountain-foreigner" (1.1.133).

[97] Michael Neill argues that "the 'native garb' of Welsh English is after all no more than the cover for an Englishness paradoxically more essential than Pistol's 'counterfeit' chauvinism"; "Broken English and Broken Irish: Nation, Language, and the Optic of Power in Shakespeare's Histories,"

In its complexity, the scene distills the ideological paradox of British nationalism, as propounded by writers from Somerset to Spenser: the advancement of recognizably English interests by means of the vehement renunciation of Englishness itself.

Shakespeare Quarterly 45 (1994), 20. But David Baker (in an analysis that takes full account of the Welsh dimension of Tudor ideology) argues that Fluellen's actions and utterances provoke "a troubling of, even a collapsing of, categories that does not comport with a uniformly English nationalism"; *Between Nations*, p. 46.

CHAPTER 2

Bale's books and Aske's abbeys: nostalgia and the aesthetics of nationhood

Since the Tudor era, blood has remained central to most versions of English and British nationalism. As Edmund Burke would explain in his *Reflections on the Revolution in France*, "we have given to our frame of polity the image of a relation in blood."[1] Yet, in spite of his commitment to the figure of the nation-as-family, Burke recognizes that blood alone is never enough. Indeed, however essential it may be, it remains only an "image." What really binds the nation together, then, is something still more fundamental: a mode of collective introspection, a way of seeing. Like Narcissus, the nation finds its proper object of contemplation in itself, and its survival depends on ceaselessly sustaining that self-constituting gaze. Therefore, argues Burke, it must always be sure of liking what it sees. "To make us love our country, our country ought to be lovely."[2]

Disgusted by what he saw as Burke's dainty aestheticism in the face of an epoch-making struggle, Thomas Paine fired back a bitter riposte: "he pities the plumage, but forgets the dying bird."[3] The lines were thereby drawn in a controversy that has persisted into the present day. Nationalists the world over have come down firmly on Burke's side of the question. A host of patriotic songs, from "America the Beautiful" to "O Lovely Zimbabwe," testify to the central place of the aesthetic in nationalist thought and feeling.[4] Scholars of nationalism, on the other hand, have tended to follow Paine in minimizing or dismissing the question of beauty. Lists of the features fundamental to nations (e.g., myths of origin, common laws,

---

[1] Edmund Burke, *Reflections on the Revolution in France*, introduction by A. J. Grieve (London: Dent, 1967), p. 32.
[2] Burke, *Reflections*, p. 75.
[3] Thomas Paine, *The Rights of Man*, introduction by Arthur Seldon (London: Dent, 1969), p. 24.
[4] The assertion of peculiar national beauty also occurs in the anthems of Australia ("Our land abounds in Nature's gifts / Of beauty rich and rare"), Brazil ("More flowers put forth in thy fair, smiling fields / Than in the most gorgeously reputed lands"), Denmark ("A lovely land is ours / With beeches green about her"), Mauritius ("Sweet is thy beauty, Sweet is thy fragrance"), and The Philippines ("Beautiful land of love, oh land of light"), to name but a few.

a public culture) rarely if ever make mention of aesthetic appeal.[5] The grounds for this indifference are implicit in Paine's chosen metaphor. Like "plumage," beauty is seen as something merely external, as opposed to the "meat" of the matter. Like the feathers on a fashionable hat, it is regarded as too frivolous (and perhaps too feminine) to merit serious consideration. And, like a handful of down, it is hard to grasp – resistant to analysis, impervious to refutation. (One might with effort convince a nationalist that he was misinformed about Bannockburn or the Treaty of Trieste, but one could hardly hope to prove him wrong in his idea of the beautiful.) Yet, whatever our larger sympathies with Paine, it must be apparent that in this case Burke's insight is too important to belittle or ignore. Given the many and notorious failings of nationalism on a practical level, it is questionable whether it would have survived so long as an ideology, were it not for the fact that nations – all of them – are enduringly, achingly beautiful.

The loveliness of nations had been noticed long before the advent of Edmund Burke. A debate crucial to the English Reformation centered on what constituted the beauties of the land. Robert Aske, leader of the Pilgrimage of Grace, applied the phrase "the beauties of this realm" to the abbeys and monasteries he fought determinedly and unsuccessfully to save. On the opposing side, the Protestant polemicist John Bale argued that the ancient manuscripts previously hidden in monastic libraries were the true "beauty of our nation." These differing aesthetic judgments spring from fundamentally opposed imaginings of the national space. Aske's concept of beauty is embedded in a vision of timeless feudal harmony. Bale, by contrast, discovers in the legacy of Petrarch the means of conceiving of a new kind of a national community, one born out of shared experiences of disruption, loss, and nostalgia.

As I shall argue, Bale and Aske differ not only in their very different ways of imagining the nation, but in the nations they imagined. In hindsight, Aske can be seen as the first in a long line of English patriots to mourn the death of medieval England. In spite – and indeed because – of his profound Yorkshire regionalism, Aske gives voice to an identity that is

---

[5] Two of the most influential definitions of the nation today are those of Anthony D. Smith, as "a named human population sharing an historic territory, common myths and historical memories, a mass, public culture, a common economy and common legal rights and duties for all members," and of Benedict Anderson, as "an imagined political community . . . imagined as both inherently limited and sovereign." Differing in so much else, these definitions are equally blind to the aesthetic. See Smith, *National Identity* (Harmondsworth: Penguin, 1991), p. 14; Anderson, *Imagined Communities*, p. 6.

unmistakably and quintessentially English. John Bale, on the other hand, was the leading ideologue of post-Reformation British nationalism. The nation whose beauties Bale praised, and which he exhorted his readers to adore, was not a land anyone could inhabit in the sixteenth century. It belonged, rather, to the distant pre-Saxon past. Paradoxically, it is in the very irrecoverability of Britain's ancient beauties that Bale locates the basis of a new British nation.

ASKE'S ABBEYS: "THE BEAUTIES OF THIS REALM"

The spark that would ignite the greatest rebellion of the Tudor era was lit by a few men who wanted to hold on to their beautiful things. Since the late fifteenth century, the prosperous artisans of Louth had spared no effort or expense to add luster to their parish church. In the 1530s, the church's beauties included a magnificent spire of almost 300 feet, raised in the previous generation, no fewer than four silver crosses behind which the townsfolk marched proudly in procession, and – the most recent acquisition – a costly new organ.[6] In the early autumn of 1536, the people of Louth were agitated by alarming rumors that the king was planning to confiscate church ornaments, and even to pull down many parish churches. On Sunday, October 1, they rose in arms to defend their church from despoilment. The rising spread quickly through much of Lincolnshire. By October 7, Lincoln had been taken by the rebels, whose forces had swelled to 20,000 men. Although the Lincolnshire movement dissipated a few days later, word of the revolt had by then spread north to Yorkshire, where other insurgents launched what would become the Pilgrimage of Grace.

In Yorkshire, the movement quickly fell under the military and ideological leadership of the lawyer Robert Aske; it was he who gave the Pilgrimage its name and devised the oath all Pilgrims were to swear. The city of York surrendered to Aske's forces without resistance on October 16. By the end of the month, with allied or parallel insurgencies erupting in Richmondshire, Durham, Cumberland and Northumberland, most of the north of England was in the hands of the rebels. Unable in the short term to respond militarily, Henry VIII agreed to a truce, which held for several months. In December, Aske and his fellow leaders issued their manifesto, the "Pontefract Articles," in which they demanded, among other things, the stamping out of Luther's heresies, the recognition of the Pope as head

---

[6] For further detail on the ongoing "work of beautification" at Louth, see R. W. Hoyle, *The Pilgrimage of Grace and the Politics of the 1530s* (Oxford: Oxford University Press, 2001), pp. 101–2.

of the church, punishment of Thomas Cromwell and other corrupt royal councillors, and "to have the abbeys suppressed to be restored unto their houses, lands, and goods."[7] Still biding his time, the king offered the rebels some minor concessions, and a universal free pardon.

Historians remain divided over both the nature and causes of the Pilgrimage of Grace. Was it a spontaneous and genuinely popular rebellion, or the fruit of a conspiracy hatched by members of the northern nobility whose faction was out of favor at court? Were the motives of the rebels primarily religious or economic? The Pilgrimage undoubtedly presents a complex picture.[8] But while we can only guess at the motives and feelings of the majority of Pilgrims, we can describe with some clarity those of their Captain, Robert Aske. For Aske, no issue took precedence over the defense of the monasteries threatened with dissolution. As I shall argue, the principles that impelled Aske to lead a desperate fight to save the monasteries were, on a deep level, aesthetic.

In the spring of 1537, Henry VIII capitalized on a few isolated outbreaks of fresh rebellion to cancel the truce and arrest the ringleaders. But, having broken his word and the Pilgrimage of Grace at one blow, he did not rush to execute the movement's leaders. First he wanted their opinions. Under the direction of Thomas Cromwell, Aske and his associates were subjected to long days of meticulously recorded interrogation. Who was responsible for spreading rumors that the churches would be stripped of their goods, and but one parish church within seven miles left standing? Where, when, and upon what occasion was Aske made captain of the commons in Yorkshire? Was he chosen because he was the initiator of the rebellion, or merely the most enthusiastic once it had begun? Which of the King's acts had Aske and the rebels resented ("grudged against"), and why?[9]

With little hope of preserving his own life, Aske was determined to put the best case possible for the Pilgrimage in written answers which, he must

---

[7] Hoyle, *Pilgrimage of Grace*, p. 461.

[8] The debate among historians is reviewed in Hoyle, *Pilgrimage of Grace*, pp. 13–17. Hoyle and C. S. L. Davies have presented compelling evidence that the Pilgrimage was a genuinely popular revolt, at least at the outset, and vitally though not exclusively concerned with religion (see C. S. L. Davies, "Popular Religion and the Pilgrimage of Grace," in Anthony Fletcher, John Stevenson, eds., *Order and Disorder in Early Modern England* [Cambridge: Cambridge University Press, 1985], pp. 59–91). The lack of consensus among the Pilgrims themselves about the scope and priority of their aims is demonstrated by Ethan H. Shagan, *Popular Politics and the English Reformation* (Cambridge: Cambridge University Press, 2003), pp. 89–128.

[9] "The Pilgrimage of Grace and Aske's Examination," ed. Mary Bateson, *English Historical Review* 5 (1890), 552. All further quotations of Aske are from this text, unless noted otherwise.

have hoped, might yet have some influence on the King.[10] In response to the 23rd article, regarding the King's acts, Aske asserted that he and "the holl contrey" grudged against the dissolution of the abbeys of the north by the Act for the Suppression of the Smaller Monasteries of 1536. Aske's ensuing defense of the abbeys is impassioned and occasionally incoherent, but the arguments are well rehearsed, and they are deployed for maximum effect. Aske was a lawyer before he became a rebel, and he was careful in constructing his last case.

Aske's strategy in responding to Cromwell's query is to emphasize first the spiritual and then the economic importance of the abbeys, without losing sight of the ways in which these are intertwined.

[F]urst, to the statut of subpressions, he dyd gruge ayenst the same & so did al the holl contrey, because the abbeys in the north partes gaf great almons to pour men and laudable servyd God; in wich partes of lait dais they had but smal comforth by gostly teching. And by occasion of the said suppression the devyn seruice of the almightie God is much minished, great nombre of messes unsaid ... the temple of God russed and pulled down, the ornamentes & releques of the church of God unreverent used, the townes [tombs] and sepulcres of honorable & noble men pulled down & sold, non hospitalite now in thos places kept, but the fermers for the most parte lettes and taverns out the fermes of the same houses to other fermers, for lucre and advauntage to them selfes. And the profites of thies abbeys yerley goith out of the contrey to the Kinges highnes ... Also diverse & many of the said abbeys wer in the montaignes & desert places wher the peple be rud of condyccions & not well taught the law of God, & when the said abbeys stud, the said peple not only had worldly refresshing in ther bodies but also speritull refuge ... & many ther tenauntes wer ther feed servaundes to them, & servyng men, well socored by abbeys: & now not only theis tenants & servauntes wantes refresshing ther, both of meat, cloth & wages, & knowith not now wher to have any liffing, but also strangers & baggers of corne as betwix Yorkshir, Lancashir, Kendall, Westmoreland & the bischopreke ... [W]herefore the said statut of subpression was greatly to the decay of the comyn welth of that contrei, & al those partes of al degreys greatly groged ayenst the same, & yet doth, ther dewtie of allegieance alwais savyd. (561–62)

Aske depicts the consequences of the dissolution in terms of spiritual and material deprivation; souls and stomachs have suffered in equal measure. Only once these points have been thoroughly established does Aske introduce a new and different argument: "Also the abbeys was on of the bewties of this realme to al men & strangers passing threw the same" (562).

[10] Madeleine Hope Dodds and Ruth Dodds, *The Pilgrimage of Grace, 1536–1537, and the Exeter Conspiracy, 1538* (London: Frank Cass and Co., 1915, new impression 1971), vol. 2: 207.

Up to this point Aske has been speaking to his interrogators, to Cromwell, and through Cromwell to the king; now, suddenly, he speaks in terms that seem to resonate down the ages, demanding our sympathy and agreement. Almost five centuries after their dissolution, the shells of the great English and Welsh abbeys still rank very high among the beauties of the realm; they attract the gaze not only of natives but of millions of strangers – or tourists – passing through the land. There is, of course, a painful irony in this, for the beauty discerned today at a Fountains or a Rievaulx depends in large part on the very conditions Aske gave his life to forestall. Today, these sites offer the stranger the melancholy "pleasure of ruins," a pleasure bound up with the isolation and contemplative silence which are increasingly rare commodities.[11] For Aske, on the other hand, the abbeys were hubs of life and hospitality, a refuge *from* isolation in "the montaignes & desert places." The beauty he took up arms to defend did not consist in architecture only, but in divine service and sacred song, in the brightness and fascination of "ornamentes and releques," in simple bustle and prosperity. Aske's abbeys would have stimulated all of the five senses, not, as today, the eyes alone.

Yet in spite of this strange and ironic reversal, there remains at least one feeling or perception common to the sixteenth-century Pilgrim and the modern tourist. Today, as then, the beauty of the religious houses seems peculiarly national: they are still "beauties of this realm." The phrase is particularly striking as used by Aske, for up to this point his concern has been wholly with the "country" (Yorkshire) or more generally with "the north parts." His only reference to a wider realm has been to complain that the rents on monastic lands now "goith out of the contrey to the Kinges highnes" (561). Suddenly, with the invocation of beauty, Aske's horizons enlarge.

Aske's vision of the abbeys was, to some extent, a personal one. Other participants in the Pilgrimage would probably not have ranked the suppression of the smaller monasteries so highly among its causes.[12] As for Aske's aesthetic sentiments, they appear to find no echo in the recorded testimony of other Pilgrims.[13] But while Aske may have had a special

---

[11] The phrase is taken from Rose Macaulay, *The Pleasure of Ruins* (London: Weidenfeld and Nicolson, 1953).

[12] See Hoyle, *Pilgrimage of Grace*, pp. 48–50; Shagan, *Popular Politics*, pp. 99–102.

[13] Almost a century later, however, William Lithgow in his *Comments upon Scotland* (1628) lamented that "Mr. Knoxe did with our glorious Churches of Abbacies and Monasteries (which were the greatest *beauty of the Kingdome*) knocking all downe to desolation" (cited in Macaulay, *Pleasure of Ruins*, p. 355; my italics). The coincidence of phrase and context seems too close to be accidental.

enthusiasm for the abbeys, he never saw their plight in isolation from the other traumatic events of the 1530s; and though he laid stress on their beauty, the terms of his answer make it clear that his vision was not *narrowly* aesthetic. His difference from his fellows was perhaps more a matter of emphasis and expression than of ideology. When Aske spoke of "beauties," he had in mind a whole pattern of social and national life, which he together with thousands of others had risked everything to defend.

In his response to the 23rd article, Aske carefully positions the abbeys within an intricately patterned world, structured by cycles in space and time. Interspersed in the "mountaignes and desert places," the abbeys bring a human design to an otherwise hostile and formless landscape. They are attuned to the reliable rhythms of the year, both liturgical and agricultural (offering succor to itinerant "baggers of corne"), and are also bound up with the longer cycles of generations, housing the "sepulcres of honorable & noble men," ensuring that the sons and daughters of the gentry are "brought up in vertuee" (562), and guarding "mony left to the usses of infantes" (562). Aske concludes his defense by pointing out how the beauties of the realm help maintain its very shape, preserving sea walls, bridges, highways, and "such other thinges for the comyn welth" (562). Aske's recourse to the aesthetic occurs at the pivotal moment in which he shifts from the regional to the national, and from the yearly cycles of masses and migrating labor to the greater historical patterns of human generations and the shape of the land itself. The beauty of the abbeys is intimately bound up with their role in preserving these cycles, and providing the links between one and another. They are keys to the land's unchanging pattern, and it is for this reason that they must be recognized as not only beautiful in themselves, but as beauties of the realm.

Aske's intensely ideological answer to Cromwell's question amounts to an ideal vision of late-feudal agrarian society with all its traditions and customary rights. One fundamental feature of this vision is uniformity across historical time; society in Yorkshire is structured as it always has been and as, were it not for the suppression of the abbeys, it would always be. Equally fundamental to this vision, however, is an understanding of time as highly variegated with respect to the calendrical year. Inside the abbeys, the religious follow the pattern of the liturgical calendar; outside, agricultural

---

Since Lithgow can hardly have consulted the record of Aske's interrogation, this may indicate that this way of describing the suppressed houses had become something of a commonplace, and not in England alone.

laborers migrate with the changing seasons "betwix Yorkshir, Lancashir, Kendall, Westmoreland & the bischopreke" (561). As this varied group of place names indicates, this late feudal world was also highly variegated with respect to space. The physical topography of the north with its "montaignes & desert places" was overlaid with a complex tapestry of overlapping and incommensurate jurisdictions: crown lands, monastic estates and lordships; manors, parishes and wapentakes; commons, wastes and forests; boroughs, honours, and liberties.[14] Yorkshire itself was for some purposes a single county, for others three autonomous Ridings; to the north, the "bischopreke" of Durham had long possessed the unique status of a county palatine ruled by a prince bishop.

Aske saw himself as defending not only the smaller religious houses, but the whole world he describes in his answer. In the mid-1530s, that world had come under an unprecedented attack coordinated by the man who was now his chief interrogator, Thomas Cromwell. The traditional religious calendar had been subjected to rationalization with the elimination of many holidays, especially in the harvest season; one particularly offensive order required all churches to celebrate their patronal festivals on the same day, October 1st.[15] On a grander scale, Cromwell had embarked on the rationalization of national space, with the aim of ensuring that the king's writ ran evenly throughout his dominions. In the same year, 1536, that saw the suppression of the smaller religious houses, the first act of union between England and Wales was passed; closer to the scene of the Pilgrimage of Grace, the Archbishop of York's liberties of Beverley, Ripon, and York were eliminated, and the county palatine of Durham was stripped of its special status, with judicial supremacy passing from the Bishop to the King. The ultimate tendency of Cromwell's reforms was the transformation of his master's dominions into a realm where the state's sovereignty would be, in the words of Benedict Anderson, "fully, flatly, and evenly operative over each square centimeter of a legally demarcated

---

[14] On the complex pattern of lordship, jurisdiction, and political power in Yorkshire in this period, see R. B. Smith, *Land and Politics in the England of Henry VIII: The West Riding of Yorkshire, 1530–46* (Oxford: Oxford University Press, 1970). The landscape described by Aske exemplifies the traditional "landscape of custom" which in the sixteenth century would be increasingly challenged by the new "landscape of absolute property"; see Garrett A. Sullivan, Jr., *The Drama of Landscape: Land, Property, and Social Relations on the Early Modern Stage* (Stanford: Stanford University Press, 1998), p. 12.

[15] See Davies, "Popular Religion," p. 71; Hoyle, *Pilgrimage of Grace*, p. 85. Some churches, with important patrons, were exempt. Davies notes that one unintended effect of the new system was to bring together large and potentially disgruntled crowds at the beginning of October, a factor which may have contributed to the outbreak of the Lincolnshire rising.

territory" – in Wales as it was in Durham, in Dublin as it was in Calais.[16] A consequence of these transformations would be the abolition of a host of local customary rights upon which English people of all classes had been able to rely for as long as local memory could recall. It is little wonder that, as Aske had sought to warn Henry VIII months before, "ther is non erthly man so evill belevyd as the said Lord Cromwell is with the comyns" (343).[17]

Most of Cromwell's reforms were undertaken piecemeal, in opportunistic response to contingent pressures and events, and perhaps with no grander ends in view than to fill the royal coffers and secure his master's political and religious supremacy. Yet they did not lack for ideological underpinnings. As I argued in the previous chapter, a common thread runs through the radical legislation of the mid-1530s, a thread best defined as British nationalism. Thus, Cromwell's 1536 "Act for Recontinuing of Certain Liberties and Franchises Heretofore Taken From the Crown," which revolutionized local jurisdiction in counties like Yorkshire and Durham, rested on the same ideological basis as Henry VIII's assertion of imperial status and the annexation of Wales. In each case, what were in fact radical innovations were presented rather as pious restorations. What was supposedly being restored was the political and religious order of an imperial Britain in the early Christian era, before the arrival of pagan invaders and papal emissaries. Since then, the story went, the realm had languished in a state of ever-deepening corruption, awaiting its rescue by a Tudor king. If the people had in the meantime come to regard certain forms of corruption as "customary," it was time they were taught to see with better eyes.

By 1537, Aske's vision of the nation as variegated over space and the calendrical year but uniform across historical time was thus open to challenge from a vision which held the nation to be opposite in each respect. Whereas Aske's idyllic feudal realm was on the verge of vanishing forever (to the extent that it had ever existed), the Cromwellian agenda held

---

[16] Anderson, *Imagined Communities*, p. 19; see also Swen Voekel, "'Upon the Suddaine View': State, Civil Society and Surveillance in Early Modern England," *Early Modern Literary Studies* 4.2/ Special Issue 3, September, 1998 (journal online); available from http://purl.oclc.org/emls/04-2/ voekupon.htm; Internet.

[17] On Cromwell's drive for a "uniform legal order," see B. W. Beckingsale, *Thomas Cromwell: Tudor Minister* (London: Macmillan, 1978), pp. 79–91; for parallels between the crown's actions in the far north of England and in Ireland, see Steven G. Ellis, *Tudor Frontiers and Noble Power: The Making of the British State* (Oxford: Clarendon Press, 1995); on the transfer of power in the County Palatine of Durham, see Gaillard Thomas Lapsley, *The County Palatine of Durham: A Study in Constitutional History* (New York: Longmans, Green & Co., 1900), pp. 196–98; and on the Archbishop of York, see Smith, *Land and Politics*, p. 176.

the seeds of a world-view that is familiarly modern: one in which there is no
fundamental (in the sense of being institutionally recognized) difference
between one part of the nation and another, or between February and
October, but in which change is the constant condition of the present, and
the past is a foreign country.[18] But the gulf between Aske and Cromwell
cannot be understood solely in terms of medievalism and (early) modernity. The two men did not only look at the nation differently. They were
also looking at different nations.

Cromwell's nation, as I have argued, was the imperial Britain of
Reformation-era British nationalism. But what of Aske's? Should someone
whose references to the "realm" are so glancing, and often so uncompli-
mentary, be said to have a national identity at all? As we have seen, the
"country" (Yorkshire / the north) is generally far more prominent in Aske's
mind than anything resembling a nation. Yet at crucial moments in his
testimony – for instance, when he unexpectedly invokes beauty – the larger
"realm" suddenly emerges as a site of loyalty and concern. And in the
proclamation Aske made to the city of York before the Pilgrims entered in,
he was for once unambiguous about his loyalties: "for this pilgrimage, we
have undertaken it for the preservation of Christ's church of this realm of
England, the king our sovereign lord, the nobility and commons of the
same . . ."[19]

In some respects, then, Aske can be seen as expressing an English
national identity, and even as a kind of English nationalist. Many of his
utterances and attitudes resonate powerfully with those of certain English
writers in the nineteenth and early twentieth centuries who located the
national essence in the organic community of a "merry" medieval England.
There are elements in Aske's defense which could easily have come from
the pen of a William Cobbett, William Morris, or G. K. Chesterton, who
in different ways pined for that lost world, and hoped to see at least some

---

[18] Here Benedict Anderson, following Walter Benjamin, would speak of the rise of "homogenous
empty time" (*Imagined Communities*, p. 24). It would of course be absurd to trace the origins of
modernity to the machinations of a Thomas Cromwell. The economic and social changes which
gathered pace in England from this point probably owed less to Cromwell's rationalization of
Tudor governance than to that new breed of agricultural entrepreneur or "fermer" noticed with
dismay by Aske. The flooding of the Tudor land market in the wake of the dissolution would
greatly accelerate the transformation of the agrarian economy and, ultimately, the English
economy as a whole. See Robert Brenner, "The Agrarian Roots of European Capitalism," in
T. H. Aston and C. H. E. Philpin, eds., *The Brenner Debate: Agrarian Class Structure and Economic
Development in Pre-Industrial Europe* (Cambridge: Cambridge University Press, 1987), p. 298;
Andrew McRae, *God Speed the Plough: The Representation of Agrarian England, 1500–1660*
(Cambridge: Cambridge University Press, 1996).

[19] Quoted in Hoyle, *Pilgrimage of Grace*, pp. 456–57.

elements of it restored.[20] Even Aske's intense regionalism harmonizes with the vision of later English nationalists, since fierce pride in the region would come to be seen as a central aspect of English identity. It can thus be tempting to see Aske as an early exponent of a powerful strain of English patriotism. Yet there is one crucial difference. Aske, in declaring his aims at York, was still able to speak in terms of "preservation." For him, everything essential to the idea of "England" was still a living part of the land, though under serious threat. No later English nationalist would be able to speak in quite this way. They would speak instead in terms of "restoration." In the form of their ideology, then, they are closer to the British nationalist Cromwell than to the Englishman Robert Aske.

Yet even Aske's national vision would come, under the pressure of events, to resemble in unsettling ways that of his nemesis. There is an unmistakable shift in tone from the York proclamation and the Pilgrim's Oath, both composed in October 1536, to the testimony given in the Tower of London in the spring of 1537. In the earlier utterances, Aske speaks of those institutions the Pilgrims wished to preserve as existing in the present day, and he speaks in the present tense; the abbeys *are*, and they are under threat. In the Tower testimony, there is a shift to the past. "Also the abbeys *was* on of the bewties of this realme." (The ungrammatical form of the verb gives added prominence to the shift in tense.) Aske here seems to be lapsing into a kind of proleptic nostalgia – for it is worth bearing in mind that in 1537 most of the major monasteries were not yet under threat. The full idealization of the world for which he fought goes hand in hand with consigning it to the irrecoverable past. And it is precisely in the moment that Aske effectively acknowledges the defeat of his cause that he makes his first recorded mention of beauty. In his final utterance, Aske verges on the insight that John Bale would develop and place at the center of his national vision: that the beauty of the nation is always and by definition out of reach, belonging to a world we have lost.

---

[20] Compare Cobbett's account of what was lost with the monasteries, from the standpoint of the 1820s: "Love of country, that variety of feelings which all together constitute what we properly call patriotism, consists in part of the admiration of and veneration for ancient and magnificent proofs of skill and of opulence. The monastics built as well as wrote for posterity.... [I]n the whole of their economy, they set an example tending to make the country beautiful, to make it an object of pride with the people, and to make the nation truly and permanently great. Go into any county, and survey, even at this day, the ruins of its perhaps twenty abbeys and priories, and then ask yourself, 'what have we in exchange for these?'" William Cobbett, *A History of the Protestant Reformation*, new edition (London: R. & T. Washbourne, n.d.), pp. 114–15.

BALE'S BOOKS: "THE BEAUTY OF OUR NATION"

As Dom David Knowles concluded in his history of the monasteries, "the loss to what may be called the aesthetic capital of the nation was very great."[21] In the long run, as I have suggested, that loss seems to have been redeemed, and the abbeys are once again the beauties of the realm. Yet this transformation did not occur overnight. For at least a century after the dissolution, almost no one saw anything beautiful or sublime in the shattered husks of the religious houses. To succeeding generations they must have appeared "like the gashes in an urban landscape continuing long after the Second World War."[22] For Sir John Denham, in the middle of the seventeenth century, the ruins of Chertsey Abbey seen from Cooper's Hill remained "dismal heaps," hideous witnesses to a deed of wanton destruction.[23] The immediate effect of the dissolution, then, was to make England appear a much uglier place. The image of the broken monasteries must have flashed before the minds of many who heard Shakespeare's John of Gaunt lament, "That England that was wont to conquer others / Hath made a shameful conquest of itself" (*Richard II*, 2.1.65–66).

We need not imagine that those involved in the destruction of the abbeys were somehow blind to their beauty. The commissioner Sir Arthur Darcy, present at the suppression of Jervaulx, cast an admiring and frankly covetous eye over "one of the fairest churches that I have ever seen, fair meadows, and a river running by it." What especially attracted Darcy's admiration was the lead-covered roof which, needless to say, was swiftly stripped.[24] Whether his role in the dismantling of this fair place caused Darcy any disquiet we do not know; but there is no doubt that the loss in national beauty weighed heavy on the minds of some of the chief supporters of the dissolution. Thomas Starkey favored the suppression of the smaller houses for the good of the commonwealth, but some months before the outbreak of the Pilgrimage he issued a strikingly prescient warning to the king: "pity it were that so much fair housing and goodly building . . . should be let fall to ruin and decay, whereby our country

---

[21] Dom David Knowles, *The Religious Orders in England, Volume 3: The Tudor Age* (Cambridge: Cambridge University Press, 1959), p. 387.

[22] Margaret Aston, "English Ruins and English History: The Dissolution and the Sense of the Past," in *Lollards and Reformers: Images and Literacy in Late Medieval Religion* (London: Hambledon, 1984), p. 325.

[23] Sir John Denham, "Cooper's Hill," in *The Poetical Works of Sir John Denham*, ed. Theodore Banks, second edition (New Haven: Yale University Press, 1969), p. 73.

[24] G. H. Cook, ed., *Letters to Cromwell and Others on the Suppression of the Monasteries* (London: John Baker, 1965), p. 131.

might appear so to be defaced as [if] it had been lately overrun with enemies in time of war."[25] But neither a Starkey nor an Aske could stand in the way of the political juggernaut that – almost accidentally – reduced the ancient beauties of the realm to ruins in a remarkably short space of time. As the antiquarian William Lambarde wrote of Canterbury, the monasteries "came soudenly from great wealth, multitude of inhabitaunts, and beautiful buildings, to extreme poverty, nakednes, and decay."[26] It was an aesthetic loss from which there appeared to be no hope of recovery – unless, that is, "the beauties of the realm" could somehow be rediscovered elsewhere, safe from the catastrophe that had blighted the realm's physical landscape.

In the years before the suppression began, one of the "strangers passing through" the religious houses of north and south was John Leland. He had received his warrant from the king in 1533 "to peruse and dylygentlye to searche all the lybraryes of monasteryes and collegies of thys ... noble realme, to the entent that the monumentes of auncyent wryters ... myghte be brought out of deadly darkenesse to lyvelye lyght."[27] Leland visited more than 100 libraries, cataloguing their contents and often bringing ancient writers "to light" by appropriating them for the royal library, or his own. Significantly, the volumes he selected for the king were concentrated disproportionately in the field of early British history.[28] Leland seems to have been genuinely seduced by the vision of Henry VIII as an enlightened monarch bent on restoring the British nation to its ancient and imperial glory. He promised his king, "I trust so to open this wyndow, that the lyght shall be seane ... by the space of a whole thousand yeares stopped up, & the old glory of your renoumed Britaine to reflorish through the worlde."[29] The reference to "a whole thousand yeares" is by no means merely rhetorical. According to Geoffrey of Monmouth, King Arthur had departed for Avalon in 542, leaving his realm at the mercy of the Saxons. So when Leland, writing in the 1540s, speaks of "a whole thousand years," he means it quite literally and specifically; at the same time, the never-insignificant figure of a round millennium must have heightened the confidence of

[25] Joyce Youings, *The Dissolution of the Monasteries* (London: George Allen and Unwin, Ltd., 1971), p. 169.
[26] William Lambarde, *A Perambulation of Kent* (London, 1570), p. 236.
[27] John Bale and John Leland, *The Laboryouse Journey and Serche of Johan Leylande, for Englandes Antiquitees* (London, 1549), sig. B8r.
[28] See Jennifer Summit, "Monuments and Ruins: Spenser and the Problem of the English Library," *ELH* 70 (2003), 9.
[29] Bale and Leland, *Laboryouse Journey*, sig. E7r.

British nationalists like Leland that their generation was indeed destined to witness the long-prophesied restoration of British glory. The role Leland had assigned himself in bringing about this restoration was the recovery of documents from the Arthurian era which, he firmly believed, lay moldering on the shelves of monastic libraries.[30]

But while Leland was struggling to "open this wyndow," others were tearing down the walls. With the dissolution underway, his task became a hopeless race against time. No official provision was made to safeguard the contents of the monastic libraries. Manuscripts were robbed or bought up for use as rags, wrapping, or toilet paper. Some were simply cast to the winds; as the visitor Dr. Layton exultingly reported to Cromwell, "the second time we came to New College after we had declared your injunctions, we found all the great quadrant court full of the leaves of Dun, the wind blowing them into every corner."[31] In the midst of this continuing catastrophe, Leland preserved what he could, and devoted himself to his commentaries on British writers, compiling nearly 600 entries. And, in the late 1540s, he went insane – perhaps, as Anthony á Wood thought, because of the impossibility of the task he had set himself, and because "at the time of the dissolution of the monasteries, he saw with very great pity what havoc was made of ancient monuments of learning."[32]

The task of carrying forward Leland's many unfinished projects was left largely to John Bale, the dramatist, antiquary, and famously vituperative enemy of monks and monasteries. Bale was no stranger to the insides of monastic libraries. In his twenty years as a Carmelite friar he had compiled a history of the order, consulting libraries across England and France. Now, as Leland's literary executor, Bale set about expanding the catalogue of British writers, incorporating numerous legendary figures from the pre-Saxon era.[33] He also put into print Leland's progress report of 1546, the "New Year's Gift" to Henry VIII. Published in 1549 as *The Laboryouse*

---

[30] Leland was not alone. "The desire for positive proof of Arthur's historicity suffused post-Reformation library making" (Summit, "Monuments and Ruins," 15). Unfortunately, as Leland's own *Assertio inclytissimi Arturii Regis Britanniae* (1544) would demonstrate, there was not enough such positive evidence to fill even a single volume.

[31] Cook, ed., *Letters to Cromwell*, p. 48. On the dispersal, see C. E. Wright, "The Dispersal of the Libraries in the Sixteenth Century," in *The English Library Before 1700*, ed. Francis Wormald and C. E. Wright (London: Athlone Press, 1958), pp. 148–75.

[32] Quoted in James Simpson, "Ageism: Leland, Bale, and the Laborious Start of English Literary History," in *New Medieval Literatures, Volume I*, ed. Wendy Scase, Rita Copeland, and David Lawton (Oxford: Clarendon Press, 1997), p. 222. Simpson further suggests that Leland must have suffered a "divided consciousness," being "himself an agent of the destruction of the very past he [sought] to recuperate" (p. 222).

[33] On Bale's catalogues, see Trevor Ross, "Dissolution and the Making of the English Literary

Journey and Serche of Johan Leylande, for Englandes Antiquitees the book includes an introduction, conclusion, and frequent interpolations by Bale, all devoted to stressing the vital necessity of saving England's bibliographical heritage.

Convincing his readers to place a value on the books once housed in monastic libraries presented Bale with a tricky task. He was genuinely horrified by the fate suffered by so many volumes in the immediate aftermath of the dissolution.

A greate nombre of them whych purchased those superstycyouse mansyons, reserved of those lybrarye bokes, some to serve theyr jakes, some to scoure theyr candelstyckes, and some to rubbe their bootes. Some they solde to the grossers and sope sellers, & some they sent over see to the bokebynders, not in small nombre, but at tymes whole shyppes full, to the wonderynge of the foren nacyons.   (B1r)[34]

The market economy which took over in the wake of the desacralization of monastic property had left nothing exempt from commodification and recognized no form of value beyond immediate practical utility. Yet appalled as he was by this spectacle, Bale himself had played a leading role in demystifying monastic life and denouncing the superstitious veneration of objects. He now found himself caught, as it were, between the monks and the soap-sellers, between two opposing and equally intolerable ways of valuing manuscripts. To save his beloved books, Bale had to reinvest them with a form of value distinct from both the idols of the monastery and those of the marketplace. This value turns out to be aesthetic value.

Not once, but several times in *The Laboryouse Journey*, Bale employs a phrase that hauntingly echoes Robert Aske's description of the abbeys as "one of the beauties of this realm." But he refers not to the buildings themselves, but to the books once housed within their walls. For Bale, in other words, the destruction of the supposed beauties of the realm has brought to light the *true* beauties of the realm. These manuscripts are variously described as "precyouse antiquytees, whych are the great bewtie of our lande" (E7v), and "the landes antiquitees whyche are a most syngulare bewtye in every nacyon" (B8v). The pillaging of the libraries

---

Canon: The Catalogues of Leland and Bale," *Renaissance and Reformation* 15 (1991), 57–80; Simpson, "Ageism"; and Anne Hudson, "*Visio Balei*: An Early Literary Historian," in *The Long Fifteenth Century*, ed. Helen Cooper and Sally Mapstone (Oxford: Clarendon Press, 1997), pp. 313–29.

[34] See also John Bale, Letter to Matthew Parker, 20 July 1560, in *The Recovery of the Past in Early Elizabethan England: Documents by John Bale and John Joscelyn from the Circle of Matthew Parker*, ed. Timothy Graham and Andrea G. Watson, Cambridge Bibliographical Society Monograph 13 (Cambridge: Cambridge University Library, 1997), p. 17.

"is hyghly to be lamented of all them that hath a naturall love to their contrey, eyther yet to lerned antiquyte, whyche is a moste syngular bewty to the same" (A7v). What has survived must be preserved and published; Bale calls on every nobleman to finance the printing of an ancient manuscript, for "a more notable poynt of nobylyte can ye not shewe, than in suche sort to bewtifie your contrey" (B2v). Likewise, "lete one ryche merchaunt brynge one worthye worke of an auncyent wryter to lyght, and another put forth another, to the bewtie of our nacyon" (F6v).[35]

It is striking to find so-called "bilious" Bale, among the coarsest and most brutal of Protestant controversialists, writing so insistently of beauty. This is not to say that he writes of it in a beautiful manner. As Polonius says, "that's an ill phrase, a vile phrase, 'beautified' is a vile phrase" (*Hamlet*, 2.2.111–12). Vile or not, the phrase was in 1549 a relatively newfangled one – the first recorded instance of "beautify" in the *OED* dates only from 1526 – and this too is something of a surprise in a work by Bale, known for his "old and rude English."[36] His incessant repetition of this wooden if not vile phrase suggests that, however alien to his own style, the beautiful is central to his understanding of antiquity, and the nation. But what does he mean by "beauty" and "to beautify"?

To clear the ground, there is no difficulty in specifying what he does not mean. Bale is not celebrating the beauty of illuminated manuscripts as art objects; he repeatedly insists on the necessity of having these works printed, and he seems to have the widest and cheapest dissemination in mind. Nor is he thinking of the beauty and grace of literary language. While normally careful to harmonize his project with Leland's, he rejects Leland's call for the chronicles to be revised and embellished with humanist eloquence, preferring that they "apere fyrst of all in their owne simplycyte or native colours without bewtie of speche" (C3v).[37] Whatever the beauty of ancient manuscripts may be, it has nothing to do with either the physical pages themselves or the prose style of the words written upon them.

Bale's preferred method of defining and praising the beautiful is to contrast it with its opposite, which is not sheer ugliness so much as false

---

[35] See also Bale and Leland, *Laboryouse Journey*, sigs. A2r, B6v.

[36] Anthony á Wood, quoted in John N. King, *English Reformation Literature: The Tudor Origins of the Protestant Tradition* (Princeton: Princeton University Press, 1982), p. 59. King offers a sympathetic account of Bale as an English stylist. Bale's Latin catalogues of authors are far less concerned with the beautiful, though he occasionally praises a writer for having beautified (*ornavit*) the English language; see Hudson, "*Visio Baleii*," 327–28.

[37] On Bale's attempts to create an appearance of harmony between his own and Leland's rather different agendas, see Simpson, "Ageism," 232–33.

and transient beauty. He is in his element – and at his most bilious – as he denounces the sins and vanities, the "belly bankettes and table tryumphes" (B2r) which distract the English from contemplation of their own past. He begs his countrymen to belie their reputation abroad: "I have hearde it amonge straungers reported, that Englysh men are fryndely in thinges which lasteth not, as in bankettes and late suppers" (F8v). To this spiritual distaste for worldy luxuries, Bale adds the economic patriotism of an Edwardian commonwealth-man:

We sende to other nacyons to have their commodytees, and all is to lyttle to feade our filthye fleshe. But the syngular commodytees within our owne realme, we abhorre and throwe fourth as most vyle noysome matter. Avydyously we drynke the wines of other landes, we bye up their frutes and spyces, yea we consume in apparell their silkes & their velvettes. But alas our owne noble monumentes and precyous Antiquytees, which are the great bewtie of our lande, we as little regard as the parynges of our nayles. (E7v)

Here the beauties of the land are defined equally against all that is fleeting and all that is foreign.[38]

Yet to qualify as a "bewtie of our lande" requires more than a record of durability and a domestic origin. Bale's notion of national beauty also stands opposed to that part of the nation that is visibly manifest in landscape and in buildings.[39] Where Robert Aske had seen "the beauties of this realm," Bale recognizes only "thinges which lasteth not." No doubt with the architectural devastation of the dissolution in mind, he cautions his readers against placing faith in built structures, however ancient: "neyther the labyrinth of Dedalus, nor yet the great pyllers of Hercules, neyther yet here in England the Stoneheng of Salysbury playne" (F7v) can preserve fame as reliably as a book. Bale's impatient dismissal of the physical nation is all the more striking in that he is required to print and comment upon

---

[38] Bale's remarks on commodities find a close parallel in the *Discourse of the Commonweal of this Realm of England*, attributed to Thomas Smith, also 1549: "What number first of trifles comes hither from beyond the seas that we might either clean spare or else make them within our realm, for the which we either pay inestimable treasure every year or else exchange substantial wares and necessary for them ... What grossness of wit be we of ... that will suffer our own commodities to go and set strangers awork and then to buy them again at their hand ..."; *A Discourse of the Commonweal of This Realm of England*, ed. Mary Dewar (Charlottesville: The University Press of Virginia, 1969), pp. 63–65. The example is that of wool being exported and then bought back dearly as cloth, but Bale's example of precious manuscripts going abroad only to return in the binding of foreign books would have served just as well.

[39] "As far as landscape and architecture were concerned, Bale would never demonstrate much sensitivity"; Leslie P. Fairfield, *John Bale: Mythmaker for the English Reformation* (West Lafayette: Purdue University Press, 1976), p. 6. This is an understatement.

Leland's plans to produce a topographical description of England. Bale's tone is brisk and businesslike on the subject of Leland's *Itinerary*: such a tome would be "profytable" to men in "their necessary affayres" (D5r). There is no suggestion that either the work or the land it describes could qualify as beautiful. But the very moment the subject turns from contemporary to antiquarian geography, Bale returns eagerly to the aesthetic: "for the syngular bewtye of Englande, he calleth agayne to lyvely memory, the auncyent names of cyties, townes, castelles, hylles, havens, ryvers, and suche lyke, which have bene longe buryed in oblivion" (E7v–D8r).

If we take Bale at his word, it appears that nothing that is to be seen in England, no building, hill, or haven, ranks as a thing of beauty. Beauty resides instead only in their long-disused names. The beauty of London, for instance, is not to be found in its streets, bridges, and towers, but rather in its ancient name of Troynovant. This radical approach reveals the extent to which Bale's vision of the nation is diametrically opposed to Robert Aske's. For Bale, the nation is an entity uniform across physical space. Recognizing the tendency of Cromwell's reforms (perhaps even more clearly than did Cromwell himself), Bale writes as if the national territory were not only jurisdictionally homogenous, but effectively (and ideally) featureless and flat. To depart from this stance and recognize the possibility of topographical beauty would be to locate beauty in a part rather than in the whole, and thus to invite the confusion of national and regional loyalties.[40] (The danger of this would have been particularly apparent in 1549 when the Western Rising, to which Bale refers, reinforced the lessons of the Pilgrimage of Grace.) Even Leland's *Itinerary* would seem to be useful primarily in that it allows travelers and merchants to anticipate and circumvent the obstacles posed by inconveniently variegated topography, and so to traverse the nation as if it were indeed a uniformly flat space.

In contrast to his effective leveling of topography, and in further opposition to the ideological vision of Robert Aske, Bale presents the nation as highly differentiated across historical time. Of all Tudor reformers, Bale was the most devoted to the exhaustive periodization of British history, subdividing the standard Reformation narrative (purity–corruption–regeneration) into a sequence of distinct ages. Already in the first part of *The Actes of English Votaryes* (1546), Bale had divided the history of the English clergy into four periods whose names are suggestive of both landscape and architecture – "rising, building, holdynge, and

---

[40] See Helgerson, *Forms of Nationhood*, pp. 131–39.

falling."[41] In his celebration of Leland's "journey," Bale seems determined to substitute chronological for topographical terrain, timescape for landscape.

In his rapturous response to the revival of moribund topographical nomenclature, Bale deploys a phrase which offers a further key to his aesthetic ideology. Beauty, he makes clear, is not a property inhering in the disused names themselves but rather a consequence of their being summoned to "lively memory." Variations on this phrase recur throughout the text, as when Bale terms antiquities "lyvelye memoryalles of our nacyon" (A7v). The peculiar "liveliness" of these memorials is a crucial feature. For when Bale describes an ancient text as "lively" he does not mean that it has a vigorous style or an action-packed plot. He is using the word in its original and most literal sense: "lifelike."

That the beauty of representations consists in their truth to nature, their lifelikeness, is an ancient notion.[42] It is epitomized in Pliny's famous story of the painter Zeuxis, who depicted grapes so realistically that birds came to feed on them, and who then lamented that the boy he had painted was not lifelike enough to scare the birds away.[43] The long-lost art of lively representation was restored at the dawn of the Renaissance by Giotto – that, at least, was the story the Renaissance liked to tell about itself. As the fourteenth-century Florentine Filippo Villani wrote of Giotto, "images formed by his brush agree so well with the lineaments of nature as to seem to the beholder to live and breathe; and his pictures appear to perform actions and movements so exactly as to seem from a little way off actually speaking, weeping, rejoicing, and doing other things, not without pleasure for him who beholds."[44] The language employed to describe the pleasure derived from Giotto is the same as that applied in this period to the art of antiquity. Thus the Byzantine humanist Manuel Chrysolaras marveled at the figures depicted in relief "as if really alive" on Roman triumphal arches: "one seems to see a real man, horse, city or army . . . and real people captured or fleeing, laughing, weeping, excited or angry."[45]

[41] Fairfield, *John Bale*, p. 95. On Bale's periodization of church and national history, see Fairfield, pp. 50–120, and Andrew Hadfield, *Literature, Politics and National Identit*, pp. 51–80.
[42] And a very modern one; see Elaine Scarry, *On Beauty and Being Just* (Princeton: Princeton University Press, 1999), pp. 68–70, 80, 89–90.
[43] The story is first told in Pliny's *Natural History* and retold in the early modern era by (among others) Thomas Nashe; *The Works of Thomas Nashe*, ed. R. B. McKerrow, revised by F. P. Wilson (Oxford: Blackwell, 1958), 2.96.
[44] Villani, *De origine civitatis Florentiae et eiusdem famosis civibus* (1381–2), quoted and translated in Michael Baxandall, *Giotto and the Orators: Humanist Observers of Painting in Italy and the Discovery of Pictorial Composition, 1350–1450*, corrected edition (Oxford, 1986), p. 70.
[45] Chrysolaras, letter to John VIII Palaeologus (c. 1411), quoted and translated in Baxandall, *Giotto and the Orators*, p. 81.

Francis Petrarch also saw ancient Romans moving and speaking "as if really alive." He saw them not on triumphal arches, however, but in his mind's eye, stirred by the sad spectacle of Rome's crumbling ruins. "Here was the dwelling of Evander . . . here the cave of Cacus, here the nourishing she-wolf."[46] The vestiges of ancient greatness fill Petrarch with an almost intolerable longing to recapture the past, to make the Rome that is lost forever live again. Similarly, in Mantua he searches for signs of the poet Virgil: "Constantly I wonder where it was that you rested upon the sloping sward, or that, reclining in moments of fatigue, you pressed with your elbow the grassy turf or upon the marge of a charming spring. Such thoughts as these bring you before my eyes."[47] It is not the landscape itself which succeeds in conjuring the image of Virgil but rather the poet's own impossible desire, expressed in fruitless questioning of hill and stream. Petrarch is blessed – or cursed – with what Bale would later term a "lively memory." Desire works upon his mind so powerfully that its eternally lost object, be it Evander or Virgil or his beloved Laura, seems almost to live again.

Longing for the lost object of desire, longing so intense that it seems almost capable of making what is absent present or conjuring the dead, is the thread that unites Petrarch's humanist writings with his poetry of love. In sonnet 78, he experiences the familiar surge of yearning when faced with Simone Martini's wonderfully lifelike portrait of Laura:

If he had given to his noble work voice and intellect along with form, he would have lightened my breast of many sighs that make what others prize most vile to me. For in appearance she seems humble, and her expression promises peace; then, when I come to speak to her, she seems to listen most kindly: if she could only reply to my words! Pygmalion, how glad you should be of your statue, since you received a thousand times what I yearn to have just once![48]

---

[46] Petrarch, Letter to Giovanni Colonna (*Rerum familiarum*, VI.2), in *Rerum familiarum libri I–VIII*, trans. and ed. Aldo S. Bernardo (Albany: State University of New York Press,1975), p. 291. See Thomas Greene, *The Light in Troy: Imitation and Discovery in Renaissance Poetry* (New Haven: Yale University Press, 1982), p. 88; Giuseppe Mazzotta, "Antiquity and the New Arts in Petrarch," in *The New Medievalism*, ed. Marina S. Brownlee, Kevin Brownlee, Stephen G. Nicholls (Baltimore: Johns Hopkins University Press, 1991), pp. 46–69. Erwin Panofsky's assertion that "Even the ruins of Rome failed to evoke in [Petrarch] what we would call an 'aesthetic' response" is true in the literal sense that Petrarch did not find the ruins themselves aesthetically appealing – but the visions they prompted in his mind were undoubtedly aesthetic; *Renaissance and Renascences in Western Art* (New York: Harper & Row), p. 11.

[47] Petrarch, to Publius Virgilius Maro (*Rerum familiarum*, XXIV.11), *Letters on Familiar Matters / Rerum familiarum libri XVII–XXIV*, trans. and ed. Aldo S. Bernardo (Baltimore: Johns Hopkins University Press, 1985), p. 341. See Greene, *Light in Troy*, p. 90.

[48] From *Rima* 78, in *Petrarch's Lyric Poems: The* Rime Sparse *and Other Lyrics*, trans. and ed. Robert M. Durling (Cambridge, MA: Harvard University Press, 1976), p. 178.

The artwork remains as silent and uncompliant as the Mantuan landscape. But this is by no means a criticism of Martini's painting, which Petrarch praises in sonnet 77 for its unearthly beauty. The painting's success – its beauty – lies precisely in its power to excite longing in the beholder's breast; fulfilling that desire is not part of its business. This was the most important lesson that Renaissance artists and aesthetes derived from Petrarch. As Elizabeth Cropper has argued of the High Renaissance, "Petrarchan aesthetics and ideals . . . were integrally bound up with the production of beautiful images . . . At the turn of the century, the expression of desire for the impossible object . . . became both the means and ends of painting, as it was for poetry."[49] The traditional compliment paid to the lifelike figure, that it lacks nothing but the power of speech, was more and more often expressed as longing that the image would, in fact, speak.[50] Vasari reports of Donatello that while working on his greatest statue he kept muttering, "Speak, damn you, speak!"[51] But what Donatello sought was not the actual fulfillment of Pygmalion's desire so much as to bring to the marble the imprint of that impossible yearning. For Donatello and his audience, frustrated longing for the irrecoverable was another name for beauty. By the second half of the sixteenth-century, such a response would come naturally to an English humanist such as Daniel Rogers, who wrote of Veronese's portrait of Philip Sidney, "When I look at that image, so like your own nature, it looks back at me with eloquent eyes. But oh, why is it muter than a silent fish, why does it not speak?"[52]

Such sophisticated if not masochistic Petrarchan pleasures may seem a long way from the world of Bale – and even further, surely, from the world of Robert Aske. Yet there are unmistakable resonances between High Renaissance aesthetic theory and late medieval popular piety. The longing gaze that worshipers fixed on images of the Virgin and various saints provoked the rage of Protestant reformers, culminating in the burning of

---

[49] Elizabeth Cropper, "The Place of Beauty in the High Renaissance and its Displacement in the History of Art," in *Place and Displacement in the Renaissance*, ed. Alvin Vos, Medieval & Renaissance Texts & Studies 132 (Binghamton: Medieval & Renaissance Texts & Studies, 1995), p. 192.

[50] See Giorgio Vasari, *Lives of the Artists: Volume 1*, trans. George Bull (Harmondsworth: Penguin, 1987), for the compliment paid to Masaccio (128), Donatello (189), Bramantino (193), and Fra Filippo Lippi (222).

[51] Vasari, *Lives of the Artists*, p. 178.

[52] Quoted in J. A. Van Dorsten, *Poets, Patrons and Professors : Sir Philip Sidney, Daniel Rogers and the Leiden Humanists* (Leiden: Leiden University Press, 1962), p. 56. For the English translation of Rogers's "In effigiem illustrissimi iuvenis D. Philippi Sydnaei" (1577?), see pp. 55–56, and for the Latin original, pp. 174–75.

a number of famous and venerated images as "idols" at Smithfield in 1538.[53] There was undoubtedly a significant aesthetic element in popular devotion to such images, as evidenced by Roger Martin's memory of the pre-Reformation furnishings of the church at Long Melford, which included a representation of Christ's passion, "lively and beautifully set forth," and an image of Our Lady, "the tears as it were running down pitifully upon her beautiful cheeks."[54] Nor was Martin alone in imagining, as he clearly did, that those tears might really flow. Late medieval Christianity abounds with pious versions of the Pygmalion story, in which holy statues come wonderfully to life.[55] The Protestant response was to trace such tales to monkish trickery. At the suppression of Boxley Abbey, its venerated Rood of Grace was found to contain "certain engines and old wire, with old rotten sticks ... that did cause the eyes ... to move and stare in the head thereof like unto a living thing; and also the nether lip in likewise to move as though it should speak."[56] Such mechanical effects were clearly designed to facilitate and intensify the same longing gaze which worshipers elsewhere fixed on less animated images, a gaze which could surely have expressed itself in the words of Daniel Rogers: "When I look at that image, so like your own nature, it looks back at me with eloquent eyes. But oh, why is it muter than a silent fish, why does it not speak?"

Bale was anything but unaware of the power of this gaze. As recently as 1536 he had been Prior of the Carmelite house at Doncaster, whose Image of Our Lady, among the most venerated in the country, was one of those burned at Smithfield just two years later. Now a confirmed and radical Protestant, Bale recognized the need to find a new and worthier object for the gaze that could no longer fix on images and abbeys. He found this object in the literary records of British antiquity. In classic Protestant manner, Bale sought to replace the false shows and spectacles of Catholicism with the truth of texts – texts viewed, in this case, through the lens of Petrarchan desire.

---

[53] John Phillips, *The Reformation of Images: Destruction of Art in England, 1535–1660* (Berkeley: University of California Press, 1973), p. 75.

[54] Roger Martin, "The State of Melford Church and our Ladie's Chappel at the East End, as I did know it," in *The Spoil of Melford Church: The Reformation in a Suffolk Parish*, ed. David Dymond and Clive Paine (Ipswich: Salient Press, 1992), pp. 1, 2. See also Eamon Duffy, *The Stripping of the Altars: Traditional Religion in England, c. 1400–c. 1580* (New Haven: Yale University Press, 1992), p. 38.

[55] Michael Camille, *The Gothic Idol: Ideology and Image-Making in Medieval Art* (Cambridge: Cambridge University Press, 1989), pp. 220–41, 317–37.

[56] Letter of Geoffrey Chamber to Thomas Cromwell, 7 February 1538, in Cook, ed., *Letters to Cromwell*, p. 145.

At the time of writing *The Laboryouse Journey* Bale was immersed in Petrarchan ideas, perhaps more than he realized. He was John Leland's literary executor during his madness, and Leland, more than anyone then alive in England, could respond to Petrarch's legacy in all its complexity. As a close friend of Sir Thomas Wyatt and a mediocre versifier himself, Leland knew Petrarch as a poet. In a sequence of funeral songs on his friend's death, he names Wyatt as England's Petrarch, and one poem in particular seems to echo Petrarch's praise of Simone Martini:

> Holbein, the chiefest of that curious Art,
> Drew Wiat's *lively image* in each part
> With matchlesse skill; but no Apelles can
> Pourtray the witt and spiritt of that man.[57]

Leland was also an admirer of Petrarch the antiquarian and preserver of manuscripts. *De viris illustribus*, the title Leland gives to his catalogue of English authors in his *New Year's Gift*, is borrowed from Petrarch, as is the ubiquitous metaphor of antiquarian study as illumination ("out of deadly darkness to lively light").[58]

It is unlikely that Bale's spirit could ever have warmed to Petrarch as a poet. Indeed, he regarded poor Leland's "poetycall wytt" (B4r) as a principal cause of his madness. He may, in spite of a deep anti-Italian bias, have had more time for Petrarch as an antiquarian, sharing his love of manuscripts and his conviction that one should honor the ancients "by making their obscure names well known."[59] But Bale's principle debt to Petrarch lies in a simple realization. The gaze that fixes on a beautiful and lifelike work of art and the gaze that bores into the ancient past are one and the same. Both produce aesthetic gratification out of a longing for the irrecoverable, both fix on those who must be forever silent, and yearn for them to speak. The Petrarch who wished for the painting of Laura to reply to his words is the same man who clasped to his bosom a manuscript of Homer in Greek (a language he never mastered), and sighed "Oh great man, how willingly would I listen to you!"[60] The force of this impossible longing still

---

[57] Kenneth Muir, *Life and Letters of Sir Thomas Wyatt*, (Liverpool: Liverpool University Press, 1963), p. 261 (my emphasis). Muir's edition includes all of Leland's funeral songs for Wyatt (Appendix A).

[58] Ross, "Dissolution," 64.

[59] Greene, *Light in Troy*, p. 312, n. 29.

[60] Petrarch, Letter to Nicholas Sygeros (*Rerum familiarum*, XVIII.2), in *Letters on Familiar Matters / Rerum familiarum libri XVII–XXIV*, p. 46.

resonates down the centuries. "I began with the desire to speak with the dead."[61] "Speak, damn you, speak!"

Bale recognized that the "lively memorials" of antiquity could serve as objects of beauty in the desiring gaze, in the manner of the lifelike painting of Laura or an Image of Our Lady. Of course, he must also have recognized that these textual beauties differed from paintings, images and physical ruins in one crucial way. They *could* speak. No thinker of the Reformation era could fail to be alert to the unique power of language, unlike all other modes of representation, to render the object of its representation present.[62] Possibly, then, in his program for the beautification of the nation through the publication of these beauties, Bale hoped to combine the pleasures of Petrarch with the joys of Pygmalion. If only these books were in print! Then, at last, the image would speak, the statue would move, the irrecoverable object of desire could be and would be recovered.[63]

This would be a relatively straightforward way of understanding what Bale means by "beautify." The project of recovering and restoring Britain's beauties through the dissemination of texts would harmonize with the optimistic (or naïve) British nationalism of Thomas Cromwell and John Leland. Yet there are reasons for doubting whether Bale's intentions were ever so straightforward. For one thing, if he truly believed that the nation could be transformed through the printing of ancient texts, he would presumably have done something about it. Bale was extraordinarily prolific, and his historical and bibliographical writings, including the massive *Catalogus*, run to thousands of pages. Not one printed page of Gildas, Nennius, Asser, Bede, or any other ancient author can be set in the scales

[61] Stephen Greenblatt, *Shakespearean Negotiations: The Circulation of Social Energy in Renaissance England* (Berkeley: University of California Press, 1988), p. 1. As Greenblatt's opening remark suggests, Petrarchan preoccupations continue to inform the project of literary studies.

[62] As Erasmus wrote in his *Paraclesis*, the treatise that inspired William Tyndale, "If anyone shows us the footprints of Christ . . . how we adore them! But why do we not venerate instead the living and breathing likeness of Him in these books? . . . [A]ny paltry image . . . represents only the form of the body – if indeed it represents anything of Him – but these writings bring you the living image of His holy mind, and the speaking, healing, dying, rising Christ Himself, and thus they render Him so fully present that you would see less if you gazed upon Him with your very eyes"; *Christian Humanism and the Reformation: Selected Writings of Erasmus*, ed. John C. Olin, 3rd edition (New York: Fordham University Press, 1987), p. 108. To substitute "England" for "Christ" is to come (almost sacrilegiously) close to Bale's tone in *The Laboryouse Journey*.

[63] Such visions are, as Katherine Eggert argues in relation to *Henry V*, characteristic of *supernostalgia*, "the fantastic irrational desires to which nostalgia, when intensified to the point of supersaturation, gives way: that the past may return, that the dead are indeed alive"; Katherine Eggert, "Nostalgia and the Not Yet Late Queen: Refusing Female Rule in *Henry V*," *ELH* 61 (1994), 537.

against this weight. Bale did nothing, in other words, to gratify the desire which so much of his writing is calculated to heighten.

At different points in his career, Bale offered various excuses for his failure to produce the goods in terms of published memorials of antiquity. Yet while there can be no denying that he suffered terrible setbacks – including the dissolution itself, the loss of his personal library when he fled his post as Bishop of Ossory at the accession of Mary Tudor, and years of subsequent exile – this succession of crises cannot quite account for his failure to carry through with the publication project envisioned in *The Laboryouse Journey*. The fact that he continued to work on his catalogues while in exile in the mid-1550s demonstrates that he retained both his antiquarian interests and access to old books. The real reason for his reticence may lie in the fact that he never had the *right* old books. Even in 1549, Bale may have begun to suspect that the texts dearest to the heart of any British nationalist – the Bible in the old British vernacular, records of the ancient empire, the lost "source" of Geoffrey of Monmouth – simply did not exist. Publishing them was therefore out of the question. But desiring them, longing for them with a painful patriotic ardor, was another matter altogether.[64] In short, Bale's project of national beautification in *The Laboryouse Journey* may have less to do with the production of printed texts than with the production of nostalgia.

"Nostalgia," the name we now give to the yearning for the irrecoverable past, was not yet a word in 1549, but as many scholars have emphasized, it had a constant place in early modern thought – more particularly after the traumatic break with the customary past entailed by the Reformation and the dissolution of the monasteries.[65] The term aptly describes what Petrarch feels when he thinks of Laura or Evander, as well as what Bale feels when he muses on learning in the age of Alcuin and sighs, "Muche altered are we from that golden worlde, now adayes" (F2v). But Petrarch and Bale were both well aware that it is in the nature of nostalgia to misidentify the object of its desire. As David Lowenthal argues, nostalgia

---

[64] In his last years, Bale was associated with the circle of Matthew Parker, which finally succeeded in publishing a small handful of ancient books, more than a decade after Bale's death. In his letter to Parker (op. cit.), Bale recounted the succession of public and private catastrophes which had stood in the way of his antiquarian pursuits.

[65] See Phyllis Rackin, *Stages of Histoy: Shakespeare's English Chronicles* (Ithaca: Cornell University Press, 1990); Eggert, "Nostalgia"; Richard Hillman, *Intertextuality and Romance in Renaissance Drama: The Staging of Nostalgia* (London: Macmillan, 1992). For Erwin Panofsky, a "nostalgic vision born of a sense of estrangement as well as a sense of affinity . . . is the very essence of the Renaissance"; *Renaissance and Renascences*, p. 210. For the history of the term, see Jean Starobinski, "The Idea of Nostalgia," *Diogenes* 54 (1966), 84–103.

always conjures "a past that was unified and comprehensible, unlike the incoherent, divided present . . . what we are nostalgic for is the condition of *having been*, with a concomitant integration and completeness lacking in any present."[66] The nostalgic image of the past incites longing precisely because it is *not* like life, but is rather *lifelike*, or, as Bale would put it, "lively."

Even were they to be published and disseminated across the land, the ancient manuscripts Bale calls beautiful could never fulfill the desire they provoke. This is because that desire is neither for the words on the page (which can be reproduced), nor for the long-vanished world they describe (which cannot), but rather for the perceived integration of those words and that world. As Janet Sorensen argues, "the nationalist nostalgic" conjures "a mythic past where experience mystically mirrored – even joined – linguistic description."[67] In the nostalgized past, unlike the fragmented present, words are things. And this applies above all to that word which Bale is determined to present as a thing: the nation. Bale never speaks simply of the beauty of antiquity, but always of antiquity as the beauty of the land, or the country, or the nation. The ancient chronicles are beauties of the nation because in them the nation is realized as a thing and presented to the desiring, nostalgic gaze as integrated, unified, graspable, lifelike.

---

[66] David Lowenthal, "Nostalgia Tells It Like It Wasn't," in *The Imagined Past: History and Nostalgia*, ed. Christopher Shaw and Malcolm Chase (Manchester: Manchester University Press, 1989), p. 29. Once again there is a parallel with contemporary discourses of painting and lifelikeness. As Richard Halpern remarks of the famous tale of Zeuxis and his painted grapes, "the unsatisfied hunger of the birds indicates *their own emptiness* in relation to the image, which is complete unto itself. In the paradoxical ontology of the artwork, it is the real birds who are hollow and the painted grapes that are full"; Richard Halpern, " 'Pining their Maws': Female Readers and the Erotic Ontology of the Text in Shakespeare's *Venus and Adonis*" in *Venus and Adonis: Critical Essays*, ed. Philip C. Kolin (New York: Garland, 1997), p. 383.

[67] Janet Sorensen, "Writing Historically, Speaking Nostalgically: The Competing Languages of Nation in Scott's *The Bride of Lammermoor*" in *Narratives of Nostalgia, Gender and Nationalism*, ed. Jean Pickering and Suzanne Kehde (New York: New York University Press, 1997), p. 37. Similarly, Susan Stewart argues that "In order to entertain an antiquarian sensibility, a rupture in historical consciousness must have occurred, creating a sense that one can make one's own culture *other* – distant and discontinuous. Time must be seen as concomitant with a loss of understanding, a loss which can be relieved through the reawakening of objects and, thereby, of narrative"; *On Longing: Narratives of the Miniature, the Gigantic, the Souvenir, the Collection* (Durham, NC: Duke University Press, 1996), p. 142. Both Sorensen and Stewart associate this "nationalist nostalgic" or "antiquarian sensibility" with the era of Romanticism. Yet a markedly similar sensibility developed in the early modern period as a result of advances in Biblical scholarship (a subject naturally close to Bale's Protestant heart). "Humanist scholarship . . . designed to retrieve the exemplary past from the ravages of time, unearthed alien cultures fixed in time. Yet although unfamiliar, the rediscovered visage remained . . . the matrix of early modern identity. The estrangement of the past did not destroy the longing for it"; Debora Kuller Shuger, *The Renaissance Bible: Scholarship, Sacrifice, and Subjectivity* (Berkeley: University of California Press, 1994), p. 53.

Throughout *The Laboryouse Journey,* Bale insists that antiquity will be honored by "all them that hath a naturall love to their contrey (A7v).[68] The implication is that these people constitute the vast majority. Bale's confidence seems remarkable, considering that twelve years before Robert Aske had used "the country" to mean his county (a usage that survived long after), and that for many people in 1549 the nation would still have seemed a less natural repository for affections than either Kent on the one hand or Christendom on the other. In fact, Bale is quite wittingly reversing cause and effect. For him, love of country emerges out of a longing for antiquity, not the other way around. British antiquity holds out the promise of making love of Britain natural, by presenting the lost nation as an object of desire in the nostalgic gaze.

As Edmund Burke had it, "To make us love our country, our country ought to be lovely." He need only have added, "to make our country lovely, it must be forever lost." An approach to nationalism founded in the unfulfillable longing for an irrecoverable object may seem needlessly convoluted and, indeed, perverse. In fact, however, it is this very aspect of Bale's British nationalism that is most prescient of modern forms. As Eric Hobsbawm remarks, "nationalism comes before nations."[69] From the historian's point of view, this means that nations are invented and brought into being by nationalists. From the nationalist's own point of view, it means that the nation which anciently existed but which has more recently been dead or sleeping must be revived (through the restoration of ancient liberties, dignity, customs, borders, etc.). Nationalism is the project of bringing a nation into being, and one of its prerequisites is thus the *absence* of a fully realized nation. (A nationalism that accomplished its project would presumably wither away, but this has never happened.) To be a nationalist, then, is to experience forever the longing of Petrarch, and to be forever denied – perhaps fortunately, after all – the joys of Pygmalion.

[68] For variations of this phrase, see also sigs. A2ᵛ, B6ʳ⁻ᵛ, B7ʳ, D8ʳ, E3ᵛ, E7ʳ.
[69] E. J. Hobsbawm, *Nations and Nationalism since 1780,* p. 10.

CHAPTER 3

"Awake, lovely Wales":
national identity and cultural memory

In February of 1574, the young Philip Sidney, at rest in Padua in the course of his continental tour, received a letter from his mentor, Hubert Languet. Having dispensed the usual stiff dose of moral and scholarly advice, the Huguenot intellectual adopted a more playful tone to report his reading of a certain author who

would think he had received great injury at my hands if I should call him English, because he again and again declares that he is Welsh, not English. His name is Humphrey Lhuyd, and he is, if not really learned, at any rate well read, though he occasionally makes judgments which seem to lack common sense...You are fortunate that your ancestors came from France, for he says that the Saxons from whom the English descend were nothing but pirates and robbers.[1]

The book Languet had been reading was Humphrey Llwyd's recently published *Commentarioli Brittanicae descriptionis fragmentum* (Cologne, 1572; translated into English by Thomas Twyne in 1573 as *The Breviary of Britain*). The unfinished final work of the esteemed Welsh humanist, geographer, and antiquarian, Llwyd's survey of Britain had been undertaken at the request of the atlas-maker, Abraham Ortelius. The *Fragmentum* included a robust defense of Geoffrey of Monmouth against the skepticism of two foreign historians, the Italian Polydore Vergil and the Scot Hector Boece. It was one aspect of this defense which particularly incensed Languet. As he complains in the letter to Sidney, Llwyd had "stolen" from the French their ancient Gaulish leader Brennus and turned him into a Welshman. In other words, Llwyd followed Geoffrey in insisting that the Brennus who sacked Rome in the fourth century BC was in fact

---

[1] Translated from the Latin in James M. Osborn, *Young Philip Sidney* (New Haven: Yale University Press, 1972), p. 140.

"a perfect Britayne."[2] Languet had not been slow in exacting revenge for this national insult, albeit unconsciously:

> While I was drowsily extending my reading of the good Welshman deep into the night, it somehow happened that my candle ignited the book, and since it had not yet been bound, a good part of it was burned before I could extinguish the fire ... I was on the point of sending you the scorched remains of my poor Welsh man so that you might have your Griffin, his countryman, conduct his funeral; you would, however, solemnize it with a laugh. So, I entreat you, commission Griffin to write an epicede for him in Welsh, and send it to me.[3]

As far as we know, Griffin Madox, Sidney's Welsh serving-man, did not take up the pen on this occasion. Nevertheless, he was on hand, as a good valet must be, to help his master out of a tight spot. Languet's letter placed Sidney in an awkward position. Sidney himself was never an avowed British nationalist, and would probably have been more than willing to accept the intellectual case against Geoffrey of Monmouth.[4] He knew as well that the continued allegiance of the English to Brutus the Trojan, at a time when other European peoples had relinquished their own mythical Trojan founders, made them a laughing-stock among continental scholars. On the other hand, he was the son of Sir Henry Sidney, who as Lord President of the Council in the Marches of Wales displayed a pronounced interest in British antiquity and Welsh scholarship such as Llwyd's. He understood the national insult entailed when a foreign scholar (such as Polydore Vergil) dared to question Britain's hallowed historical traditions. And he knew as well how central the figure of Brennus in particular had become to England's imperial claims and to militant English Protestantism. This, after all, was the very "Englishman" (in the Duke of Norfolk's phrase) "who had conquered Rome."[5]

---

[2] Humphrey Llwyd, *The Breviary of Britaine*, trans. Thomas Twyne (London, 1573), fol 53[r].

[3] Osborn, *Young Philip Sidney*, p. 141.

[4] Katherine Duncan-Jones suggests of Sidney that "like many Elizabethans of his generation and later, he may have regarded the earlier Tudor cult of ancient Britain as a bit of a joke"; "Sidney in Samothea Yet Again," *RES* 38 (1987), 227. But in another place, and with no necessary contradiction, Duncan-Jones observes that "Languet seems to have been unimaginative about how deeply even the most sophisticated Elizabethans were attached to Tudor claims for the Celtic roots of British culture, and his attempt to make Sidney laugh may have served only to make him bristle"; *Sir Philip Sidney: Courtier Poet* (London: Hamish Hamilton, 1991), pp. 72–73.

[5] See chapter 1. Throughout the sixteenth century and well into the seventeenth, Brennus remained a figure for Britain's independence from, rivalry with, and primordial superiority to Rome. Spenser devotes a stanza to his and his brother's conquests in *The Faerie Queene* (II.x.40). In Jasper Fisher's *Fuimus Troes, or The True Trojans* (1633), the ghost of Brennus watches over the British resistance to the Roman invasion and boasts of his earlier and greater conquest: "Rome, proudest Rome / We cloath'd in skarlet of patrician blood" (sig. A3r). See see Curran, *Roman Invasions*, pp. 125–29.

In his reply to Languet, Sidney sets about the delicate task of redeeming Llwyd (whom he terms "our poor Cambro-Briton") and, more importantly, Brennus without appearing to care very much about either. His anxiety to disassociate himself from the whole business is clear despite the affected breeziness of his tone. "Where he maintains that the Saxons were pirates and robbers, you see, I readily grant him everything, strong in the awareness of my French heritage." Next, in a laboriously witty passage, Sidney warns Languet that the Welsh magician John Dee will take supernatural vengeance for this mockery of "his blood brother." Finally, and with evident relief, he invokes the testimony of his Welshman-in-waiting, Griffin Madox.

Griffin has spoken many things in Master Lhuyd's memory and has given a kind of funeral oration which I solemnized with laughter. In order to efface the brand of stupidity with which you stamp the good Lhuyd, he says, among other things, that so far as Brennus is concerned, Lhuyd was wholly correct, and he proves this from Brennus's name; for in their ancient British language, Brennus meant king and was as common among them as Pharaoh or Ptolemy among the Egyptians ... By this perhaps feeble reasoning he concludes that the celebrated robber was his countryman. Let me prevail upon you to concede this.

But I have written all this in jest. Joking aside ...[6]

And with that Sidney shifts the subject to more ostensibly serious matters.

Griffin Madox offers Sidney his last and best hope of wriggling out of Languet's trap. It is the Welshman, not his master, who speaks in Llwyd's memory and offers the proof that Brennus was indeed a Briton. Sidney, meanwhile, represents himself as laughing indulgently and accuses his servant of "feeble reasoning" before abruptly asking Languet to concede the point. The comic Welshman is called upon to draw fire, defending the crucial yet indefensible position of the Matter of Britain and heroically sacrificing his own dignity for the sake of his English master. Yet Sidney ultimately robs Madox of more than his dignity. He also robs him, paradoxically, of Brennus. In his reply, Languet is diplomatic enough to bow to Sidney's request and concede the point of Brennus' nationality. Yet in archly offering "a few other robbers of this sort from French history to adopt into *your nation*," Languet makes it clear that he recognizes the

[6] Osborn, *Young Philip Sidney*, p. 145.

Englishman's stake in the debate.[7] Sidney has saved Brennus, not for Madox's Welsh nation, but for an English-authored, English-dominated Britain.

There is, of course, no way of knowing whether Griffin Madox ever spoke the words reported in Sidney's letter. English writers have a long history of "ventriloquizing" Welsh voices where required to negotiate a sticky patch of national self-definition.[8] Nevertheless, Madox's predicament in the letter is representative in several respects of the problems and possible courses confronting Welsh intellectuals in the Tudor era. Welsh scholars were all too familiar with finding themselves exposed to foreign ridicule on the one hand and English appropriation on the other. Humphrey Llwyd offers a case in point. His *Breviary of Britaine* contains what has been identified as the first use of the soon-to-be famous phrase "British Empire." Llwyd was also the first to record the tradition of the Welsh prince Madoc and his discovery and settlement of America in the twelfth century. Both "British Empire" and the Madoc story were swiftly disseminated and popularized in England, initially by the border-straddling John Dee and subsequently by a host of imperially minded British nationalists.[9] Yet while key elements of British imperial ideology were lifted from his work (and twisted out of recognition in the process) by English writers, it was Llwyd who became the butt of mockery abroad. Like Madox, part of the service he performed was to draw foreign fire. Not far behind Languet in pouring scorn on "our poor Cambro-Briton" was the Scot George Buchanan, who derided "all the Hodge-Podge trash of *Llud,* raked by him out of the Dunghil, Collections good for nothing but to be laughed at, and to disparage the Collector."[10]

The deeper dilemma confronted by Griffin Madox is again representative of the problem faced by all Welsh scholars in this era. How do you demonstrate a credible relationship between the present and the ancient past when the books you need for the purpose have gone up in flames? The task imposed upon the Welsh intellectual community in reassembling their nation's bibliographical heritage was even more daunting than that facing

[7] Osborn, *Young Philip Sidney,* p. 150. Italics mine.
[8] See Schwyzer, "British History."
[9] Bruce Ward Henry, "John Dee, Humphrey Llwyd, and the Name 'British Empire,'" *Huntington Library Quarterly* 35 (1971–72), 189–90. See also Gwyn A. Williams, *Madoc: The Making of a Myth* (Oxford: Oxford University Press, 1987), pp. 39–40; Gwyn A. Williams, *Welsh Wizard and British Empire: Dr. John Dee and a Welsh Identity* (Cardiff: University College Cardiff Press, 1980); and Sherman, *John Dee.*
[10] George Buchanan, *Buchanan's History of Scotland* (London, 1735), p. 6.

the English after the Reformation. Indeed, a Welsh reader of Bale's lament at the destruction of the monastic libraries might have taken some grim satisfaction in reflecting that now the English, too, knew how it felt for a nation to lose its books. As Richard Davies lamented, "never was there a nation so badly off for books and knowledge in their own language as the Welsh."[11]

For the Welsh, as for Bale, the discovery of just two books would have made up for the loss of all the rest. But these two books did not exist – and in all probability never had. The first book was the Bible in the British vernacular, which Protestant scholars argued must have existed in the centuries before the British church was tainted by the corruption of Rome. If recovered, it would prove beyond doubt that the early British church had been the true church, and that the English Reformation was not an innovation but a restoration. The second book was the famous *vetustissimus liber*, that very ancient book in the British tongue which, Geoffrey of Monmouth claimed, he had translated into Latin as the *Historia Regum Britanniae*. If discovered, it would confute the skeptics by demonstrating that Geoffrey was not a cunning fabulist but the faithful translator of a true history.

Needless to say, neither of these books was recovered in the sixteenth century, nor has there been any sign of them since. Yet the desire for them was constitutive of both Welsh and Anglo-British nationalism in the Tudor era, and deeds performed in the name of that desire had a crucial impact on the subsequent development of Welsh national identity. Although the recovery of Welsh antiquity was a joint project in which several generations of scholars were engaged, often in collaboration, this chapter will be chiefly concerned with the efforts of two individuals, the antiquarian Sir John Prise of Breconshire, and Richard Davies, Bishop of St. David's.[12] The former focused his attention on the lost *vetustissimus liber*, while the latter pursued the recovery (through re-translation) of the Welsh Bible. In their works, we find the Welsh nation conceived and

---

[11] Richard Davies, "Address to the Welsh People" translated in Albert Owen Evans, *A Memorandum Concerning the Legality of the Welsh Bible and the Welsh Version of the Book of Common Prayer* (Cardiff: William Lewis, 1925), p. 95. Except where noted, all translated passages from the addresses by Davies and Salesbury prefixed to the Welsh New Testament of 1567 follow Evans's translations. References to the original Welsh are to *Testament Newydd* (London, 1567).

[12] On Welsh historical and antiquarian scholarship in the sixteenth century, see R. Geraint Gruffydd, "The Renaissance and Welsh Literature," in *The Celts and the Renaissance: Tradition and Innovation*, ed. Glanmor Williams and Robert Owen Jones (Cardiff: University of Wales Press, 1990), pp. 17–39; Ceri Davies, *Latin Writers of the Renaissance* (Cardiff: University of Wales Press, 1981).

constituted as a community of longing, united by a collective orientation toward its own vanished antiquity.

THE SHADOW OF YSGOLAN

To sixteenth-century Welsh scholars, their nation's history had the appearance of a succession of bibliocausts. As early as the sixth century, the British monk Gildas had lamented that "literary remains from this country . . . such as they were, are not now available, having been burnt by enemies or removed by our countrymen when they went into exile."[13] A second and more systematic destruction of British books was thought by Protestants to have occurred after St. Augustine's conversion of the Saxons to the Roman faith. The third occasion came when, according to bardic tradition, Edward I imprisoned all the vanquished nobility of Wales in the Tower of London; the bored nobles gathered a great collection of Welsh books in their prison where, in the course of time, they were burned. The humanist William Salesbury, who records this tradition, goes on to explain that even those books that escaped this disaster were reprieved for a short time only, for in the course of Owain Glyndwr's rebellion they were "in like maner destroyed & utterly devastat, or at the least wyse that there escaped not one, that was not uncurablye maymed, and irrecuparablye torne and mangled."[14] Still to come, less than a century and a half later, was the general destruction of libraries in the course of the dissolution of the monasteries, which was at least as devastating for Wales as it was for England. Hubert Languet can hardly have suspected, when he let Humphrey Llwyd's treatise to go up in flames, that he was simply adding insult to a relentless string of historical injuries.

At some point, the repeated immolation of the books of Wales became associated with the deeds of a single legendary malefactor, the mysterious Ysgolan.[15] The earliest surviving version of the Ysgolan legend in Welsh, in the twelfth-century Black Book of Carmarthen, describes him as a sinister

---

[13] Gildas, *The Ruin of Britain and Other Documents*, ed. and trans. Michael Winterbottom (London: Phillimore, 1978), p. 17.
[14] William Salesbury, *A Briefe and a Playne Introduction, teachyng how to pronounce the letters of the British tong* (London, 1550), sig. E2ᵛ.
[15] See A. O. H. Jarman, "Cerdd Ysgolan," *Ysgrifau Beirniadol* 10 (1977), 51–78. See also Gruffydd, "The Renaissance and Welsh Literature," pp. 19–20. The Ysgolan tradition is also found in medieval Breton literature.

black scholar on a black horse who suffers eternal punishment for a trio of sins:

> O losgi eglwys, a lladd buwch ysgol,
> A llyfr rhodd ei foddi
> Fy mhenyd ys trwm gyni.
>
> For burning a church, and killing a school cow,
> And causing a book to drown,
> My penance is wretched adversity.[16]

By the fifteenth century, the first two of Ysgolan's crimes seem to have been forgotten or forgiven, while the third had been enlarged from the drowning of a single book to the burning of an entire library. Two couplets by the bard Guto'r Glyn indicate that he had become associated with the legendary conflagration in the tower of London:

> Lhyfreu Kymry ai llofrudd,
> Ir twr gwyn aythant ar gudd,
> Ysceler oedd i Scolan
> Vwrw'r twr o lyfreu ir tan.
>
> Murdering the books of the Welsh,
> Concealed in the White Tower,
> It was infamous of Ysgolan
> To throw the stack [tower] of books in the fire.[17]

Ysgolan also seems to have become associated at some point with the destruction of books in the Glyndwr rebellion and even, following the Reformation, with the eradication of ancient British Christianity by the papacy. A late-sixteenth-century song, of which at least two versions survive, makes Ysgolan the book-burning emissary of the Pope:

> Gynt ydd oedd gair Duw'n ein mysg
> Yn rhoddi dysg i'n llywio,
> Rhoes Duw hwn o'i nefol ddawn
> Yn gynnar iawn i'r Cymro
> 'Dd oedd ar hynn y Pab ai wg,
> Annuwiaeth drwg oedd ynddo

---

[16] Jarman, "Cerdd Ysgolan," 54 (my translation).
[17] Quoted in the margin of Salesbury's *A Briefe and a Playne Introduction*, sig. E2v (my translation).

A danfon Scolan, gythraul gau,
I losgi llyfrau'r Cymro.

Once the word of God was among us,
Giving knowledge for our guidance,
God gave this heavenly gift
Very early to the Welshman.
The Pope frowned at this,
Evil ungodliness was in him,
And he sent Ysgolan, false devil,
To burn the Welshman's books.[18]

This version of Ysgolan bears a striking resemblance to the contemporary black legend of Polydore Vergil, who was charged with having ransacked the libraries of Llandaff and Hereford, burning or shipping back to Rome all the books which would have proved the veracity of the British History.[19]

In spite of the late development of an anti-Romanist variant of the Ysgolan tradition, in most versions he is clearly a Welshman, and thus a figure for the wounds the Welsh inflict upon themselves.[20] Of the six historical occasions when the books of the Britons were supposed to have been destroyed, only two could be blamed solely on foreigners (the Roman emissaries Augustine and Polydore Vergil), while in the other four cases, the Welsh themselves were at least partly responsible: Gildas pointed an accusatory finger at those Britons who had taken books into exile, the blame for the conflagration in the White Tower fell in part on the Welsh nobles who sent for the volumes, the Glyndwr rebellion was remembered as an internecine conflict, and the destruction of the monastic libraries was, for the Welsh as for the English, a self-inflicted wound. To paraphrase Lady Bracknell, for a nation to lose its libraries once may be counted a misfortune; to lose them six times looks like carelessness, or something worse. The stern humanist Salesbury went so far as to suggest that the bards secretly delighted in the destruction of the libraries, for it gave them unchallenged control over the Welsh historical memory. In the absence of a reliable written record, how could one confute "the phantasticall

---

[18] Jarman, "Cerdd Ysgolan," 61 (my translation).
[19] Denis Hay, *Polydore Vergil: Renaissance Historian and Man of Letters* (Oxford: Clarendon Press, 1952), p. 159.
[20] The memory of great traitors is of course often an important feature of nationalist narrative. Consider the importance of Diarmaid MacMurrough, Malintzin / Malinche, and Benedict Arnold to Irish, Mexican, and US nationalism respectively.

vanities of theyr prophecies"?²¹ As enemies of historical truth, Salesbury implies, the bards were in fact abettors of Ysgolan.

The history of successive bibliocausts summed up in the figure of Ysgolan could be regarded as advantageous to bards and scholars alike insofar as it offered a convincing explanation for the absence of the old Welsh Bible and the *vetustissimus liber*. To put it rather differently, Ysgolan ensured that the Welsh past would remain irrecoverable, and thus that there would be no end to the nostalgic longing constitutive of nationalism. At the same time, however, there is an element of excess in the Ysgolan tradition – what might be called a surplus of loss – that threatens to overbear the impulses of nationalist nostalgia, consuming the same desire it provokes. When national history amounts to nothing but an endless series of conflagrations, what is there to be nostalgic *for*?

The problem of the missing books was thus experienced and responded to by Welsh scholars in a very different way than by their English counterparts. While English writers from Bale to Michael Drayton might lament the lost books of the Britons and yearn for their recovery, their practical contribution amounted to little more than a flood of crocodile tears.²² Indeed, the very absence of these books facilitated the English appropriation of British antiquity. Had the Welsh Bible and the *vetustissimus liber* miraculously resurfaced, English scholars would have been disadvantaged by their inability to read them; but a loss is equally legible to nostalgists of every nationality. And, after all, weren't the Welsh and the English all Britons together now? If Ysgolan's final legacy was the blotting out of distinctively Welsh traditions in favor of inclusively British ones, this, from the point of view of the Anglo-British nationalists, was not necessarily a bad thing.

There is a curious contradiction at the heart of sixteenth-century Welsh scholarship. Men like Llwyd and Prise provided the raw materials for the construction of a British national ideology which was ultimately hostile to a separate sense of Welshness. They were not, however, poor dupes like Griffin Madox, powerless to prevent the absolute appropriation of their utterances. They were instead among the first scholars in Europe to grasp that there was more to national history than books and artifacts. Emphasizing oral tradition and collective memory, they set out to rescue from the wreck of history a distinctively Welsh set of practices and attitudes

²¹ Salesbury, *A Briefe and a Playne Introduction*, sig. E2ᵛ.
²² On Drayton, see John E. Curran, Jr., "The History Never Written: Bards, Druids, and the Problem of Antiquarianism in *Poly Olbion*," *Renaissance Quarterly* 51 (1998), 498–525.

which could be held safe from immolation on the one hand and appropriation on the other.

A MEMORIOUS PEOPLE

In the course of writing this book, I have sometimes had the sense of being haunted by Sir John Prise. The author of *Historiae Brytannicae Defensio* had a habit of turning up in the most unlikely places. He has already been encountered as the conduit whereby the image of the Tudor spark bursting into flame found its way from Dafydd Nanmor to Edmund Spenser – the passage occurs near the beginning of the *Defensio*, which I will discuss more fully here. But Prise also turns out to have been present when Robert Aske gave his last impassioned defense of the abbeys; he was acting as secretary to the team of interrogators. Owing to his strangely varied career, Prise's name crops up in histories of the Reformation and the dissolution of the monasteries, in studies of antiquarianism, Welsh literature and theology, book history, and early modern agriculture.[23] He was, in the fullest sense of the term, a Renaissance man.

In the major historical developments of the 1530s and 1540s, Prise played an agile, if generally unobtrusive, role. A lawyer and the husband of Thomas Cromwell's niece, he probably assisted Cromwell in drafting the legislation of the first Act of Union. More prominently, he was one of the visitors sent out in 1535–36 to inspect the monasteries and prepare the ground for their dissolution. Prise's large personal library undoubtedly contained many volumes "rescued" from the monasteries (including the renowned Black Book of Carmarthen, in which he would have encountered the earliest version of the Ysgolan legend). He was also the recipient of monastic estates in Breconshire and Herefordshire which he diligently sought to improve. In the same years, Prise served as an MP and wrote a number of books and treatises in three languages, including the first

---

[23] On the various facets of Prise's career, see Knowles, *The Religious Orders in England, Volume 3*; Glanmor Williams, *Wales and the Reformation* (Cardiff: University of Wales Press, 1997); Davies, *Latin Writers of the Renaissance*; N. R. Ker, "Sir John Prise," *The Library*, 5th ser. 10 (1955), 1–21; Hoyle, *Pilgrimage of Grace*, pp. 3, 26; and Joan Thirsk, "Making a Fresh Start: Sixteenth-Century Agriculture and the Classical Inspiration," in *Culture and Cultivation in Early Modern England: Writing and the Land*, ed. Michael Leslie and Timothy Raylor (Leicester: Leicester University Press, 1992), p. 24. The difficulty in grasping the shape of Prise's career as a whole – that is, in recognizing that it is again and again the same man – is enhanced by the fact that Prise's name occurs in published studies in at least four different spellings, as Prise, Price, Pryse, and ap Rice.

printed book in Welsh, *Yny Lhyvyr Hwnn* (1546) and *A Description of Cambria, now called Wales* (1584), as well as the *Defensio*.

I call Prise a Renaissance man not simply because he turned his hand to a wide range of pursuits with assurance and success. The more important point is that in all his activities Prise was dedicated to bringing about the Renaissance – that is, rebirth – of Britain. As church reformer, government servant, farmer, book collector, and writer, Prise was perennially pre-occupied with the preservation and recovery of antiquity.[24] Both the Act of Union and the dissolution of the monasteries were, as we have seen, underwritten by this ideology of restoration. As an improving farmer, Prise saw himself as reintroducing the wisdom of Palladius and other ancient authorities. The cult of improvement which seemed to Prise (and many others) to be a restoration of ancient practice was in fact the engine propelling early agrarian capitalism in this period.[25] In an irony which may also be the master-irony of his era, this apparent devotee of the past was consistently engaged in processes of radical innovation.

Historiae Brytannicae Defensio (written c. 1545, published 1573) is the most ground-breaking of all Prise's works, though the author never acknowledges this, and may not have realized it.[26] The ostensible purpose of the book is to defend Geoffrey of Monmouth, the *vetustissimus liber*, and British antiquity generally against the skepticism of Polydore Vergil. As historians have noted, Prise's *Defensio* is the most capably argued, as well as the least violent, of all the Tudor defenses of Geoffrey.[27] With the advan-tages over Vergil of a training in law and a knowledge of Welsh, Prise sets out to prove that native Welsh records are superior to those of the Roman colonists, to demonstrate that Geoffrey's history is a translation, and finally to defend the fame and exploits of King Arthur and of Brennus, conqueror of Rome. In the course of this defense, he anticipates Bale's call for the printing of medieval histories (though Prise would have this done not by

[24] As Prise proudly and characteristically noted in a copy of Bede's *De tabernaculo* in 1553, "John Prise saved this book from destruction by bookworms" (*Jo. Prise vindicavit hunc librum a tinearum morsibus*); Ker, "Sir John Prise," 5.
[25] Prise's notes in a manuscript of Palladius' *Of Agriculture*, now in the British Library, demonstrate his interest in emulating ancient farming practice; see Thirsk, "Making a Fresh Start," p. 24. On improvement, see also Andrew McRae, "Husbandry Manuals and the Language of Agrarian Improvement," in *Culture and Cultivation*, ed. Leslie and Raylor, pp. 35–62.
[26] A rough draft of the work was in existence by 1545, while the finished version is dedicated to Edward VI. Prise's *Historiae* was only printed, by his son, in 1573, almost twenty years after the author's death.
[27] Davies, *Latin Writers of the Renaissance*, pp. 16–20. T. D. Kendrick called the *Defensio* "the first of the great books on the subject of the antiquity of the British" (*British Antiquity*, p. 88).

merchants and lords but at royal expense – an even less plausible sce-nario).[28] The most remarkable part of the work, however, is the first chapter, which simply seeks to show "that Britain at no time from its first being inhabited has ever lacked in records of deeds."[29]

The gist of Prise's argument in this chapter is that the Welsh as a people are and have always been peculiarly devoted to preserving their past, and are thus hardly likely to have forgotten their origins, even if they have mislaid the *vetustissimus liber*. He is not concerned at this point with the specific content of Welsh records, but rather with demonstrating that record-keeping has been constant. Prise argues that a repertoire of cultur-ally specific arts of memory has been in continuous use among the Welsh since remotest antiquity.[30] These include patronyms, which preserve the memory of as many as five previous generations, and genealogies, whereby the living maintain an honorable link to their most distant ancestors. But the most effective custodian of memory is bardic lore and poetry:

Now in the last thousand years, more or less, no time can be seen in which are not found at least some British writers who have made mention of national affairs. In particular, those poets who are also called bards ... never cease cultivating this, celebrating both the deeds of ancestors and the genealogies of those more recent, and the praise of heroes, in both verse and prose, preserved in written texts as well as in memory.[31]

Prise makes an illuminating reference to Chaucer's *House of Fame*, where the names of those ancient heroes whose memory remains flourishing are written clearly on the walls, while the names of those whose fame has dwindled are faded and practically illegible. (In Chaucer, the latter names have been "molte awey with hete," while the former have survived in the

---

[28] Sir John Prise, *Historiae Brytannicae Defensio* (London, 1573), p. 129.

[29] "Quod Brytannia rerum in ea gestarum monumentis nullo unquam tempore a primo eius incolatu, caruisse videatur"; Prise, *Historiae*, p. 1.

[30] On arts of memory, see Patrick H. Hutton, *History as an Art of Memory* (Hanover, NH: University Press of New England, 1993); and Frances Yates, *The Art of Memory* (Chicago: University of Chicago Press, 1966). The cultural practices described by Prise bear little relation to the formal mnemonic arts which are Yates's concern – though it is interesting to note that two of the foremost practitioners of these arts in early modern Britain were John Dee and Robert Fludd, both of Welsh descent.

[31] "Nam a mille plus minus proxime elapsis, nullum tempus est videre, quo non aliqui scriptores saltem Brytannici reperiantur, qui de rebus patriis aliquam mentionem fecerint. In hoc enim potissimum Poetas, illos quos Bardos etiam nunc appelari inter eos ... semper colere non cessarunt, qui & maiorum res gestas & recentiorum genealogias, atque Heroum laudes tum carmine tum prosa celebrarent, ac scriptis pariter & memoria conservarent"; Prise, *Historiae*, pp. 9–10.

cool shade of Fame's mansion.[32]) The chief cause of such fading, Prise thinks, is language change, a phenomenon to which Chaucer's tongue is peculiarly susceptible, just as Welsh is peculiarly resistant. While books in English become impenetrable to readers after a mere three hundred years, the Welsh can still understand poetry written in their language a thousand years ago.

Nearly all our English are so addicted to new names of things, that they hold neither a fixed or certain method of speaking or writing the language of their fathers. However, the case is far otherwise with that most ancient British language. For they both hold correct and constant spelling in writing and abhor all license in manner of speech.[33]

This linguistic stability is due in part to the custodial diligence of the bards, and in part to the fact that the Welsh have never migrated from their ancestral seats or been forced into exile, "which would have forced them to let their language slip absolutely, and from there on to suffer the oblivion of their antiquities, in company with nearly all other nations . . ."[34] Prise's argument neatly reverses the terms of the Ysgolan tradition; now it is the English whose links with antiquity have been burned (or, as Chaucer has it, melted) away in the heat of linguistic change, while Welsh historical memory has survived in the cooling shade of a stable language.

   The ostensible aim of all this is to prepare the ground for a defense of Geoffrey of Monmouth's British History. In fact, however, Prise increasingly invites the reader to marvel at the sheer fact of Welsh historical memory, rather than its content. What other people have preserved their

---

[32] Geoffrey Chaucer, "The House of Fame," ed. Larry D. Benson, *The Riverside Chaucer* (Boston: Houghton Mifflin, 1987), line 1149.

[33] "Adeo novandis rerum vocabulis nostri Angli pene omnes indulgent, neque aliquam certam fixamue rationem loquendi aut scribendi patrium sermonem tenent. Atqui in vetusta illa Brytannica lingua longe alia est ratio. Nam & in scribendo rectam & constantem tenent orthagraphiam, & in loquendo omnem novandi licentiam abhorrrent"; Prise, *Historiae*, pp. 10–11. Prise ascertained by experiment that four educated Englishmen spelled the same English words in four different ways; ten Welshmen, by contrast, all spelled Welsh words in the same way. See Prise, *Historiae*, p. 5; Ker, "Sir John Prise," 9. The tactic of highlighting Welsh memoriousness by contrasting it with English amnesia would also be adopted by Humphrey Llwyd, who abrasively demanded, "let suche disdaynfull heades as scant knowe ther owne grandfather leave there scoffinge and tauntinge of Welshmen for that thinge that all the worthye nations in the world do glory in"; Llwyd, *Cronica Walliae*, p. 90.

[34] "Certum quidem est, Brytannos nostros multis hic annorum centenariis ante Romanorum adventum floruisse, nec ullo unquam tempore sedibus omnes pulsos alio migrasse, quo & linguam suam prorsus omittere coacti sint, atque inde suae antiquitatis oblivionem capere, quum caeteris nationibus pene omnibus hoc semel atque iterum per id temporis usu venisse comperiamus"; Prise, *Historiae*, p. 19.

language largely unchanged for the last thousand years, and after "so many great and memorable disasters"?[35] What other people still occupy the territories inhabited by their ancestors before Roman times? Prise frankly admits that for a people in a region so barbarous and so remote from the rest of humanity to have preserved the memory of their origins is "incredible" – but how much more incredible would it have been for "a people clinging so much to all ancient things" to have done otherwise![36]

At the end of his first chapter, Prise is really no closer to proving the point that Geoffrey of Monmouth was a faithful translator, or that the events recorded in the *Historia Regum Britanniae* ever really took place. But he has achieved something of at least equal significance, producing on the basis of literary and ethnographic analysis a vision of the Welsh as an *intrinsically* ancient people. The Welsh are not defined as a community of people descended from Troy, nor even as a linguistic community, but rather as a community of desire, whose stubborn habit of "clinging so much to all ancient things" is expressed in a range of distinctively Welsh arts of memory. It is this common will to preserve and pass on their history, rather than any aspect of that history *per se*, that binds them together.[37] Though chapter 1 of *Historiae Brytannicae Defensio* purports to provide the basis for an argument that the *vetustissimus liber* actually existed, it in fact comes close to doing away with the need for the *vetustissimus liber*, placing Welsh historical consciousness and Welsh identity beyond the reach of Ysgolan.

SLEEPING BEAUTY, AWAKE

Yny Lhyvyr Hwnn (1546), the only one of John Prise's works printed in his lifetime, offered its Welsh readers translations of the Creed, Paternoster, and the Ten Commandments. For Prise, as might be expected, this act of translation was not an innovation but a first step toward the restoration of a lost text. In common with other Welsh and English reformers of his era, Prise was convinced that all of holy scripture had once been available to the

---

[35] "post tot tamque memorabiles gentis illius clades"; Prise, *Historiae*, p. 10.
[36] "Et quamvis incredibile sit tam barbaram usquam, tamque ab omni humanitate remotam fuisse gentem aliquam, quin suae gentis originem atque progressus...Multo minus credendum est gentem illam usque adeo antiquitatis omnis tenacem, & tandiu literarum subsidio adiutam, id maxime omisisse"; Prise, *Historiae*, pp. 17–18.
[37] Here we may see both the truth and the limitations of Ernest Gellner's observation that "The cultural shreds and patches used by nationalism are often arbitrary historical inventions. Any old shred and patch would have served as well"; *Nations and Nationalism*, p. 56.

Britons in their own language, before the devastation wreaked by Augustine and Ysgolan. From the 1540s, the call for a new translation of the Bible into Welsh began to resound ever more strongly. In *Oll Synnwyr Pen Kembero Ygyd* (All the Wisdom in a Welshman's Head, 1547) William Salesbury exhorted the Welsh "to obtain the scriptures in your own language as they once existed among your fortunate ancestors, the early Britons."[38] The same argument was repeated by the Puritan John Penry 1587, on the eve of the publication of William Morgan's translation of the complete Bible.[39]

F. J. Levy's assertion that "Of all the 'reformations' of Europe, the English was, in terms of its justification, the most historical," is inaccurate only in that it fails to note that the Welsh theater of that Reformation was even more preoccupied with history.[40] The representation of the (re)translation of the Bible into Welsh as an essentially antiquarian enterprise was partly tactical; it was by appealing to Archbishop Parker's and William Cecil's interest in British antiquities, as much as to their concern for Welsh souls, that Richard Davies and William Salesbury at last won statutory backing for a Welsh translation of the Bible in 1563.[41] But appeals to antiquity also had a peculiar force within Wales itself. The Reformation for the Welsh was not just a restoration of true religion but a return to the "the faith of their forefathers, the ancient Britons" (*ffydd ei hen deidieu y Brytaneit gynt*).[42] Genealogy, that classically Welsh art of memory, provided the structuring principle of the Welsh Reformation.

Published in 1567, the Welsh New Testament (*Testament Newydd*) included addresses to the Welsh people by the two chief translators, Davies and Salesbury. Much the longer of the two, Davies's "Epistol at y Cembru" is notable for barely discussing the translation to which it is prefaced. Instead, Davies devotes all his rhetorical skill to reminding the

---

[38] Williams, *Wales and the Reformation*, p. 176.

[39] Williams, *Wales and the Reformation*, p. 308.

[40] Levy, *Tudor Historical Thought*, p. 79. Passion for British antiquity ran equally high among Welsh recusants and counter-reformers. As Owen Lewis, who rose in exile to become bishop of Cassano, exclaimed to an envoy of Mary, Queen of Scots, "my lord, let us stick together, for we are the old and true inhabitants of the isle of Britain. The others be but usurpers and mere possessor"; Williams, *Wales and the Reformation*, p. 276.

[41] Robin Flower, "William Salesbury, Richard Davies, and Archbishop Parker," *National Library of Wales Journal* 2 (1941), 7–14; and "Richard Davies, William Cecil, and Giraldus Cambrensis," *National Library of Wales Journal* 3 (1943–44), 11–14; Williams, *Wales and the Reformation*, 237.

[42] "Address to the Welsh People by William Salesbury," in Evans, *A Memorandum*, p. 125; *Testament Newydd*, sig. c3ᵛ. The same phrase could be employed by Catholics, who urged the Welsh to remain true to "the faith of the old Britons, their dear progenitors" (Williams, *Wales and the Reformation*, p. 270).

Welsh of the Bible which existed in their language many centuries ago. As Glanmor Williams has pointed out, this approach serves a threefold purpose: it appeals to Welsh pride in their nation's antiquity, disposes of the charge that Protestantism is an innovation, and brands Catholicism, by contrast, as a Saxon imposition.[43] In addition, in a manner John Bale would have well understood, Davies's address insistently provokes nostalgic longing for the lost Bible of the ancient Britons – a longing which the new translation seems ideally designed to salve. And yet, as I will argue, the address intentionally produces a surplus of nostalgia in excess of anything the new *Testament Newydd* can hope to satisfy.

The nation to which Davies addresses his epistle is (like all nations) exceptionally beautiful. Wales, however, has for too long been a sleeping beauty:

> it grieves me to see thee, Wales, which was at one time foremost, but now the last in such a glorious triumph as this: awake thou now lovely Wales [*Cymbro glan*], my dear and fond brother in Jesus Christ: do not denationalize thyself [*paid ath ddigenedlu*], do not be indifferent . . .[44]

These lines from the opening sentence of the epistle could belong to a much later period in the history of nationalism. The trope of national "awakening from sleep," which Benedict Anderson associates with the "second-generation" nationalisms of the nineteenth century, is already fully fledged in this precocious passage of sixteenth-century Welsh prose.[45] Yet Davies's language is rooted in Petrarch, and his central themes are all borrowed from John Bale: the beauty of the nation, "natural love of country," and the lost glory of antiquity. The source of the nation's beauty is to be found not in the visible world but in the depths of time. "[T]he true religion of Christ and the word of God beautified [*hardday*] the Britons of old and brought them pre-eminence and dignity."[46] What sunders Wales in its present slumber from the beauty of its antiquity is not merely a

[43] Glanmor Williams, "Some Protestant Views of Early Church History," p. 213.

[44] Evans, *Memorandum*, pp. 83–84; *Testament Newydd*, sig. a3^r . The literal sense of *Cymbro glan* is "lovely Welshman." Evans's translation of "ddigenedlu" as "denationalize" seems slightly anachronistic in a sixteenth-century context. The closest translation of "ddigenedlu" in this case might be "degenerate," or better still "degender," in the sense employed by Spenser when he complains that the Old English in Ireland "have degendred from their auncient dignities" (Spenser, *A View*, p. 70).

[45] Anderson, *Imagined Communities*, pp. 194–96.

[46] Evans, *Memorandum*, p. 88; *Testament Newydd*, sig. a4^v. The literal sense of *hardday*, which Evans translates as "adorned," is "beautified," and as used here is clearly cognate to Bale's "beautify."

millennium, however, but the sundry depredations of Ysgolan, whom Davies invokes by name:

Next to this recall the loss which the Welsh sustained in whatever books they had, in their art, their histories, their pedigrees, and their Holy Scriptures: for the whole of Wales was entirely despoilt of them. For since Wales was subjected to the crown of England by the force of arms, without a doubt many of their books were destroyed under such treatment. And of those that escaped, the bards say, that the nobility of Wales being taken as prisoners for life to the White Tower, collected as many as they could carry with them, to read them for their own comfort in the prison, and these in the end were burnt in the White Tower: therefore the poet sang, *It was wicked of Scolan, to throw the heap of books into the fire.*[47]

For Davies as for other writers of his generation, the Ysgolan tradition serves the dual function of explaining the absence of the ancient Welsh Bible and provoking nostalgic desire for the irrecoverable. Significantly, however, Davies is not content to suppose that the Bible perished in the seventh century or the thirteenth. Instead, he traces the survival of at least parts of the Welsh Bible down to the very threshold of the present age, producing nostalgia in its most profound and intimate form as he captures the lost text in the rosy glow of childhood memory:

Truly I was never fortunate to see the Bible in Welsh: but when I was a lad I remember that I saw the five books of Moses in Welsh, in the house of an uncle who was a learned man: but no one had any conception of the book, neither valued it. It is doubtful (as far as I know) whether it is possible in the whole of Wales to see one old Bible in Welsh since the Welsh were robbed and spoilt of all their books as I have before mentioned.[48]

The losses mourned by the nationalist nostalgic are always recent, just as they are always absolute. The same refrain has been heard in many times and places: "Our grandparents still preserved some link, however attenuated, to the good, old ways. Fifty years ago there would still have been time to save the national essence [the greenwood, the gaucho, Gaelic]. But now it is too late." Employing the device of the childhood memory, Davies brings the Welsh Bible through the storms of Saxon invasion and papal persecution, the conflagration in the White Tower and the destruction of the Glyndwr rebellion, brings it so close to the present that one could almost – almost! – reach out and touch it. Yet that Bible is nonetheless as irrecoverably lost as if the last copy had been burned by Augustine himself.

---

[47] Evans, *Memorandum,* pp. 94–95.
[48] Evans, *Memorandum,* p. 103.

The readers of Davies's "Epistol" could, of course, reach out and touch the word of God in Welsh – they were holding it in their hands. There is something paradoxical in Davies's insistence on the impossibility of recovering the Welsh Bible when he has every justification for celebrating its recovery. The Welsh people must be made to remember that once they possessed the Bible in their own language. But equally, they must not be allowed to forget, now that it has been restored to them, that once they lost it forever. Davies insists upon this because, as he will seek to demonstrate, consciousness of loss is integral to a distinctively Welsh kind of Christian spirituality. [49]

If the first half of the "Epistol" is a nostalgic meditation on the beauty of antiquity in the manner of Bale, the second half is a celebration of the Welsh arts of memory in the manner of Prise. Davies's attitude to the bards is far more positive than that of some of his humanist contemporaries, who saw them as liars in league with Ysgolan. He regards bardic lore as a valuable mnemonic device. Seeking to demonstrate the deep roots of anti-Romanism in Wales, Davies quotes "a piece of work by Taliesin the chief of the bards which will help thee to remember something of the old world of long ago."[50] Later, citing an anti-papal couplet by Iorwerth Fynglwyd (fl. 1460), he notes in the margin, "This stanza was written before a word was said in England against the Pope."[51]

For Davies, the most important of the Welsh arts of memory is one that went unnoticed by Prise, the proverb. In ancient times, he argues, knowledge of scripture "was so general among them that it gave rise to proverbs and learned well-arranged sayings which contained the gist of the whole of the Holy Scripture and sound teaching about many an article of the religion of Christ."[52] Blandly pious proverbs such as "With God with plenty: without God without anything" may not seem like convincing evidence of familiarity with the gospels, but pages of exegesis reveal that

---

[49] Of course, in 1567, only the New Testament in Welsh had been "recovered." Davies may thus have had another motive in reminding his people of their loss, namely, to encourage longing for a more complete recovery. Davies and Salesbury did indeed embark subsequently upon a translation of the Old Testament, but abandoned it (having quarreled, by one account, over the translation of a single word). Only in 1588 would a complete Welsh Bible appear, and it would be the work of another translator, William Morgan. No doubt real impediments, temperamental or otherwise, prevented Davies and Salesbury from completing their task. But their failure to produce a Welsh Old Testament is curiously reminiscent of John Bale's failure to print any of the old books which might assuage the longing he sought to instill.

[50] Evans, *Memorandum*, p. 117. The verses, admirably suited to Davies's purposes, read in part: "*Woe to him who does not protect with his pastoral staff his sheep from the Roman wolves.*"

[51] Evans, *Memorandum*, p. 120.

[52] Evans, *Memorandum*, p. 122.

they contain much essential scriptural wisdom. Thus the proverb "Son of Grace" [*Y Mab rhad*] is "but three short words and each word consists of one syllable," yet it encapsulates the vital teaching that salvation is achieved not through merit but by Christ's grace alone.[53] Although Davies admits that without recourse to scripture the Welsh have strayed far from the truths memorialized in their proverbial lore, he nevertheless exalts memoriousness – in the face of overwhelming loss – as a central facet of Welsh spirituality. His address reverberates with repeated calls to the Welsh to "remember" (*coffa*) or "call to mind" (*galw ith cof*).[54] By the time he issues this call for a final time in the peroration, he is calling upon his countrymen to remember not only the Bible they once possessed and lost, but their own identity as a memorious people.

> Call to mind [*Galw ith cof*] thy old privilege and thy great honour on account of the faith of Christ and God's word which thou didst receive before the islands of the world. The religion of Christ beautified [*harddai*] thee for thou didst obtain it true and pure as Christ taught it to His Apostles and Disciples... Therefore fall thou on thy knees and thank God who today visits thee in his mercy, and begins to exalt thee to thy old privilege and thy former very great dignity, by making thee a partaker of His blessed word, in sending thee the sacred Testament, which shows that thy proverbs and sayings above mentioned were old friends.[55]

From their new New Testament, then, the Welsh will imbibe Christ's pure doctrine, but they will also learn something about themselves. The oral traditions which they have long valued and preserved are even older and more precious than they might have suspected. If the value of proverbs lies in demonstrating the existence of the ancient Welsh Bible, the reverse of the equation also seems, however perversely, to hold true: the value of the Bible itself lies in testifying to the antiquity and usefulness of the proverbs. This is the sort of implication one might expect to encounter in Prise's *Defensio*. But it is one thing to suggest that folk traditions can stand in for the lost *vetustissimus liber*, and quite another to make the same suggestion about holy writ. Even if it comes across as an afterthought or aside, Davies's

[53] Evans, *Memorandum*, p. 112; *Testament Newydd*, sig. b3ᵛ.
[54] e.g., Evans, *Memorandum*, pp. 84, 94, 96, 105, 116, 122. The oft-repeated imperative "remember" echoes in the annals of many nationalisms (e.g., "Remember the Alamo"). In Wales today it manifests in the graffito, "Cofiwch Tryweryn" ("Remember Tryweryn" – the village and valley drowned in the late 1950s to make a reservoir providing water for Liverpool.)
[55] Evans, *Memorandum*, pp. 122–24 (again, Evans translates *harddai* as "adorned"); *Testament Newydd*, sig. c2ᵛ.

apparent wavering as to the sufficiency of scripture is nonetheless astonishing in this paradigmatically Protestant context.

Why would the Bishop of St. David's, committed to the reconversion of his people, risk even for a moment undermining the fundamental principle of *sola scriptura*? The answer must be that while scripture may contain all that is necessary for the salvation of individual souls, it may still not be sufficient to save a nation. Davies shares with Prise the recognition that books alone can neither contain the essence nor guarantee the survival of national life. Texts are fragile things, vulnerable to flames, bookworms, and appropriative readings. The Welsh had already lost their Bible on one occasion. They had also arguably lost the rights to much of their native history, thanks to the English, who borrowed the British past for their own uses. By emphasizing oral traditions and collective memory, Davies and Prise chart a course for their nation between the Scylla and Charybdis of Ysgolan and England – between, that is, the risks of utter oblivion and of total co-optation. Proverbs, patronyms, bardic lore, a stable language, are the "old friends" by whose aid it is possible to maintain a genuinely Welsh connection with the genuine past of Wales.

This chapter has been devoted to a Welsh paradox: that within those Welsh texts that provided the key materials for the development of British nationalism there is also encoded a resistance to such acts of appropriation, a refusal to relinquish a separate Welsh identity. In conclusion, let me suggest what may be the accompanying English paradox: that one of the elements of Welsh writing that English nationalists appropriated most successfully, if unconsciously, was this very spirit of anti-colonial resistance. Literary historians have sometimes noted the "oddly colonized quality of historically based nationalism in early modern England."[56] English voices speaking of their nation in the sixteenth century can sound more like those of Latin Americans in the nineteenth century or Africans and Asians in the twentieth than like Europeans in the eighteenth. One explanation for this no doubt lies in the sense among English Protestants that their nation had only recently and incompletely escaped from the domination of an evil (Roman) Empire. Yet other influences may also be at work in the case of, say, Edmund Spenser.

Consider the world in which Spenser places his national heroes, and the challenges with which they are confronted – a world in which beguiling false friends pose an even greater threat than open enemies, in which one

[56] Mikalachki, *The Legacy of Boadicea*, p. 11. See also Richard Helgerson's comparison of Elizabethan writing with postcolonial African writing (*Forms of Nationhood*, p. 17).

must be ever vigilant to maintain control of one's own meanings and resist mutability, in which the greatest temptation is to forget oneself, to forget and to sleep. Holding to one's truth is no easy task, as Redcrosse is the first to discover, especially when beguiled by seemingly authoritative and all-too-accessible simulacra. One's very name and history can be appropriated, as we learn with Florimell; how then to preserve and demonstrate an authentic identity? The poem's *milieu* has of course been read as mirroring the situation of the New English settlers in Ireland, fending off the temptation to forget their origins and "go native."[57] But do not the challenges facing Redcrosse, Guyon, Britomart, and Artegall also smack of another colonial situation, one in which it was the colonized who faced the lure of abandoning their separateness, of letting themselves be subsumed within the dominant culture? Spenser, I would argue, took rather more from Prise's *Defensio* than the bare image of a spark kindling into flame.

[57] See, e.g., Stephen Greenblatt, *Renaissance Self-Fashioning: From More to Shakespeare* (Chicago: University of Chicago Press, 1980), pp. 157–192.

CHAPTER 4

Ghosts of a nation:
A Mirror for Magistrates *and the poetry of*
spectral complaint

In the last week of 1915, the Irish poet and nationalist Patrick Pearse issued a pamphlet, *Ghosts*, in which he summoned the shades of Ireland's dead patriots to his side.

Here be ghosts that I have raised this Christmastide, ghosts of dead men that have bequeathed a trust to us living men ... There is only one way to appease a ghost. You must do the thing it asks you. The ghosts of a nation sometimes ask very big things; and they must be appeased, whatever the cost.[1]

Four months later, on Easter Monday, Pearse and a contingent of rebels seized control of the Dublin General Post Office and proclaimed the rebirth of Ireland "in the name of God and of the dead generations from which she receives her old tradition of nationhood."[2] Appropriate to its date, the Easter Rising witnessed a blurring of the boundaries between this world and the next, with spirits crossing over in both directions. For a few days under English bombardment, a mundane public building played host to an eerie gathering of living men on the threshold of death and dead men – Wolfe Tone, Parnell, Cuchulainn – who on that day of national resurrection had duly risen.

As W. B. Yeats would later wonder, "When Pearse summoned Cuchulainn to his side / What stalked through the Post Office?"[3] Whatever name we give to this uncanny presence (whose mode of locomotion irresistibly recalls the Ghost in Hamlet), it has stalked through the imagination of many nations, and has not yet been laid to rest. Nationalism would appear to depend on a form of legitimized necromancy – a "magical

---

[1] *Collected Works of Padraic H. Pearse: Political Writings and Speeches* (Dublin: Maunsel & Roberts, 1922), p. 221. For a fascinating – if somewhat one-sided – account of Pearse's "mystical nationalism," see Conor Cruise O'Brien, *Ancestral Voices: Religion and Nationalism in Ireland* (Chicago: University of Chicago Press, 1995), pp. 96–117.
[2] Quoted in O'Brien, *Ancestral Voices*, p. 111.
[3] W. B. Yeats, "The Statues," in *The Collected Works of W. B. Yeats, Volume 1*, ed. Richard J. Fineman, (London: Macmillan, 1983), p. 337.

harnessing of the dead" – by means of which those who have already given one life for their country are called up for another tour of duty.[4] The paradox is that these ghosts are often (like Pearse's Cuchulainn) far more ancient than the nation for which they purportedly died – and indeed were in some sense already haunting the nation before it came into being. Whereas houses (and post offices) can become haunted, nations are made that way.

All of these importunate ghosts and demanding "dead generations" are, of course, no more than figures of nationalist speech. The nation may be, in Stephen Kemper's phrase, "a conversation that the present holds with the past" but at the end of the day we can rest assured that "those who live in the present speak both parts."[5] Yet while common sense would seem to dictate that the dead can only say what the living permit, it is not always so easy to tell who is the ventriloquist, and who is the dummy. As Marx memorably observed, history itself can be viewed as an ongoing struggle for supremacy waged between the living and the dead.

Men make their own history, but not of their own free will; not under circumstances they themselves have chosen but under given and inherited circumstances with which they are directly confronted. The tradition of the dead generations weighs like a nightmare on the minds of the living. And, just when they appear to be engaged in the revolutionary transformation of themselves and their material surroundings, in the creation of something which does not yet exist, precisely in such epochs of revolutionary crisis they timidly conjure up the spirits of the past to help them; they borrow their names, slogans and costumes so as to stage the new world-historical scene in this venerable disguise and borrowed language.[6]

---

[4] Michael Taussig, *The Magic of the State* (New York: Routledge, 1997), p. 3. The necromantic magic of the state is potent enough to conscript even those who died fighting against it. Witness Douglas Macarthur's warning to the cadets at West Point that, should they fail in their trust, "a million ghosts in olive drab, in brown khaki, in blue and gray would rise from their white crosses, thundering those magic words: Duty, honor, country." On the face of it, nothing could be less appropriate than the presence at this spectral rally of ghosts in the gray of the Confederacy. But their presence testifies to what Benedict Anderson memorably calls "the reassurance of fratricide"; *Imagined Communities*, pp. 9 n. 2, 199.

[5] Steven Kemper, *The Presence of the Past: Chronicles, Politics and Culture in Sinhala Life* (Ithaca: Cornell University Press, 1991), p. 7.

[6] Karl Marx, *The Eighteenth Brumaire of Louis Bonaparte*, trans. Ben Fowkes, in *Surveys From Exile: Political Writings, Volume 2*, ed. David Fernbach (Harmondsworth: Penguin, 1992), p. 146. Marx's nightmarish "tradition of the dead generations" finds a remarkable and ironic echo in the Irish Volunteers' invocation "of the dead generations from which she receives her old tradition of nationhood." Can this be a coincidence? While it is unlikely that Pearse, who drafted the bulk of the Proclamation, was familiar with Marx, his socialist compatriot James Connolly may well have known *The Eighteenth Brumaire*. But if Connolly remembered this phrase, he clearly ignored Marx's warning that the socialist revolution "cannot begin its own work until it has sloughed off all its superstitious regard for the past" (p. 149).

Thus the balance of power shifts uneasily back and forth between the living and the dead. At times the dead generations seem capable of imposing an almost crushing burden on the living, as difficult to shake off (and as insubstantial) as a bad dream. At other times, the living seem thoroughly in control, cynically manipulating the voices of the dead in pursuit of their own new world-historical ends. Yet, Marx suggests, the living are driven to this shift out of their timidity – out of awe and fear, that is, of the same ghosts they shamelessly personate.[7] In this complex interplay between the living and the dead, whose ends are ultimately being served? Who is speaking whom?

This chapter will explore how Britain became a haunted nation – and how ghosts helped bring Britain into being. As I shall argue, ghosts came to inhabit the national space only after – and as a consequence of – their exclusion from traditional social life. In one of the crowning acts of the Reformation, the old ghosts of Catholic England and Wales were exorcized, not with bell, book, and candle (for these too had been proscribed), but by order of Parliament. Their banishment was one effect of the Chantries Act of 1547, which abolished a wide range of practices designed to alleviate the sufferings of the dead in Purgatory. That Act had far-reaching effects which were at once psychological – robbing the bereaved of any means of communicating with the departed – and social – dissolving the organizations which existed to serve the dead and which, I shall argue, provided a model for subsequent imaginings of the nation. In readings of the *Mirror for Magistrates* and related works of "Complaints" literature, I will show how the ghosts driven out in 1547 gradually re-infiltrated Tudor literature and life, now in the guise of distinctively national spirits. The nation from which large numbers of these ghosts emanated, to which they addressed themselves, and on whose behalf they asked some very big things, was the long-vanished nation of Britain.

THE BANISHMENT OF GHOSTS

Whereas Patrick Pearse regarded Christmas as a fitting season for the summoning of ghosts, Edward VI's first parliament chose the same festival to enact their banishment. Passed and ratified on Christmas Eve, 1547, the Chantries Act decreed the immediate dissolution of all those institutions

---

[7] Jacques Derrida argues that a similarly anxious and ambiguous relation to ghosts is characteristic of Marx himself; *Specters of Marx: The State of the Debt, the Work of Mourning, and the New International*, trans. Peggy Kamuf (New York: Routledge, 1994).

whose function was to pray for the dead in Purgatory: chantries, colleges, and free chapels, obits, lamps, and lights, fraternities, brotherhoods, and gilds. The assets of these intercessory institutions were seized by the crown.[8] If the monasteries had provided a feast for the royal maw, the chantries were now served up as a light dessert. The stated rationale for the dissolution was not, of course, royal insatiability, but sound Christian doctrine. As the preamble to the Chantries Act made clear, "superstition and errors in Christian religion" had arisen through "devising and fantasying vain opinions of purgatory and masses satisfactory to be done for them which be departed."[9] Since Purgatory was nothing but a popish superstition, institutions devoted to easing the sufferings of the souls in torment there were manifestly useless.

It was the end of more than one old song. The dissolution of the chantries had an enormous and undeniably traumatic impact on religious and communal life, an impact arguably even greater than that of the dissolution of the monasteries.[10] Purgatory, the middle space between heaven and hell, whose reality had been accepted for centuries and whose qualities were food for both scholastic disputation and vivid poetic imagining, was dismissed as nothing more than a fable.[11] The vast sums given over the years to provide for masses and prayers ("suffrages") for the dead imprisoned there were declared to have served no purpose other than to fatten lazy monks and chantry priests and enhance the power of the papacy. The Chantries Act put an end to the expression of solidarity between the living and the dead, and also to various forms of solidarity among the living expressed through and around the intercessory institutions. Finally, at least as far as church and state were concerned, it put an end to the visitations of

---

[8] The timing of the Act reflects the government's desire to rush the controversial legislation through with as little debate as possible, but also resonates with the belief expressed by Marcellus in *Hamlet* that in the Christmas season "no spirit can walk abroad" (1.1.142). An alternative view, championed by Patrick Pearse, is that Christmas is precisely the season for ghostly visitations.

[9] Alan Kreider, *English Chantries: The Road to Dissolution* (Cambridge, MA: Harvard University Press, 1979), p. 190. The explicitly doctrinal basis of the 1547 Chantries Act distinguishes it from an earlier act of 1545 (never enforced), which proposed to dissolve only those institutions which were found to be corrupt or moribund, and which was frank in acknowledging that the money was needed for the royal purse.

[10] See Shagan, *Popular Politics*, p. 241.

[11] On the doctrine of Purgatory and the beliefs and practices associated with it, see Jacques Le Goff, *The Birth of Purgatory*, trans. Arthur Goldhammer (London: Scolar Press, 1984); Jean-Claude Schmitt, *Ghosts in the Middle Ages: The Living and the Dead in Medieval Society*, trans. Teresa Lavender Fagan (Chicago: University of Chicago Press, 1998); Eamon Duffy, *The Stripping of the Altars: Traditional Religion in England, c. 1400–c. 1580* (New Haven: Yale University Press, 1992), pp. 299–376; Stephen Greenblatt, *Hamlet in Purgatory* (Princeton: Princeton University Press, 2001).

ghosts. Believers in Purgatory generally accepted that from time to time spirits might return from beyond the grave to plead with their loved ones for intercessory prayers, to condemn those who had betrayed their trust (e.g., by embezzling bequests intended for chantries), or even to torment the living in order to spare them greater torment in the world to come. Protestants countered that such apparitions could only be the work of the devil, or else illusions created by cunning priests. "God hath shut up that way, neither doth he suffer any of the dead to come again hither."[12]

The psychological repercussions of the abolition of Purgatory were inevitably profound, perhaps even more so than its institutional and social effects. Protestant foes of Purgatory hoped to free the living from their superstitious and morbid obsession with the souls of the departed, to remove from their shoulders the nightmarish weight of the dead generations. Arguably, they accomplished just the opposite. Elizabethan theologians might tussle over what form of words was permissible in the funeral sermon, but for ordinary men and women undergoing the intimate agony of bereavement, the problem was not how to remember the dead – it was, as it has always been, how to let go of them.[13] One function of the elaborate set of intercessory practices surrounding the doctrine of purgatory – funerary masses, month minds, annual recitations of the parish bead-roll – was to enable a gradual and emotionally tolerable separation of the dead from the living.[14] As Marx recognized, the balance of power between the living and the dead shifts subtly back and forth and is not always what it seems: what looks like slavish service to the departed may in fact be a way of denying them excessive power over living minds. Thus, while the Chantries Act purported to banish the spirits of the dead from this world, its actual effect may have been

---

[12] Archbishop Cranmer, cited in Greenblatt, *Hamlet in Purgatory*, p. 145. Protestant views on the relationship between the living and the dead could be more nuanced and ambivalent than Cranmer's flat pronouncement suggests, though few were willing to depart from the basic principle that the door was shut. See Bruce Gordon, "Malevolent Ghosts and Ministering Angels: Apparitions and Pastoral Care in the Swiss Reformation," in *The Place of the Dead: Death and Remembrance in Late Medieval and Early Modern Europe*, ed. Bruce Gordon and Peter Marshall (Cambridge: Cambridge University Press, 2000), pp. 87–109; and Peter Marshall, " 'The Map of God's Word': Geographies of the Afterlife in Tudor and Early Stuart England," in the same volume, pp. 110–130.

[13] On the funeral sermon, see Frederic B. Tromly, " 'Accordinge to Sounde Religion': the Elizabethan Controversy over the Funeral Sermon," *Journal of Medieval and Renaissance Studies* 13 (1983), 293–312.

[14] As Jean-Claude Schmitt argues, "this word 'remembrance' is in fact misleading, for the goal of the *memoria* was to help the living separate from the dead, to shorten the latter's stay in purgatorial punishment... and finally, to enable the living to forget the deceased"; *Ghosts in the Middle Ages*, p. 5. See also Anthony Low, "*Hamlet* and the Ghost of Purgatory: Intimations of Killing the Father," in *English Literary Renaissance* 29 (1999), 443–467.

to set loose the ghosts of the departed in a newly terrifying form, inchoate and apparently unappeasable.[15]

Much to the outrage of Puritan polemicists, the traditional practice of praying for the dead persisted for many years, and not only among recusants and crypto-Catholics.[16] But the intercessory institutions which had organized the expression of solidarity between the living and the dead were no more, and people caught openly engaging in superstitious practices (such as lighting candles and singing psalms over the corpse) were liable for prosecution; by the 1580s, such practices were inevitably in steep decline. Some Protestant preachers, such as John Donne, attempted to reassure their flocks that a certain form of solidarity still prevailed:

> though death have divided us, and though we never receive our dead raised to life again in this world, yet we do live together already, in a holy Communion of Saints . . . the dead, and we, are now all in one Church, and at the Resurrection shall be all in one Quire.[17]

But this solidarity, unlike that which had prevailed before 1547, had to remain entirely tacit, for Protestants must not give way to "unlawful desires of communication with the Dead."[18] Indeed, it is not an exaggeration to say that Protestant teaching on death and bereavement consisted largely of instructing people in what they must not do:

> Concerning the living, they must see that their mourning be moderate, and such as may well express their affection and love for the departed . . . They must avoid superstition, and not surmise that funeral ceremonies are available to the dead . . . They ought to take heed of superstitious pomp and solemnities. For of all ostentations of pride, that is most foolish, to be boasting of a loathsome and a deformed corpse.[19]

How in the face of these proscriptions did the people of Protestant England and Wales cope with the experience of bereavement? How did they appease or otherwise attempt to silence the dead fathers, mothers, children, and friends whose voices still whispered or clamored in their heads? One method of harnessing grief was to discern in the death of

---

[15] This point is made in relation to French Protestantism by Natalie Zemon Davis, "Ghosts, Kin, and Progeny: Some Features of Family Life in Early Modern France," *Daedalus* 106 (1977), 96.

[16] See David Cressy, *Birth, Marriage, and Death: Ritual, Religion and the Life-Cycle in Tudor and Stuart England* (Oxford: Oxford University Press, 1997), pp. 398–403.

[17] *The Sermons of John Donne*, ed. Evelyn M. Simpson and George R. Potter, vol. 7 (Berkeley: University of California Press, 1954), pp. 383–84.

[18] *Sermons of John Donne*, vol. 7, p. 375.

[19] William Perkins, *The Golden Chaine* (1600), cited in Cressy, *Birth, Marriage, and Death*, p. 415.

others a lesson in the art of dying well; by this means, the dead could still be made to serve the living, though reciprocal assistance was of course impossible.[20] Another outcome of the abolition of purgatory was probably to strengthen emergent bourgeois perceptions of the family as an economic entity persisting across time; the dead could best be served by preserving and augmenting the capital they had bequeathed to the living.[21] Proscribed customs and beliefs about the dead were also infused into the practices of the Elizabethan stage, above all, as Stephen Greenblatt has argued, in the ghost-ridden plays of William Shakespeare.[22] Finally, there were those who began to believe that the dead could be served and appeased through service to the nation.

This last transition was facilitated by a number of important correspondences between the emergent idea of the nation and the time-hallowed conception of Purgatory. Both, first of all, are vividly imagined spaces whose real existence cannot be verified by normal means and must therefore be a matter of faith (a faith enhanced, in both cases, by the testimony of the dead). Secondly, both Purgatory and the nation involve people in organized rites of service to the dead (ancestors, ancient heroes, unknown soldiers), thereby offering some relief from the psychological burdens shouldered by the yet-living. Finally, there is a remarkable similarity between the forms of solidarity characteristic of these two systems. One of the most striking features of the nation is its social and temporal spaciousness, incorporating as it does members of all classes and genders on an ostensibly equal basis (whatever their objective status in society), and incorporating the dead generations on a roughly equal footing with the living. The liberality of this embrace is often taken to be a sign of the nation's distinctive modernity.[23] But there is in fact a remarkable precedent of the nation-form to be found in one of the intercessory institutions which had grown up in the late middle ages to serve the souls in Purgatory.

[20] "Deprived of the Catholic remedy of prayers for the dead, these self-conscious protestants harnessed the process of grief to the art of living and dying"; Cressy, *Birth, Marriage, and Death*, p. 395.
[21] See Zemon Davis, "Ghosts, Kin and Progeny."
[22] Greenblatt, *Hamlet in Purgatory*.
[23] As Benedict Anderson notes, "regardless of the actual inequality and exploitation that may prevail, the nation is always conceived as a deep, horizontal comradeship" (*Imagined Communities*, 7). Anthony Smith includes on his checklist of fundamental aspects of nationhood "common legal rights and duties for all members" (14), and it is on the basis of such inclusiveness that he distinguishes the nation from older and more exclusive formations such as class-based "lateral *ethnies*" and culture-based "vertical ethnies"; *National Identity* (Harmondsworth: Penguin, 1991), pp. 52–53.

Although Protestants liked to claim that Purgatory only served to strengthen the grip of the corrupt church, it was also the foundation of secular solidarity in the form of the hundreds of religious gilds, fraternities, or fellowships. These organizations, "poor men's chantries" as one historian has called them, existed to provide their members with good funerals upon their demise, and regular prayers and masses thereafter to hasten the soul's journey to salvation.[24] Some gilds confined their other activities to the keeping of a single light; but the larger and wealthier ones might also run schools and almshouses, and even offer loans, insurance, and legal services to their members. Large and small, the gilds were unique among late medieval social institutions in their openness (in other words, their catholicity). In most cases, women were allowed to join on an equal basis with men, and even – at least in theory – to hold office. The gilds were also open to members of all social classes, provided they could afford to pay the annual subscription (which ranged from a few pence for the smaller and poorer gilds to much higher sums for the more fashionable and exclusive societies). Above all, their membership included both the living and the dead, whose bond was continually reaffirmed in the performance of gild activities.[25] It was even possible to join a gild after one's death; at Stratford-on-Avon, the dead joined at half-price.[26]

In abstract terms, a religious gild can be defined as a horizontal community that incorporates both the living and the dead, binding them together in a common project worked out across many generations. The same terms are obviously applicable to the community of which nationalists feel themselves to be a part. Moreover, it is precisely because the nation is perceived to possess these qualities that it attracts such extraordinary loyalty from people like Patrick Pearse. The conclusion of one historian that the dissolution of the gilds created "a vacuum which could never be completely filled" thus seems open to question.[27] Nations abhor a vacuum.

---

[24] J. J. Scarisbrick, *The Reformation and the English People* (Oxford: Basil Blackwell, 1984), p. 20. On the gilds, see also Virginia R. Bainbridge, *Gilds in the Medieval Countryside: Social and Religious Change in Cambridgeshire, c. 1350–1558* (Woodbridge: Boydell Press, 1996); and Duffy, *Stripping of the Altars*, pp. 141–54.

[25] "The annual general obit . . . displayed the concept that the complete fraternity was a communion of the living and the dead. Both enjoyed the succour of the gild"; David J. F. Crouch, *Piety, Fraternity and Power: Religious Gilds in Late Medieval Yorkshire, 1389–1547* (York: York Medieval Press, 2000), p. 247.

[26] Scarisbrick, *The Reformation and the English People*, p. 25. On the important Stratford gild, of which Shakespeare's grandfather was a member, see Park Honan, *Shakespeare: A Life* (Oxford: Oxford University Press, 1998), pp. 4–5.

[27] Crouch, *Piety, Fraternity and Power*, p. 251.

It is true that after 1547 the lights – those lights the gilds had kept burning in churches and chapels as a service to the dead – went out all over England and Wales. But well before the Tudor era drew to an end, a new flame would be burning in their place.

THE GHOST IN THE MIRROR

In spite of Protestantism's stubborn refusal to acknowledge their existence, ghosts of a sort did reappear in English literature not long after their banishment by the Chantries Act. Indeed, ghost stories were among the most popular kinds of reading matter for two generations of Elizabethans. The great repository of such stories was the famous (for some, infamous) *Mirror for Magistrates*, with its numerous additions, supplements, and imitations. As I shall argue, these literary ghosts would eventually offer their living readers a substitute, in the form of service to the nation, for the service once performed for souls in Purgatory. But this development was both subtle and gradual, and could hardly have been predicted on the basis of the original *Mirror*. Though the work was begun no more than seven years after the dissolution of the chantries, the immediate roots of the *Mirror* did not lie in discredited Purgatorial doctrine. Instead, as William Baldwin explains in the preface to the first extant edition of *A Mirror for Magistrates* (1559), the collection was initially intended as a companion to John Lydgate's fifteenth-century *Fall of Princes*, itself a translation of Boccaccio's *De casibus illustrium virorum*.[28]

Lydgate's enormous poem describes how a succession of dead people – beginning with Adam and Eve and ending with Italian rulers of the fourteenth century – appear to "Bochas" [Boccaccio] to recount their unfortunate falls. The poem leaves it hauntingly unclear whether the beings that appear are spirits from beyond the grave, or products of the poet's imagination, or something else again. Adam and Eve seem less like ghosts than superannuated human beings who have somehow never died; they appear to the poet's "inward syght . . . full pitiouslye tremblynge, / Quaking for age, and for lack of myght."[29] None of the dead people who appear to Bochas in the poem are identified explicitly as ghosts, though

---

[28] For a politically contextualized account of the *Mirror*'s inception and subsequent publication history, see the chapter "Literature and History – 'A Mirror for Magistrates'" in Andrew Hadfield, *Literature, Politics and National Identity: Reformation to Renaissance* (Cambridge: Cambridge University Press, 1994), pp. 81–107.

[29] John Lydgate, *The Tragedies, gathered by Jhon Bochas, of all such Princes as fell from theyr estates . . .* (London, n.d), p. 1.

some of them are certainly spooky enough – especially when, like Thyestes, they sneak up behind the poet and give him a fright:

> But at his back Bochas did one se
> Which cryed loude, and bade he sholde abide . . .
> "Leave Theseus and take of hym none lede,
> But first my tragedy . . . discryve."

As this uninvited appearance and importunate demand indicate, the dead in the poem are not simply at the living's beck and call. The *Fall of Princes* portrays a classic power struggle between the living, who desire an orderly and exemplary narrative, and the dead generations, who cannot stop fighting the battles of yesteryear. Ultimately, of course, the living write both parts of this dialogue – or, in the last resort, refuse to write at all. Frustrated by the lies of Thyestes and his brother Atreus, each of whom tries to place all the blame on the other, Lydgate's Bochas finally "Put up his pen, & wrote not more a word, / Of their fury, ne of their false discorde." The only dead man capable of really controlling Bochas is his instructor Daunt (Dante), whose role, though brief, is reminiscent of Virgil's in Dante's own *Commedia*.

In 1555, the printer John Wayland commissioned a group of seven writers, led by Baldwin, to produce a supplement to Lydgate's poem covering the tragic falls which had taken place in England since the fourteenth century. Baldwin reports how he convened a planning meeting with his fellow poets, "bering with me the booke of Bochas, translated by Dan Lidgate, for the better observacion of his order: whiche although we lyked well, yet woulde it not cumlily serve, seynge that both Bochas and Lidgate were dead." The writers obviously could not stomach the notion of a dialogue between the dead and the dead. Hence, "they all agreed that I should usurp Bochas rowme, and the wretched princes complayne unto me."[30] The complaints of these "unfortunate Englysh princes," intended for Wayland's Lydgate, were suppressed by the Marian authorities for reasons that remain murky to this day. When they finally appeared in 1559 it was under separate cover as *A Mirror for Magistrates*.[31]

---

[30] Lily B. Campbell, ed., *The Mirror for Magistrates* (New York: Barnes & Noble, 1938), p. 69. Further references are given in the text.

[31] For a full discussion of the complex textual history of the suppressed first edition, see the introduction to Campbell's edition of *The Mirror*. On the relation of the *Mirror* to Boccaccio and Lydgate, see Paul Budra, "The Mirror for Magistrates and the Shape of *De Casibus* Tragedy," *English Studies* 69 (1988), 303–12.

The dead people in the *Mirror* present themselves in gruesome postures emblematic of their deaths. The decapitated Richard, Duke of York, holds his head in his hands and speaks in "a shrekyng voyce out of the weasande pipe" in his neck (181), while George, Duke of Clarence, apologizes for arriving stinking and drunk, a circumstance he cannot help as he was drowned in a butt of wine. Richard II is imagined "mangled, with blew woundes, lying pale and wanne al naked upon the cold stones in Paules church, the people standing round about him, and making his mone in this sort" (111). Yet even as it draws graphic attention to the fact that the speakers of the complaints have died violent deaths, the *Mirror* (like *The Fall of Princes*) shies away from identifying them as souls returning from beyond the grave – that is, as ghosts. Instead, betraying an anxiety born of recent controversies, Baldwin and his interlocutors repeatedly go out of their way to insist that these are not real people at all. They are merely – like Simone Martini's painting of Laura – artist's renderings. As Baldwin carefully explains, each of his associates "tooke upon themselves every man for his parte to be sundrye personages, and in theyr behalfes to bewayle unto me."[32] Reformation anxieties are also evident in the scrupulosity with which the *Mirror* segregates the living from the dead, formally and typographically. Whereas in *The Fall of Princes* the voices of Lydgate, Bochas, and their dead subjects are often interwoven in a single stanza, in the *Mirror* the living speak an informal prose while the dead recite verse, and the words of the dead appear in a smaller type-size.[33]

The *Mirror*'s dead are more docile than their pre-Reformation counterparts. Their sole desire seems to be to serve the living by reciting cautionary tales. At their most vociferous, they do no more than vie with one another to demonstrate the particular profitableness of their example. As James I of Scotland intones, "If for examples sake thou write thy booke, / I charge the Baldwin thou forget me not" (155). Similarly, the corrupt Ricardian justices who head up the collection beseech Baldwin to put them first "In the rufull Register of mischief and mishap" (73). How it might profit a dead person to be recorded in this register is left unclear. Certainly, there is no sense that inclusion in the *Mirror* allows the dead either to live again, or to progress to

[32] Sherri Geller draws attention to this emphasis on poetic personation: "the poets and the ghosts are virtually equal in their authority because the *Mirror* openly acknowledges that the poets are the ghosts"; Sherri Geller, "What History Really Teaches: Historical Pyrrhonism in William Baldwin's *A Mirror for Magistrates*, in *Opening the Borders: Inclusivity in Early Modern Studies*, ed. Peter C. Herman (Newark: University of Delaware Press, 1999), p. 162.

[33] Campbell's edition prints the prose sections in smaller type but, as Geller notes ("What History Really Teaches"), the opposite is true in the original editions.

a better place in the afterlife. All the book offers its dead contributors is re-interment in a textual tomb; the Duke of Suffolk, seeking admission to the book, refers to it as Baldwin's "grave of grief" (162).

Given its licensing and publication so soon after the accession of a Protestant queen, it is no surprise that the 1559 *Mirror* adopts a clear and uncompromising policy on the dead. Departed souls cannot return to this world except in poetry, there is nothing the living can do to benefit them, nor can they do anything to help the living beyond providing awful examples of fortune's inconstancy (i.e., the kind of lessons in the art of living and dying that even strict Protestants were willing to accept from the dead). But while the dead who populate the pages of the 1559 *Mirror* have a clear and delimited task, this is less true of those introduced in the second edition of 1563, and still less of those in later editions and imitations.[34] What happens to the *Mirror* is something like what the US military calls "mission creep": the longer the project continues, the more ambiguous and unattainable become its aims. It is no longer clear whose interests are being served or when, if ever, the campaign of haunting will come to an end.

Most of the eight complaints added to the edition of 1563 violate in one way or another the strict decorum of the original project. The first of the new speakers, Lord Anthony Rivers, launches into an unprecedented kind of complaint – not against fortune's fickleness, but against Baldwin and company for leaving him out of the first edition, after cruelly raising his hopes:

> For after brute had blased all abrode
> That Baldwyn through the ayd of other moe,
> Of fame or shame fallen prynces would unloade
> Out from our graves we got without abode,
> And preaced forward with the rufull rout,
> That sought to have theyr doynges bulted out.   (246)

While Rivers is appeased once he knows he is to be included in the second edition, his impact on the doctrinal purity of the *Mirror* is not so easily effaced. No previous speaker is described as having arisen from the grave; Rivers is a literal *revenant* in that he not only speaks in the voice of the dead but returns from the place to which the dead have departed. Moreover, he comes not only to serve the living, but to seek relief for himself. He hopes

---

[34] Lawrence D. Green describes the shift that begins in the 1563 edition as one from a "preceptive" to an "attitudinal" mode of perceiving history; "Modes of Perception in the *Mirror for Magistrates*," *Huntington Library Quarterly* 44 (1981), 117–33.

that the *Mirror* writers will "unloade" him of something that weighs upon
him. By transferring the weight of his "fame or shame" to the living, the
dead Rivers hopes to rest more easily.

The other newcomers to the 1563 edition are similarly self-interested.
Seeing himself as more sinned against than sinning, Lord Hastings begs
"Baldwin, shyeld my torne name" (293). Jane Shore, the creation of
Thomas Churchyard, complains that "my good name is pluckt up by the
roote." She has heard what people have been saying about her, "though ful
dead and lowe in earth I laye," and has wished to rise up and refute them,
"But then to speake alas I was affrayed" (374). Seeing so many of her fellow
deceased making their complaints to Baldwin has given her the confidence
to tell her story among the rest. The poet, in other words, has not *invented*
Shore's Wife; he has merely helped a suffering soul to accomplish a desired
journey (much as a gild member might offer suffrages to release a soul from
Purgatory). Elsewhere in the 1563 edition, when confronted by souls less
timid than Jane Shore's, the poets seem even less in command. The last
speaker in the volume, the "Black Smith" (i.e., Michael Joseph, a leader of
the 1487 Cornish rising) roughly insists on his right to be heard alongside
his social superiors. Baldwin is struck dumb.

> Is it not truth? Baldwyn what sayest thou?
> Say on thy minde, I pray the muse no more,
> Me thinke thou starest and lookest I wote not howe,
> As though thou never sawest a man before.   (403)

Baldwin, of course, has seen plenty of men before. His reaction is that of a
man who has – for the first time – seen a ghost.

The speakers introduced in the 1563 edition describe themselves as dead
people returning to the world of the living. But where are they returning
from? Thomas Sackville's "Induction" to the *Mirror*, also new to this
edition, purports to provide an answer. In a dream vision, Sackville and
his guide Sorrow (filling the place of Dante's Virgil) pay a visit to a classical
Hell ruled over by Pluto, where the dead swarm about them, eager to tell
their stories. The theological implications of this vision unnerve some of
Sackville's fellows, as they make plain in the prose section following the
Induction:

where as he faineth to talke with the princes in Hel, that I am sure will be mislyked,
because it is most certayne, that some of their soules be in heaven. And although he
herein do follow allowed Poetes, in theyr discription of Hel, yet it savoreth so
much of Purgatory, whiche the papistes have digged thereout, that the ignorant
maye therby be deceyved. Not a whit I warrant you (quoth I) For he meaneth not

by his Hell the place eyther of damned soules, or of such as lye for their fees, but
rather the Grave, wherin the dead bodies of al sortes of people do rest till tyme of
the resurrection. And in this sence is Hel taken often in the scriptures, & in the
writynges of learned christians.   (346)

Baldwin's interpretation preserves the *Mirror* from the charge of either
slandering the dead or, worse, recreating the evacuated space of Purgatory.
Although conforming to the prevailing Protestant view of graveyards as
"the dormitories of Christians," it is not a very convincing defense.[35] Rivers
and Shore do indeed identify themselves as coming from the grave, but for
them it has clearly been no fine and private place of sleep. Rather, it is
described as a fairly lively and sociable arena, wherein the dead both
trade rumors with one another and eavesdrop on the living. "Hell" may
be glossed by Baldwin as "the grave," but "the grave" must in turn be
understood as some sort of teeming anteroom or middle space between
heaven and hell – a place which does indeed savor unmistakably of
Purgatory.

The atmosphere of later Elizabethan editions of the *Mirror* grows ever
more Purgatorial, in spite of the authors' intermittent efforts in the prose
passages to distance themselves from Catholic doctrine.[36] The dead who
once came only to offer service by example are increasingly conscious of
their own rights and needs, and unhesitant in demanding service from the
living. As the spirit of Sir Nicholas Burdet, a hero of the French wars,
demands in the 1587 edition, if the dead were deemed worthy of royal trust
when they were alive, "Why should we so keepe silence now...?"
Rebutting in advance Marx's attack on the authority of "the dead generations," Burdet proclaims the right and duty of the dead to take part in
political debate.

---

[35] Cressy, *Birth, Marriage and Death*, p. 385.
[36] "King James...wil be misliked by for his *Miserere*" remarks one in response to a poem included in
the 1587 volume, in which James IV of Scotland is portrayed suffering what can only be purgatorial
torments:

> By mine owne foly, I had a great fall.
> Wherefore I feare mee, that now I shall
> Have payne long lasting for mine iniquity:
> Lord full of mercy yet to thee I call,
> *Miserere mei Deus & salva* mee. (p. 485)

The makers of the *Mirror* have a ready and no doubt genuine excuse in this instance, namely that the
poem in question was written "above fifty yeares agone" (p. 488).

Wee clayme as ryghte, in trueth our myndes to breake,
The rather eke wee thinke to speake we franchizde ar,
Because wee servde for peace and dyde in Prince his war.   (463)

While Burdet pursues the cause of spectral liberation polemically, other ghosts in the 1587 edition take more practical steps. Two of them, Jane Shore and Cardinal Wolsey, transgress the bounds of the verse complaint and insist on speaking their own prose introductions. Previously, the prose sections of the *Mirror* – in which the claims and careers of the dead are weighed and discussed – had been the exclusive domain of the living. The restless ghosts of 1587 tear down those barriers. Wolsey complains of the trouble he had in finding a living person to tell his story, until he happened upon the sympathetic Thomas Churchyard:

So, to the whole worlde, by his helpe and mine owne desire, I step out from the grave, where long I lay in forgetfulness, and declare in the voyce of a Cardinall, a curious discourse; yet sadly and sorrowfully tolde, as well unto Churchyard (the noter thereof) as to the rest that pleaseth to heare any peece of my misfortune.
(495)

Treating the living poet as little more than a serviceable secretary, the ghost of Wolsey speaks out of – and of – his own desire. Forty years after their banishment by the Chantries Act, England's dead have pulled off a remarkable *coup*.

THE GHOSTS OF BRITAIN

By the mid-Elizabethan period, ghosts were seemingly once again in a position to make demands of the living. But now that prayer for the dead, suffrages, and Purgatory itself had been abolished, what could these ghosts possibly demand? Now that chantries, gilds, and lay fraternities were no more, to what audience could they address themselves? These two questions have a single answer: the nation. From the 1570s onwards, ghosts return in poetry to demand remembrance from members of the national community – a community which constitutes itself in and through precisely such acts of patriotic commemoration.[37]

The dead in the original *Mirror* addressed themselves to a fairly exclusive audience, consisting of the assembled authors and the handful of powerful

[37] Hadfield, in *Literature, Politics and National Identity*, draws attention to the increasingly nationalistic tone of later editions of the *Mirror*, though he considers this development primarily in terms of a falling away from Baldwin's original ideals.

and privileged readers who might be expected to profit from their examples. It was not for nothing that Baldwin entitled the book *A Mirror for
Magistrates*. Yet as the ghosts in subsequent editions of the *Mirror* become
more conscious of their own rights, so too does their sense of audience
expand. Wolsey, as quoted above, delivers his complaint to "the whole
worlde" – though his choice of Thomas Churchyard as medium effectively
limits his audience to readers of English. As for the irrepressible Sir
Nicholas Burdet, he addresses himself not to a coterie of poets and
potentates, but to a mass audience of patriots: "Yee worthy wights alive,
which love your Countreys weale" (470).

The ghost of Burdet speaks to the nation as a whole – but what nation?
As so often in national writing of this period, the signals are mixed. On the
one hand, Burdet's oration to his troops at Poitoise is explicitly directed to
the English: "Why now my frends, for England fighte, I cryde: / Yf ever
English hearts your noble breasts posseste" (470, 481). Yet for all that his
oratory anticipates Henry V's at Harfleur and Agincourt, we should not be
too quick to assume the identity of Burdet's nation (nor, as I shall argue
later, Henry V's). Like many another Elizabethan "English" nationalist,
Burdet turns out to be a devotee of British antiquity. In a strange digression
on how national history should be written, he insists that such histories
must begin at the beginning, that is "from the *Britaynes* first antiquities"
(476). As self-appointed spokesman for the national dead, Burdet is keen to
ensure that the voices of ancient Britain are not left out.

The convergence of spectral complaint with British antiquarianism
should come as no surprise. Both modes of writing were means of achiev-
ing, or at least imagining, communion with the vanished past. Both genres,
moreover, were profoundly transformed by the abolition of Purgatory, and
with it, the time-hallowed methods of effecting such communion. Indeed,
the impact of the Chantries Act on antiquarian discourse can be observed
as early as 1549, in John Bale's *Laboryouse Journey*. Even as it responds to the
aesthetic crisis following the dissolution of the monasteries, Bale's book
also reacts to the crisis in relations between the dead and the living
following the dissolution of Purgatory.[38]

---

[38] To say that Bale's book responds to the crisis provoked by the Chantries Act is not of course to say
that he opposed it, any more than he opposed the dissolution of the monasteries. There can be no
doubt that the staunch Protestant John Bale rejoiced in the end of "popych purgatory," which he
saw as merely a pretext for the consumption of England's substance by "pristes, channons and
monkes, which do but fyll ther belly"; John Bale, *King Johan*, in *Complete Plays of John Bale,
Volume 1*, ed. Peter Happé (Cambridge: D. S. Brewer, 1985), p. 70.

As I argued earlier, Bale's nationalism was rooted in Petrarchan aesthetics. The longing gaze he encouraged his readers to fix on the vestiges of national antiquity was modeled on the gaze Petrarch fixed on the image of Laura – on the image of a woman whose death would leave him lost in a world of baffled longing and regret, a woman who could never return to him, except as a painted representation. (Although Petrarch doubtless believed in Purgatory, he also knew Laura was in heaven, and hence utterly cut off from contact with this world.) The longings and pangs that Petrarch felt were, to say the least, topical in England and Wales after Christmas, 1547. Bale's book arguably represents the first attempt to redirect the baffled desire to serve, appease, and communicate with the dead onto a respectable object, that is, the dead writers of national antiquity. All that was really required was the transposition of a few words and phrases. For suffering souls, read ancient books; for suffrages, read printing costs; for communities such as the religious gilds, read the community of the nation. When Bale appeals to his readers' "natural love," or urges them to spend money on immortal things (books) rather than "things which lasteth not," he is speaking in the borrowed accents of ghosts.[39]

For John Bale, the chaste desire for irretrievable manuscripts was or should have been enough to salve the social wounds left by the abolition of Purgatory. In practice, he was clearly not much interested in actually allowing the dead to speak, either by publishing their works or by conjuring their ghosts. Bale would probably have disapproved of *A Mirror for Magistrates*, which in its very form involves a refutation, or at least a complication, of his position.[40] Lost manuscripts, the *Mirror*-writers

[39] In several places, Bale seem to borrow phrases or images from Purgatorial writers with whose work he was familiar, notably Thomas More. In More's *Supplication of Souls* (1529), the souls in Purgatory are imagined pleading with the living not to expend their wealth on "gay gownys and gay kyrtels and mych waste in apparell," but rather to "send the money hether by masse pennys." Bale in his turn expostulates against those who waste their money on foreign commodities and "consume in apparell their silkes & their velvettes," when they might instead "brynge one worthye worke of an auncyent wryter to lyght . . . to the bewtie of our nacyon." Again, where More's souls beg their living parents, children and friends to "remember how nature & crystendom byndeth you to remember us," Bale directs his appeal to "all them that hath a naturall love to their contrey"; Thomas More, *The Supplication of Souls*, in *The Complete Works of St. Thomas More*, Volume 7, ed. Frank Manley, Germain Marc'hadour, Richard Marius, and Clarence Miller (New Haven, Yale University Press, 1990), pp. 224, 228; Bale and Leland, *Laboryouse Journey*, sigs. E7ᵛ, F6ᵛ, A7ᵛ.
[40] Ironically, Bale's own antiquarian project would eventually become the matter of a ghostly complaint. The author, the herald Ralph Brooke, claimed that much of William Camden's *Britannia* had been plagiarized from John Leland's unpublished research. To prove his point, Brooke printed Leland's "New Year's Gift," just as Bale had done half a century earlier, reiterating Bale's eternal curse on any who "in spight of his Nation" would destroy the memorials of

implicitly assert, are simply not enough; we require also the voices of the
dead, even if we know (and must from time to time acknowledge) that
these voices are really our own. This stance was expressed with particular
clarity by John Higgins who, in addition to penning Burdet's complaint,
was the author of *The First Part of the Mirror for Magistrates* (1575; reprinted
with expansions in the 1587 *Mirror*). Burdet's remarks on antiquities are in
fact a sort of plug for *The First Part*, which applies the *Mirror* treatment to a
host of specters from ancient British history.

As Higgins explains in his introduction to *The First Part*, he was
himself a collector of manuscripts, and understood something of Bale's
brand of nostalgia; he had once owned a precious copy of Geoffrey of
Monmouth's *Historia*, "which I lost by misfortune."[41] Yet as he goes on to
make clear, neither Geoffrey nor the other chroniclers in his library were
sufficient to assuage his patriotic thirst for antiquity – all of them "wrate
one thing: and that so brieflye that a whole Princes raigne, life and death
was comprised in three lines" (36). Higgins's solution to the inadequacy
of his sources was neither, following Bale, to settle for an aesthetically
productive longing, nor, with the likes of Sir John Prise, to shift the
focus from textual records to some notion of cultural memory. Instead,
he regarded it as the patriotic historians' duty to make Britain's history
"as ample as the Chronicles of any other Country or Nation." The best
way of accomplishing this, he admitted, would be to learn the
ancient languages of Britain and thereby shed new light on the island's
antiquities. In the end, however, he chose the somewhat easier course
of just making things up. "In writing the Tragedies of the first infortunate
Princes of this Isle, I was often faine to use mine own simple
invention" (36).

Higgins was no stickler for historical accuracy, but he regarded himself
primarily as a chronicler of the past, rather than as a moralist. Although his
First Part takes the form of a collection of complaints superficially resembling those in Lydgate and Baldwin, it might more accurately be described

---

antiquity. Brooke appended a poem to the end of the "New Years Gift" in which, as if in
fulfillment of the curse, Leland's ghost appears, wittily demanding to know how his labors "*Came
to be drown'd in such a thankles Denn*" (i.e., in *Cam-Denn*). Leland's Purgatory, in other words, is
the plagiarized *Britannia* itself, from which he awaits release through the efforts of an earthly
intercessor (Brooke). See York Herault [Ralph Brooke], *A Discoverie of Certaine Errours Published
in Print in the Much Commended Britannia, 1594* (London, 1596), sig. L4ᵛ, p. 4ᵛ (the "New Year's
Gift," not in all copies, is separately paginated).

[41] Lily B. Campbell, ed., *Parts Added to 'The Mirror for Magistrates'* (Cambridge: Cambridge
University Press, 1946), p. 35. Further references given in the text. Higgins seems not to have
grasped that the unanimity of the chronicles was a sign of their common source in Geoffrey of
Monmouth.

as a history of ancient Britain as told by those who were there. Building on Baldwin's hint that the *Mirror* project might usefully be expanded backwards in time, Higgins begins at the beginning, recounting the conquest of Britain by Brutus and carrying the story down to the Roman era. His book was sufficiently popular to prompt another young poet Thomas Blenerhasset, to carry the story forward to the Norman Conquest in *The Second Part of the Mirror for Magistrates* (1578). Thus, by the middle of Elizabeth's reign, almost the entirety of British history was available to a popular readership in the form of ghostly lamentations.

The critics have not been kind to Higgins and Blenerhasset. Accused of failing to grasp Baldwin's original purpose and political philosophy, as well as of plumbing new depths in the quality of their verse, they have been blamed for the "disintegration" of the *Mirror* project.[42] But in their defense it might be said that they simply develop and give expression to tendencies that were inherent in the *Mirror* from the first. We have seen, for instance, that with each new edition of the *Mirror* the dead speakers become more like the ghosts of Catholic tradition. Higgins and Blenerhasset not only recognize this trend but ratify it by daring to use the hitherto forbidden word. Higgins describes the beings introduced to him by the god Morpheus as "gryzely ghostes" (129); Blenerhasset's Cadwaladr calls for other "grizie ghosts" to come forth from their graves to help him mourn (443), while yet another "cursed ghost" emerges from a purgatorial "Limbo Lake" (485).[43]

The ghosts in these collections know what they are, and know what they want. Blenerhasset describes his *Second Part* as a "Supplication" from the dead "in which they complayne of the great injurie they suffer, because they bee excluded out of the English *Mirrour of Magistrates*" (384). This ghostly "Supplication" irresistibly and no doubt intentionally recalls Thomas More's *Supplication of Souls*, in which the dead in Purgatory complain of the great injuries they suffer because they are excluded from the prayers of the living. Though the ancient British, Roman, and Saxon ghosts in the

---

[42] Campbell, *Parts Added*, p. 13. See also Paul Budra, "*The Mirror for Magistrates* and the Politics of Readership," *SEL* 32 (1992), 1–13.

[43] Although he was an ordained minister, nowhere does John Higgins reflect on the theological implications of his summoning of ghosts in *The First Parte*. Many years later, however, he was author of *An Answer to Master William Perkins Concerning Christ's Descension into Hell* (Oxford, 1602), in which he refutes Perkins's assertion that Christ's descent took place only in a figurative sense. Higgins's determination to prove that a soul (if only that of Christ) might literally descend to Hell and return from there may reflect some lingering uneasiness about his early dabbling in literary necromancy.

parts added to the *Mirror* do not desire prayers as such, what they have in common with the souls in Purgatory is a burning need to be remembered. It is this need – more than a desire to edify the living – that prompts them to appear to Higgins and to Blenerhasset. The desire for remembrance is common to sinful ghosts and those who were models of private and public virtue. The virtuous Queen Helena complains not that her life was tragic – it wasn't – but only that posterity has failed to remember her happiness (a lapse she blames on the sexism of male historians): "I lived long, I dyde withe perfect blisse, / Yet writers will repeate no word of this" (412).

"Remember what kin ye and we be together," plead the tormented souls in More's *Supplication*; "Remember me," the ghost in *Hamlet* tells his son. In the purgatorial scheme, remembrance is a duty owed primarily by close relations (and secondarily by the surrogate family of the gild or fraternity). But the ancient ghosts in the parts added to the *Mirror* have no such audience obviously available to them. Even by the broadest definition of racial consanguinity, ancient Britons and sixteenth-century English readers do not form part of the same kinship-group. Nonetheless, Higgins and Blenerhasset insist, they are members of the same nation. It is shared nationality that obligates the latter-day readers to pay the ancient ghosts the service of remembrance. The appeal of the valiant British ghost Nennius to "you Britaynes good" (192) to spend "some tyme on mee" (191) affirms the reciprocal relation between such acts of remembrance and national identity.

If Higgins and Blenerhasset are among the first writers in the English literary tradition to use the ghost as a figure for collective historical identity, they are far from being the last. While some of the terms have changed, the Elizabethan controversy over ghosts and remembrance has carried on into the present – though today's controversialists are more likely to be literary critics than theologians. Walter Benn Michaels's remarks on spectrality, identity and remembrance, though directed at twentieth-century targets, are strikingly pertinent to the literary experiment initiated by Higgins and Blenerhasset.

It is only when [history is] reimagined as the fabric of our own experience that the past can become the key to our own identity. A history that is learned can be learned by anyone (and can belong to anyone who learns it); a history that is remembered can only be remembered by those who first experienced it and it must belong to them . . . The ghosts cannot, in other words, be explained as metaphoric representations of the importance to us of our history because the history cannot count as ours and thus can have no particular importance to us without the ghosts . . . So the ghosts are not merely the figures for history as memory, they are the technology for history as memory – to have the history, we have to have the ghosts.[44]

To possess the past, in other words, one must first imagine oneself to be possessed by it. On the face of it, the people of Elizabethan England have nothing in common – neither language, nor blood, nor faith – with ancient Britons born long before the incarnation of Christ. Yet the fact that the ghosts of these Britons choose to appear to them – and not to others – is evidence that they share a common relation to history, a common identity. Equally, it is by piously taking the time to remember these mournful ghosts that the readers demonstrate their national virtue. They are then not only Britons, but, in the words of the virtuous Nennius, "Britaynes good."

THE GHOST OF BRITAIN

The influence of *The Mirror for Magistrates* extended far beyond the additions and supplements that bore its name. In the late 1580s and early 1590s, the same years in which old Catholic mortuary practices were at last dying out with their practitioners, literary "ghosts of the nation" proliferated. Churchyard, Lodge, Daniel, Drayton, and Spenser were among the many who tried their hand at the complaint form in these years. In their contributions to the genre, it is not only the afterlife of an individual spirit that is at stake, but the possession (in both senses) of the national past.[45] The audacity with which they adapt the language and features of Purgatory increases hand in hand with their recognition of the nation as a secular substitute for Purgatory which makes it once again acceptable to believe in the solidarity of the living and the dead. Thus Daniel's Rosamond, soliciting the suffrages ("Lovers sighes") which will waft her to Elysium ("The joyfull blisse for ghosts repurified"), assures her author that the service he does her by presenting her to the English-speaking community will simultaneously be a service to that community, demonstrating once and for all that "Thames had Swannes as well as ever Po."[46] Rosamond's assumption

---

[44] Walter Benn Michaels, "'You who never was there': Slavery and the New Historicism, Deconstruction and the Holocaust," *Narrative* 4 (1996), 7.

[45] The years 1592–94 were particularly productive of literary specters. See Edmund Spenser, "The Ruines of Time," in *Complaints* (London, 1591); Samuel Daniel, "The Complaint of Rosamund," in *Delia* (London, 1592); Thomas Lodge, "The Complaint of Elstred," in *Phillis* (London, 1593); Thomas Churchyard, *Churchyard's Challenge* (London, 1593); Michael Drayton, *Peirs Gaveston Earle of Cornwall* (London, 1594), and *Matilda* (London, 1594).

[46] Samuel Daniel, *The Complaint of Rosamond*, in *Poems and A Defence of Ryme*, ed. Arthur Colby Sprague (Chicago: University of Chicago Press, 1950), ll. 2, 8–14, 728.

that the lovers who sigh for her must be of her nation, and the poet who
speaks for her must speak her language, is a measure of the distance
separating her from the dead who visited Lydgate, and an indication of
the extent to which the idea of the nation has become the enabling
presupposition of ghostly complaints.

While in some examples of late-Elizabethan complaint the national
community serves as an established and fairly unobtrusive premise, in
others it is the locus of spectral unrest. In some cases, the suppressed
contradictions of British nationalism come unusually close to the surface,
and indeed seem in large part to motivate the anguish of the revenant. The
mid-Elizabethan solution to the problem of ghostly provenance – "ghosts
do not come from Purgatory, they come out of the national past" – now
seems too pat, as the identity of the nation in question becomes no less
mired in controversy than Purgatory itself. The three complaints I will
discuss in conclusion all discover their ghosts in or on the banks of rivers, a
location which in itself suggests the difficulty of ever establishing a fixed
sense of identity, of coming home.

Nowhere is the link between ghostly possession and possession of the
British past more evident than in Edmund Spenser's sole contribution to
the genre, *The Ruines of Time* (1591). In this complaint's oft-imitated
opening, the poet is out for an innocent stroll by the river when he
encounters a ghastly vision.

> It chaunced me on day beside the shore
> Of silver streaming *Thamesis* to bee,
> Nigh where the goodly *Verlame* stood of yore,
> Of which there now remaines no memories,
> Nor anie little moniment to see,
> By which the travailer, that fares that way,
> This once was she, may warned be to say.
>
> There on the other side, I did behold
> A Woman sitting sorrowfullie wailing . . . [47]

The wailing woman soon reveals herself to be none other than the ghost of
Verlame (Verulamium) itself, the once mighty Romano-British city now
reduced to less than rubble. By making his sorrowful ghost that of a city
rather than a human being, Spenser seems to have neatly sidestepped at the

---

[47] Edmund Spenser, *The Ruines of Time*, in *The Poetical Works of Edmund Spenser*, ed. J. C. Smith
and E. De Selincourt (London: Oxford University Press, 1912), lines 1–9. Further line references in
text.

outset many of the vexed problems concerning Purgatory and the fate of departed souls. Yet these problems will soon return to haunt his long, troubled, and troubling poem.

Though she may have been a city rather than a human individual, Verlame's complaint resembles those of many of the British ghosts in later editions of the *Mirror*, such as Nennius and Queen Helena. Her paramount interest is in remembrance. Once Britain's proudest city, all her former magnificence "Is turnd to smoke, that doth to nothing fade; / And of that brightnes now appeares no shade / But greislie shades, such as doo haunt in hell . . . " (123–26). Verlame's misery can only be assuaged by the living, whose sympathetic moans, like masses for suffering souls, will ease her torments. "Yet it is comfort in great languishment, / To be bemoned with compassion kinde, / And mitigates the anguish of the minde" (159–61). Buried for so long in utter obscurity, forgotten even by those whose feet tread on her rubble, Verlame's hope of deliverance now hangs by a single thread:"Cambden the nourice of antiquitie, / And lanterne unto late succeeding age . . . " (169–70). The description of William Camden, antiquary, British nationalist, and author of the famous *Britannia* as a *nurse* is rather remarkable. It implies that antiquity is not, after all, quite dead – or at least not beyond all hope of living aid. Camden comes across as a heroic one-man gild, solacing the national dead by solemnly reciting their names, keeping, as did so many lay fraternities, a single flame alight.

The living members of religious gilds hoped the dead colleagues for whom they prayed would return the favor. For much of the poem, Verlame does just that, commemorating first her own savior Camden ("thy just labours ever shall endure," 175), and then another national hero, the recently deceased Earl of Leicester. Leicester "shall never die, the whiles this verse / Shall live, and surely it shall live for ever" (253–54). Have not poets the power to rescue souls from Hell itself, not to mention (and Spenser carefully does not) Purgatory?

> The seven fold yron gates of grislie Hell,
> And horrid house of sad *Proserpina*,
> They able are with power of mightie spell
> To breake, and thence the soules to bring awaie
> Out of dread darkenesse, to eternall day . . .   (372–76)

The Ruines of Time is in one of its aspects a crystallization of spectral British nationalism, in which the power once vested in the chantry priests who prayed souls into heaven is reinvested in the writers (poets and antiquarians) who rescue the heroes and monuments of the national past from oblivion. The poem offers a vision of a truly reciprocal relationship between the living and the dead, in which the willingness of each to serve as the other's "nourice" ensures the nation's own immortality. Yet in spite of certain intense flashes of nationalist optimism, *The Ruines of Time* is neither a cheerful nor a hopeful poem, nor even a securely patriotic one. Its presiding tone is, in more than one sense, dreary, apt to reduce the reader (as it does the poet) to "frosen horror" (483). Subject to what seem like sudden and drastic mood-swings, Verlame finds it hard to hold on to the hope that through Camden's and Spenser's efforts, she will indeed be rescued from hellish darkness. She soon relapses into the self-pitying complaints with which she began, warning others to beware her example before vanishing "with dolefull shrikes" (471).

The Ruines of Time has long puzzled its readers, when it has not simply repelled them. The poem has been variously read as optimistic and pessimistic, nationalist and anti-nationalist, painfully anxious and playfully ironic.[48] On the face of it, Verlame's complaint is self-contradictory and incoherent. Yet *The Ruines of Time* does not fail to offer answers to its mystery; it is simply that the answers are of a kind we should, after all, expect from a ghostly speaker. In place of ontological certainties, knowledge in *The Ruines* is unfixed, uncanny, and duplicitous, belonging to a spectral epistemology.[49] Even as Verlame vaunts that writers can rescue souls from Hell, she asserts that there can be no real traffic between the living and the dead: "Living, on God, and on thy selfe relie; / For when thou diest, all shall with thee die" (209–10). The two morals she draws from her plight, namely the responsibility of the living to honor the dead eternally, and the impermanence of all earthly glory, are not easy to reconcile. The

---

[48] Recent critics tend to agree that a poem that begins by the Thames, touches on the rebellion of Bonduca and the Saxon conquest, and memorializes the leading lights of sixteenth-century militant Protestantism, must have something to do with "the nation." But the identity of that nation, and the nature of the relationship, are questions that remain vexed. For Margaret Ferguson, the poem represents an English poet's anxious relationship with continental models; Verlame is to Rome as Spenser to Du Bellay; "'The Afflatus of Ruin': Meditations on Rome by Du Bellay, Spenser and Stevens," in *Roman Images: Selected Papers from the English Institute, 1982*, ed. Annabel Patterson (Baltimore: Johns Hopkins University Press, 1984), p. 34. Anne Janowitz detects a more confident nationalism, in which the ruin is successfully "English'd" in the double sense of being claimed for England and being translated into immortal verse; *England's Ruins: Poetic Purpose and the National Landscape* (Oxford: Basil Blackwell, 1990), pp. 27–30. But Huw Griffiths argues that the trope of ruin reveals the nation, with its claims to integrity and immortality, in an ironic and inadequate light; "Translated Geographies: Edmund Spenser's 'The Ruines of Time,'" *Early Modern Literary Studies* 4.2/Special Issue 3, September, 1998 (journal online); available from http://purl.oclc.org/emls/04-2/griftran.htm; Internet.

[49] As Bart van Es points out, even the poem's title is duplicitous, available to be read either "as a statement of loss or discovery"; *Spenser's Forms of History*, p. 32.

problem in unlocking Verlame's meaning, in other words, is not an absence of answers, but a surplus of them. This applies above all to the vexed question of this national ghost's own nationality.

The ghosts of a nation sometimes ask very big things, but what question could be more maddening than that implicitly asked by Verlame: what is my nation? Verlame's description of her former life commences with what sounds like a straightforward assertion of native British patriotism. "I was that Citie, which the garland wore / Of *Britaines* pride" (36–37). Yet, as happens frequently in *Ruines,* the ground shifts beneath the reader's feet before the sentence has found its period. "I was that Citie, which the garland wore / Of *Britaines* pride, delivered unto me / By *Romane* Victors, which it wonne of yore" (36–38). What sounded at first like British nationalism turns out to be an admission of participation in the Roman occupation; the poem's thorny syntax repeatedly produces such table-turning effects. Verlame goes on to boast of her role in the rebellion of the strikingly Elizabeth-like Bunduca, who "lifting up her brave heroick thought / Bove women's weakness" (109–10) was finally *defeated* at Verulamium. Though the city ultimately fell to the Saxons centuries later, Verlame's resistance was so fierce that their general was killed, "The moniment of whose sad funerall / For wonder of the world, long in me lasted" (117–18). These examples are indicative of how Verlame's assertions of patriotic steadfastness and resistance collapse repeatedly into admissions of collaboration and mutability. Whatever her resistance to the Saxon onslaught, she is helpless to prevent herself becoming in turn a monument to Saxon glory. Verlame has lost control of her own meanings, helplessly registering the identity-myths of a succession of impermanent conquerors. The true lesson of Verlame's experience seems to be neither the immortality of poetic fame nor the impermanence of earthly glory, but something more chilling, to nationalists at least, than either: the impossibility of maintaining a fixed identity in the face of history. Spenser himself, who by 1591 was something more than English and other than Irish, who was at once a leading proponent of British nationalism and foresighted enough to dread its realization in the Stuart succession, could perhaps have echoed in his own voice Verlame's sorrowful self-appraisal: "of all Nations now I am forlorne" (27).[50]

At once bitter and baggy, hectoring and wavering, *The Ruines of Time* has proved an unattractive work for most modern readers. Yet the poem

---

[50] On Spenser's antipathy to the Stuarts, see Hadfield, *Shakespeare, Spenser, and the Matter of Britain*, pp. 122–36.

was not without attentive readers and imitators in its own time. Up to the early 1590s, authors of ghostly complaints had inevitably tended to take the *Mirror* as their model. From this point onward, poets were more likely to model their complaints either on Daniel's *Complaint of Rosamond* (1592), or on *The Ruines of Time*. The poems in the latter line of influence are often those most explicitly concerned with, and troubled by, the idea of Britain.

In "The Complaint of Elstred" (1593), Thomas Lodge makes little effort to conceal his debt to Spenser. Once again, the poet starts out strolling by the river – the chief differences noticeable at the outset being that it is night rather than day, and the setting is the Severn, rather than the Thames.

> The silent shadowes with their mothers vaile,
> The brighter lampe of Heaven from Thetis hid:
> Apolloes sister in her starrie raile,
> Along her lower sphere in tryumph rid,
>   When I by Severn's beauteous banckes alone
>   Encountred with this woefull vision.
>
> A dolefull Queene in semblance and array,
> Attended by a princely looking lasse:
> Amidst the waltring wave enforced her way,
> And landed there where I lamenting was....[51]

The doleful queen is Elstred, the mistress of Brutus' son Locrine, first king of England. She is accompanied by her daughter Sabrine, from whom the Severn takes its name. Lodge listens in horror as the ghosts go on to relate how they were drowned together in the river by Locrine's vengeful wife, Gwendolen.[52]

Lodge's ghosts are chiefly interested in telling their desperately tragic story, rather than in teasing out the problem of what kind of beings they are, or what they might deserve from the living. In this, they bear some resemblance to the ghosts in the original *Mirror*, whose creators were anxious to convey the moral whilst steering clear of theological trouble-spots. But in fact they lie at the opposite end of the spectrum. As we have seen, in the first *Mirror* the poets were everything and the ghosts literally nothing – overt fictions whose sole function was to aid the living through their awful examples. What we might term the "second generation" of

---

[51] Thomas Lodge, "The Complaint of Elstred," in *Phillis* (London, 1593), sig. H4r.
[52] Combining elements of national epic and soap opera, Geoffrey of Monmouth's tragic tale of Locrine, Elstred, and Sabrine was retold many times in the sixteenth and early seventeenth centuries, by John Higgins, Edmund Spenser, Michael Drayton, and John Milton, among others. See Schwyzer, "Purity and Danger on the West Bank of the Severn."

Elizabethan ghosts, authored by the likes of Churchyard, Higgins, and Spenser, were more assertive in thrusting themselves forward and demanding their rights; yet they remained dependent on the services of a poet to bring them before the living readers who alone could ease their pain. By contrast, in "The Complaint of Elstred" the poet is little more than an agonized bystander whose presence is never explicitly acknowledged by the ghostly pair. "They sate them downe where I amaz'd remained / And thus their falls successively complained."[53] Rather than begging a hearing, they permit him to overhear. The implication is that Elstred and Sabrine are apt to appear in this place whenever the moon ("Apolloes sister") is at a certain point in the sky, regardless of whether a poet, or anyone, is passing by. These are ghosts who have become part of the British landscape.

Like other ghosts, Elstred and Sabrine are anxious not to be forgotten, and convinced that the rites of remembrance hold the key to easing their suffering. Unlike their predecessors, however, they are not primarily reliant on the poet and his readers for commemoration. The land itself remembers them – or, at least, the water does: "For floting Severne loves Sabrinaes name."

> So may he prattle still unto his wave,
> Sabrinae's name, whilst brine salt teares sea weepeth:
> And if the Gods or men compassion have,
> Compassion that with tender hearts nere sleepeth,
>   We both shall live.[54]

Here the river itself acts as beadsman, the ocean as chief mourner. Britain is capable of commemorating its own dead, and if there is still a role for compassionate readers, it is supplementary at most. Their story done, the two ghosts slip back into their watery tomb without a word to Lodge. With the ghosts, the land, and the water locked in a form of communion which the poet cannot share, Lodge finds himself relegated to the margins of his own poem. It is as if he, and by implication the whole of the living population of England, are the true ghosts, haunting a land whose identity is complete without them and does not extend to them, a land they can never truly inhabit. Never – or not yet.

The Severn had not yet given up all its ghosts. A final specter was waiting to be met with there, this one a "ghost of the nation" in the most literal

[53] Lodge, "The Complaint of Elstred," sig. H4ʳ.
[54] Lodge, "The Complaint of Elstred," sig. L4ʳ.

sense, as the Welsh poet William Harbert of Glamorgan discovered when
he took his own walk by the river in 1606.

> Adowne the oary rocke by silver lee,
> Nigh where the goodly girle was drencht of yore,
> Weeping I saw, and almost wept to see,
> A mournful queen in boat with broken oare
> Chide the stern wave, and strive aginst the Boare:
> With that she plain'd, sad ruth, it griev'd mine eye
> To see, how great and small, how all must die.[55]

The stanza is Spenser's, the location Lodge's, but the ghost is of a kind
unprecedented in the history of the genre. The poem is "The Lamentation
of Britaine." The mournful queen is Britain herself, weeping for her
vanished glory and the forgetfulness of her modern inhabitants.

Harbert's choice of the Severn as the setting of Britain's lament signifies
more than a nod to Lodge. According to Geoffrey of Monmouth, the
Severn had been appointed by Brutus as the border between the newly
created kingdoms of England and Wales. As such, the river could be
considered to be the grave not only of two unfortunate women, but of
Britain itself. The Anglo-Welsh border had long since shifted westward to
the Wye, but the Severn remained a potent and conflicted symbol for the
Welsh in the Tudor era, connoting at once an ancient Welsh identity and
the disruption of a still more ancient British one.[56] Although all of
Harbert's known work is in English (and heavily indebted to Spenser),
he was well-versed in Welsh historical and prophetic traditions, as witnessed in his earlier *Prophesie of Cadwallader, Last King of the Britaines*
(1604). In the field of spectral complaint, Harbert was necessarily reliant on
English models, there being no equivalent tradition in Welsh poetry; yet
the poem's Welsh underpinnings are evident not only in the occasional
hints of *cynghanedd* (e.g., "chi*d*e the s*t*ern wa*v*e, an*d* st*r*i*v*e"), but in its
symbolic geography.[57] Harbert's double poetic identity is reflected in the
double title he gave his work: the title-page reads *Englands Sorrowe*, yet its
contents consist, frontmatter aside, of a single poem, "The Lamentation of
Britaine." In an irony typical of British nationalism, it took a poet of such
complex and divided literary loyalties to conjure such a totalizing symbol
of unified British identity.

[55] William Harbert, *Englands Sorrowe, or A Farewell to Essex* (London, 1606), sig. B1r.
[56] Schwyzer, "A Map of Greater Cambria."
[57] See chapter 1, n. 7.

The appearance of the ghost of Britain adrift on the Severn marks, in several respects, the endpoint of the spectral trajectory traced in this chapter. As I have shown, from 1559 onwards literary ghosts grow ever more ancient, more British, and more nationally-minded. At last, Harbert comes up with the ancient British ghost no subsequent poet can trump. As I have also argued, the nationalization of spectral complaint goes hand in hand with the rehabilitation of Purgatory, now reconceived, in various ways, as the space of the nation. "The Lamentation of Britaine" pushes the parallelism of nation and Purgatory as far as it can go; in this poem, the ghost and the site of purgatorial suffering are paradoxically identical and coextensive. Britain at once complains that she is exiled to a place of torment, and reminds us that she is just where she has always been. She is "banisht by those that by my glory gaine, / Banisht by those that on my breast remaine, / Banisht by those that what they have is mine".[58] Britain, in other words, has become her own Purgatory; her sufferings stem from the borders that cruelly cut across her body (and on one of which she is found floating). At the same time, Britain – if only her name were remembered, if only she were reborn as an integral nation, as she begs to be – has the potential to become her own heaven.

The ghosts of a nation sometimes ask very big things, and Harbert's Britain asks for the biggest thing of all: a Christ-like resurrection. "As man in toombe, so I in grave was laine, / And when I rise, I'le never fall againe."[59] But Britain's deliverance cannot be brought about by prayers, or by a readerly rite of remembrance. What she needs, she explains to Harbert, is an Act of Parliament. The "Lamentation of Britaine" belongs to the period of the Jacobean union controversy, in which the Parliaments of England and Scotland came under intense pressure to accept absolute legal union between the two kingdoms. As I shall discuss in the final chapter, the union controversy led within a very few years to the implosion of British nationalism as it had developed over the course of the Tudor era. What awaited the ghosts of Britain after 1603 was not rebirth, but true oblivion.

---

[58] Harbert, *Englands Sorrowe*, sig. C2^v.
[59] Harbert, *Englands Sorrowe*, sig. C3^r.

CHAPTER 5

"I am Welsh, you know":
the nation in Henry V

Over more than a century, the Tudors had invited memorialization of their Welsh ancestry, had exploited it, had even made it the basis of a new kind of national community. But one step they had never taken. No member of the Tudor dynasty had ever claimed to be Welsh. That, they must have recognized, would be a step too far, a blunder which would expose in the eyes of their English subjects the contradictions and absurdities of British nationalism. It was not until the very twilight of the sixteenth century that an English monarch would at last overcome these inhibitions and proudly lay claim to Welsh nationality. That monarch, was not however, Elizabeth I, or any other Tudor. It was instead a king of the house of Lancaster, Henry V in Shakespeare's play.

Henry V is traditionally regarded as the most English of the histories, and hence of all Shakespeare's works. The words "England" and "English" resound through the play, occurring more than one hundred times. Henry is constantly reminding his men of what they are or should be capable of on the basis of their Englishness, and he is himself referred to by the French king as "Harry England." And yet, remarkably enough, Henry can never quite bring himself to declare unambiguously that he is English.[1] Instead, on two separate occasions in the play, the king of England identifies himself as a Welshman.

Moving in disguise through the English camp on the eve of Agincourt, Henry is accosted by Pistol, the play's representative of little English chauvinism. The king identifies himself equivocally as "Harry *le roi*" (4.1.50). Pistol then inquires if Henry is Cornish, but the king responds

---

[1] The closest he comes is to refer on a number of occasions to "our English" – a phrase that clearly does not mean quite the same thing as "we English." There is an echo here of the Welsh antiquarian Sir John Prise, who brings to the same phrase ("*nostri Anglis*") a touch of ironic acid (see chapter 3). It is true that in the final scene of the play, Henry acknowledges that his son will be part English. But given the notorious uncertainty in the play and its period more generally about the origins of ethnic identity, even this cannot be read as an unambiguous assertion of Henry's own Englishness.

"No, I am a Welshman" (4.1.52). On its own, this claim would not need to be taken very seriously, merely forming part of a game of equivocations. But Henry will go on to make the same remark the next day, this time in all apparent sincerity, to the play's representative Welshman.

FLUELLEN . . . I do believe your majesty takes no scorn to wear the leek upon Saint Tavy's day.

KING HARRY   I wear it for a memorable honour,
For I am Welsh, you know, good countryman.

FLUELLEN   All the water in Wye cannot wash your majesty's Welsh plood out of your pody, I can tell you that. God pless it and preserve it, as long as it pleases his grace, and his majesty too.

KING HARRY   Thanks, good my countryman.

FLUELLEN   By Jeshu, I am your majesty's countryman. I care not who know it, I will confess it to all the world. I need not be ashamed of your majesty, praised be God, as long as your majesty is an honest man.

KING HARRY   God keep me so.   (4.7.93–106)

If Fluellen's puppy-like eagerness to endorse the king's Welshness is understandable, Henry's own stake in laying claim to this identity is more difficult to determine. Even more obscure is the route by which "Welsh plood" has apparently found its way into the king's "pody." Although Henry was indeed born at Monmouth, on the western side of the Wye, both he and Fluellen seem to understand his assertion of Welshness to mean something more and deeper than this, something to do with blood and heritage. Yet the historical Henry V had no Welsh ancestry whatsoever.

In fact, Henry's claim to Welsh blood is not only historically premature but darkly ironic. The Tudor dynasty derived its Welsh lineage, along with its name, from Owain Tudur, the man who would take Henry's place in the bed of Katherine of France and in the pedigrees of future English kings. From the perspective of later British nationalism, Henry V has no future; he merely embodies the usurping Anglo-Saxon bloodline rushing towards its ultimate and deserved dead end. But there are exceptions to every rule. Shakespeare's heroic king is saved for the nation by a drop of blood which has somehow been permitted to flow upstream. Henry "inherits" his Welshness not from his ancestors, but from his Tudor successors.[2]

---

[2] In effect, through his claim to Welsh blood, Henry is taking Owain Tudur's place before Owain has a chance to take his. Intriguingly, this is precisely what happens in an eighteenth-century revision of Shakespeare's play, Aaron Hill's *King Henry the Fifth, or the Conquest of France by the*

Paradoxically, it is Welsh blood that must form the link between an early fifteenth-century English king and a late sixteenth-century English audience.

The secret that Shakespeare's quintessentially "English" history has important archipelagic dimensions has been out for some time. David Baker, Christopher Highley, Willy Maley, and Patricia Parker are among those who have persuasively explored the play in relation to Anglo-Welsh relations, Essex's Irish campaign, and the prospect of Anglo-Scottish union. Whether one reads the play as underwriting England's imperial domination of the British isles, or as signalling a retreat from such dreams of expansion, as marking a transitional moment between English and British identities, or as undermining all claims to a unified identity, it is no longer possible to read the nation in *Henry V* as purely and unproblematically English.[3] Applied to the play as a whole, the Irish soldier Macmorris's famous question, "what ish my nation?," yields no easy answer.

To dismiss the hundred-odd references to "England" as no more than a smokescreen masking a deeper commitment to Britishness would be too simple. The community called "England" has a real and dominant presence in the play. Yet the qualities associated with that national community, and the means by which it is brought into being – in other words, its formation and its form – have less to do with any traditional conception of Englishness than with the ways Britain came to be imagined in the Tudor era. *Henry V* is drenched in the now-familiar language of British nationalism. Whatever name the nation goes by in the play, it is not a given or customary community, but one which must be summoned out of the

English (London, 1723). In Hill's version, Katherine of France is horrified at the prospect of having to marry Henry, not only because he is the enemy of her homeland, but because she is already in love with someone else. The object of her affections is none other than Owen Tudor, a mysterious British knight who courted her on a visit to France a year before. Owen is described in terms familiar from fifteenth-century bardic poetry, and from Spenser: "an imperial offspring / deriv'd from a long line of Britain's kings." Only when the princess lays eyes on Henry V does she realize the truth: "Tis he! Tis Tudor! O amazing chance!" Henry, it transpires, has been going about France in the days of his princehood pretending to be a Welsh squire – even courting his future queen in the name of the man who will marry her when he is dead. Hill makes no attempt to fill in the gaping logical holes in this plot device; but he does, I think, pick up on something that is already happening in Shakespeare's play.

[3] See respectively Willy Maley, *Nation, State and Empire in English Renaissance Literature: Shakespeare to Milton* (Basingstoke: Palgrave Macmillan, 2003), pp. 20–29; Christopher Highley, *Shakespeare, Spenser, and the Crisis in Ireland* (Cambridge: Cambridge University Press, 1997); David J. Baker, *Between Nations: Shakespeare, Spenser, Marvell, and the Question of Britain* (Stanford: Stanford University Press, 1997); Patricia Parker, "Uncertain Unions: Welsh Leeks in *Henry V*" in David Baker and Willy Maley, eds., *British Identities and English Renaissance Literature* (Cambridge: Cambridge University Press, 2002), pp. 81–100.

distant past through the power of bloodlines, the manipulation of nostalgic memory, and, above all, the invocation of ghosts.

"ARTHUR'S BOSOM": THE GHOSTS OF *HENRY V*

Unlike several of his great tragedies, Shakespeare's histories rarely if ever feature actual ghosts. Yet from *1 Henry VI*, which begins with the repeated invocation of Henry V's ghost, to *Henry V* itself, these plays generate a diffuse and pervasive atmosphere of hauntedness.[4] Nowhere is the playwright so concerned with the ways in which the past impinges on the present and the present battens on the past; nowhere is the language of haunting so pervasive. Though no specter appears on stage in *Henry V*, no play in the Shakespearean canon (not even, I would argue, *Hamlet*) is so deeply and thoroughly preoccupied with the presence and power of the dead. Some of the ghosts that haunt the play are English, some British; what they have in common is possession of some part of the lost national essence, which the living can recapture only by entering into communion with the dead generations.

Of the many spirits that haunt *Henry V*, the first and the most regularly invoked is that of the king's glorious English ancestor and martial role model, Edward III. His ghost is initially conjured by the Archbishop of Canterbury, whose appeal to Henry combines the language of spectrality with an odd theatricality:

> Look back into your mighty ancestors.
> Go, my dread lord, to your great-grandsire's tomb,
> From whom you claim; invoke his warlike spirit,
> And your great uncle's, Edward the Black Prince,
> Who on the French ground played a tragedy,
> Making defeat on the full power of France,
> Whiles his most mighty father on a hill
> Stood smiling to behold his lion's whelp
> Forage in blood of French nobility.   (1.2.102–10)

Mingling spiritcraft with stagecraft, Canterbury figures Edward III and his son at once as ghosts and as players in a tragic drama. The task imposed on Henry is, in a double sense, that of *revival* – of the dead themselves, and of

---

[4] Although *Richard III*, uniquely among the histories, features beings called ghosts, even these are confined to the world of dreams, and come across more clearly as heralds of divine justice than as the souls of dead human individuals.

the successful theatrical production staged at Crécy. The terms of the archbishop's exhortation are recapitulated in the subsequent urgings of Ely and Exeter. The former calls on the king to "Awake remembrance of the valiant dead, / And with your puissant arm renew their feats" (1.2.115–16), and invokes the blood of Edward running in Henry's veins. Exeter reminds the king that his fellow monarchs "Do all expect that you should rouse yourself / As did the former lions of your blood" (1.2.123–24). Called upon at once to represent the dead in his living person and to re-present their past performance, Henry finds himself in a position strikingly akin to that of Shakespeare's own actors at the beginning of the play (though the king is lucky enough to have at his disposal resources for which the Chorus in the Prologue must yearn in vain: "A kingdom for a stage, princes to act, / And monarchs to behold the swelling scene" [3–4]).

Repeatedly invoked by friend and foe alike, Edward III haunts the play as the Ghost of Conquests Past. Another term for him would be the Ghost of Nostalgia. First Canterbury and later the French King (2.4.50–60) bring a remarkable visual intensity to their evocations of the vanished, irrecoverable scene of 1346, gazing back across lost time to behold the king and the Black Prince "as if really alive." In a play riddled with nostalgia, the English (and, Fluellen reminds us, Welsh) victory at Crécy is the spatial and temporal locus upon which Shakespeare's characters gaze with longing. Desperate to get back to Crécy, subsequent generations invoke Edward's spirit and re-enact his deeds, on the field of Agincourt and later on the London stage. Shakespeare's play can thus be seen as the classic object of Petrarchan aesthetics: a thing of beauty born out of frustrated longing for the irrecoverable past.

Viewed more closely, however, the nostalgia of *Henry V* turns out to go beyond familiar Petrarchan models. Normally, nostalgia takes for its object something that is supposed to have really existed (but has since been lost): "Merrie England," for instance, or the Bible in Welsh, or Laura in the flesh. Nostalgia may give rise to innumerable *simulacra* – in paint, in poetry, and in the mind's eye – but all of these are understood to refer to the long-lost "real thing." In *Henry V*, however, when we trace the nostalgia to its source what we find is simply more nostalgia. The central nostalgic tropes of haunting and playing are associated not only with Henry V's attempt to repeat the victory at Crécy, but with the original victory itself. Even when they were winning that original victory – of which all later victories are only re-enactments – Edward III and his son were already players in "a tragedy." Even when they were living and breathing, they were already ghosts who, in the French King's words, "haunted us in our familiar paths"

(2.4.52). The nostalgic desire to trace national history back to a definite moment of plenitude, before the sundering of word and thing, seems doomed to failure. This is not to say that *Henry V* is anti-nostalgic, but rather that the form nostalgia takes in the play is peculiarly radical (or, more properly, anti-radical, for it seems to have no root).[5]

Crécy may be one object of impossible desire in the play, but longing for the lost past is not confined to visions of victory in France. There is another ghost at work, another figure for lost plenitude, who in several respects looms larger than Edward III: this is the ghost of Sir John Falstaff.[6] Falstaff never appears, and his death is announced early in the play, yet his sheer absence is, for many readers, the play's defining feature. Though his demise may be as impossible to grasp, as far "out of all compass" (*1 Henry IV*, 3.3.17) as the fat knight himself, there is no doubt that he is gone for good. Gone – but gone where? The problem of the play's nostalgia – what it is, and what, in both senses, it is for – is curiously bound up with a more intimate problem, that of the fate of Falstaff's soul.

If it is difficult to accept that one so large and full of life as Falstaff could leave no trace of himself among the living, it is even harder to picture the progress of his spirit beyond the grave. Purgatory might seem an appropriate destination for a character who periodically, if with transparent insincerity, declared an intention to "purge" and "live cleanly" (*1 Henry IV*, 5.5.1556–57). But without recourse to the possibility of a third space between heaven and hell, both the audience and Falstaff's old companions find themselves in a state of some bewilderment about the location of the fat knight's soul. "Would I were with him," declares Bardolph, "wheresome'er he is, either in heaven or in hell." Hostess Quickly quickly retorts: "Nay, sure he's not in hell. He's in Arthur's bosom, if ever man went to Arthur's bosom" (2.3.7–10). In her attempt to determine the whereabouts of one ghost, the Hostess introduces us to another.

Quickly, of course, has simply confused Arthur with Abraham. What else should we expect from a character who says "adultery" when she means "assault" and "honeyseed" for "homicide"? Yet here, as elsewhere, there is a

---

[5] A similar – not identical – effect is produced in *Julius Caesar*, when the assassins imagine their deed being "acted over" on future stages. Jonathan Goldberg suggests that "the perfect reciprocity of the metaphor hints that history itself may be a series of representations." *James I and the Politics of Literature* (Baltimore: Johns Hopkins University Press, 1983), pp. 166–67. See also Marjorie Garber, *Shakespeare's Ghost Writers: Literature as Uncanny Causality* (New York: Routledge, 1987), pp. 55–56.

[6] The image of Falstaff as the play's unquiet ghost is suggested by David Quint: "Alive or dead, Falstaff haunts the play from the wings"; "'Alexander the Pig': Shakespeare on History and Poetry," *Boundary 2* 10 (1982), 52.

method to the malapropism. Just as Quickly's bawdy slips of the tongue reveal more about herself than she intends, so in substituting a British king for a Biblical patriarch she unwittingly lays bare a scandalous truth. Absurd and blasphemous as it is, Quickly's error on this occasion must have struck some of Shakespeare's audience as unsettlingly familiar. They were used to hearing the same error routinely – if rather more subtly – propagated by the organs of the Elizabethan church and state.

There is no doubt about what Quickly is trying to say. But what exactly was "Abraham's bosom"? The place is first mentioned as the destination of the soul of Lazarus in Luke 16: "And it came to pass, that the beggar died, and was carried by the angels into Abraham's bosom."[7] From this vantage point Lazarus is able to see and hear – but not to comfort – the rich man being tormented in Hell. Early Christian writers glossed Abraham's bosom as a place of "interim refreshment" where the souls of the righteous awaited their final entry into Heaven.[8] Some later theologians equated it with heaven itself, whilst others made it a kind of salubrious suburb of Hell. It was inevitable that most Protestant reformers, pledged to eradicate all middle spaces between Hell and Heaven, would regard Abraham's bosom with suspicion. Given that it had the authority of scripture, the existence of such a place could not be flatly denied, but it could be played down – even, to a certain extent, hushed up. Whereas in the old Catholic funeral service the soul of the deceased was commended to God "to be laid in the bosom of thy patriarch Abraham," from 1552 all mention of Abraham's bosom was omitted from the Book of Common Prayer.[9]

While English Protestants said as little as possible about Abraham's bosom, they were somewhat more forthcoming on the subject of King Arthur. Very early in the English Reformation, a link had been forged between Arthur and the True Church, both arch-enemies of Rome. As we have seen, the precedent of Arthur's imperial conquests was invoked – not very successfully – by the Duke of Norfolk in his interview with Chapuys in 1530. A year earlier, the Protestant Simon Fish had argued in his attack on Purgatory and suffrages that: "The nobill king Arthur had never ben abill to have caried his armie to the fote of the mountaines, to resist the coming

---

[7] See Le Goff, *Birth of Purgatory*, p. 43.

[8] Tertullian, cited in Le Goff, *Birth of Purgatory*, p. 47

[9] Cressy, *Birth, Marriage and Death*, p. 396. The 1549 service offered a halfway house, praying that the soul might "dwell in the region of light, with Abraham, Isaac, and Jacob" (pp. 396–97). Cressy notes that though Abraham's Bosom was omittted from the funeral service, "this comfortable notion persisted in popular culture and in sermons" (p. 384). But Quickly's slip, which Cressy cites, suggests that popular memory was somewhat vague.

downe of Lucius the Emporer if suche yerely exactions had ben taken of his people."[10] The choice Fish offered Henry VIII was a simple one. You may have a middle place between heaven and hell or you may have Arthur's Empire; you cannot afford both. Imperial Britain and Purgatory were effectively in economic and conceptual competition to fill a single space. It is no accident that the English crown's seizure in 1547–48 of the assets set aside for the relief of souls in Purgatory coincided with its aggressive attempt to force the Scots to participate in a renewed British Empire. England's rulers had chosen Arthur over Abraham – the same choice made in *Henry V* by Hostess Quickly.

The Hostess's slip depends on her not knowing much about Abraham, but also on her not knowing much, in a concrete sense, about Arthur. Indeed, her opportunities to discover hard information about Arthur, beyond unenlightening snatches of Falstaff's drunken songs (*2 Henry IV*, 2.4.28–29), would have been few. The Tudor fixation on Arthur as national hero-patriarch and scourge of Rome went hand and hand with a curious reluctance to tell tales about him. His was a name to conjure with, but what was conjured was rarely Arthur himself, at least not in the sense of a historical actor associated with particular deeds.[11] This reluctance to narrate does not necessarily indicate a lack of interest, but rather an awareness of Arthur's radical vulnerability to skepticism. Attempts to defend Arthur's historicity, such as John Leland's clumsy riposte to Polydore Vergil earlier in the century, probably did more harm than good.[12] Later adherents seem to have understood that keeping silence was the best way of keeping faith. The chronicler Holinshed was typical in his

---

[10] Simon Fish, *A Supplicacyon for the Beggers* (Antwerp?, 1529), p. 2v.

[11] There are, of course, several exceptions to this rule, most notably the Prince Arthur of Spenser's *Faerie Queene* (though this knight bears only the loosest relation to the Arthur of medieval tradition). Arthur featured in one Elizabethan Inns of Court play, *The Misfortunes of Arthur*, but the absence of more such plays is surprising given that other heroes and episodes from the British History were dramatized repeatedly (e.g. the stories of Brutus and his sons, King Lear and his daughters, the Roman and Saxon invasions of Britain). It is an equally curious fact that the ghost of Arthur does not appear in any volume of the Tudor *Mirror for Magistrates*, though many of his near contemporaries feature in Blenerhasset's *Second Part*. As Blenerhasset explains in the prose section following the complaint of the ghost of Cadwaladr, the "great desire ... to heare this man, hath made us to overpasse king Arthur ... But it is not much amisse, for of Arthur there be whole volumes" (450). Unlike the many parts of the *Mirror for Magistrates*, these volumes were not often reprinted in the Elizabethan era.

[12] *Assertio inclytissimi Arturi Regis Britanniae* (London, 1544), translated by Richard Robinson as *A learned and true assertion of the original, life, actes, and death of the most noble, valiant, and renoumed Prince Arthure, King of great Brittaine* (London, 1582). For a sensitive account of the dilemmas faced by later Tudor writers in relation to Arthur and his anti-Roman victories, see Curran, *Roman Invasions*, pp. 225–50.

desire to uphold the existence of the historical Arthur, without endorsing any particular story about him:

Of this Arthur manie things are written beyond credit, for there is no ancient author of authoritie that confirmeth the same: but surely as may be thought he was some woorthie man . . .[13]

Shakespeare and his contemporaries thus knew Arthur less as a historical ruler than as a haunting absence at the heart of national life. The association of Arthur with absence, otherworldliness and the afterlife dates back at least to Geoffrey of Monmouth, who records that following the battle of Camlan the mortally wounded king was transported to the Isle of Avalon. Sojourning in Avalon, poised between this world and the next, Arthur could be said to be neither living nor dead. In spite of the exhumation of Arthur's bones at Glastonbury in the twelfth century, rumors of his return continued to alternate with avowals of his demise on both sides of the Severn. In a variant tradition, found in the *mirabilia* of Gervase of Tilbury, and as far away as Italy, Arthur figures as a king of the dead holding court in a subterranean palace.[14] In England, these associations with the other- or underworld were probably enhanced by the misfortune historically attached to Arthur's name. Too often in English history, Arthur was the prince who died too soon – Arthur, the grandson of Henry II, kept from the throne and perhaps murdered by his uncle John; Arthur, Prince of Wales, struck down by sickness soon after his marriage to Catherine of Aragon. By the later Tudor era, then, the name of Arthur seemed to describe a potential which was at once powerfully British and barred from expression in British history. Arthur had a kingdom, but it was not of this world.

When Hostess Quickly invokes "Arthur's bosom," she reveals both how the theme of British Empire had come to fill the space evacuated by Purgatory, and how as a consequence Britain had itself been spiritualized and spectralized, made otherworldly. Unlocatable in either the past or the present, Britain was seemingly confined to a third space *between* the present and the past. Seen from this perspective, the task of realizing the nation

---

[13] Raphael Holinshed, *Holinshed's Chronicles*, ed. Henry Ellis (London, 1807), vol. 1, p. 574. The position adopted by Holinshed and other chroniclers with regard to Arthur resembles the compromise Martin Luther sought to reach on the question of Purgatory: "I still hold that it exists . . . My advice is that no one allow the pope to invent new articles of faith, but be willing to remain in ignorance, with St. Augustine, about what the souls in Purgatory are doing and what their condition is." Quoted in Greenblatt, *Hamlet in Purgatory*, p. 33.

[14] Schmitt, *Ghosts in the Middle Ages*, pp. 116–17.

in the present would depend less on forging a link with the past than on opening a gap within the present moment itself, through which Britain might enter in. The journey undertaken by Henry V and his followers in Shakespeare's play will be, in more than one sense, "unto the breach."[15]

"COMMUNE UP THE BLOOD": CONJURING THE NATION

Near the beginning of the play, as we have seen, the king is urged by his counsellors to summon up the spirits of the dead. In the final scene, he receives practical advice on the art of conjuration. In response to Henry's own admission that "I cannot so conjure up the spirit of love in her [Katherine] that he will appear in his true likeness" (5.2.268–69), Burgundy points out that "If you would conjure in her, you must make a circle," and goes on to joke about what might be raised in the "circle" of Catherine's genitals. Burgundy's immediate intention may be simply to use sexual humor as a means of easing the masculine tensions of the negotiating chamber – a few moments later, the treaty of peace will be agreed, deciding the fate of both Katherine and France. If the vulgar exchange has any wider resonance for the audience, it is because it at last gives name to what Henry has been doing throughout the play, that is, conjuring spirits. More specifically, he has been conjuring them *inside* living bodies – not least his own.

While he was still a prince, Shakespeare's Hal was already in the habit of exchanging identities with others, primarily through the mode of "theatrical improvisation."[16] But when he becomes king at the end of *2 Henry IV*, he goes from trading roles to trading souls. With a perverse kind of filial piety, he lets his brothers know that "My father is gone wild into his grave; / For in his tomb lie my affections, / And with his spirits sadly I survive" (5.2.123–28). Here the spirit is figured as a kind of commodity available for exchange – it is as if the living and the dead are members not only of one

---

[15] Building on Hamlet's observation that "The time is out of joint," Jacques Derrida uses the term "spectrality" to denote the "non-contemporaneity of the present time with itself" (*Specters of Marx*, p. 25). The ghost for Derrida figures the way in which the present is fragmentary and heterogeneous, shot through with what is past and what is yet to come (or come back). A homologous splitting of the present moment, creating "a temporality of the 'in-between'," has been seen by Homi Bhabha as a characteristic feature of the nation; *The Location of Culture* (London: Routledge, 1994), p. 148. Here as elsewhere, the peculiar paradoxes of British nationalism can be seen as exacerbating and highlighting tensions and themes which may also be inevitable consequences of nationalism.

[16] Greenblatt, "Invisible Bullets" in *Shakespearean Negotiations: The Circulation of Social Energy in Renaissance England* (Berkeley: University of California Press, 1988), p. 46.

community, but of a common market. In *Henry V*, however, the king no longer seems to give anything in exchange for the souls he takes, but is instead bent on a kind of "primitive accumulation" of spiritual energy. At the beginning of the play Canterbury remarks in wonder that the king's body has become "as a paradise / T'envelop and contain celestial spirits" (1.1.31–2), while in the next scene he urges Henry to accumulate still more: "Go, my dread lord, to your great-grandsire's tomb, / From whom you claim; invoke his warlike spirit . . . "

While Henry's corporeal coffers are stuffed with spirits, elsewhere in the play it is hard to discover a soul and a body inhabiting the same space. Instead, the play abounds with images of soulless (yet somehow animated) bodies on the one hand, and free-floating spirits on the other. Falstaff is again a case in point. At the beginning of the play the fat knight is still alive, but only as a physical husk: "The king has killed his heart" (2.1.79). But Falstaff is not unique – the bodies of all of Henry's subjects are equally hollow. As Westmorland tells the king, their "hearts have left their bodies here in England / And lie pavilioned in the fields of France." Canterbury pleads "O let their bodies follow" (1.2.128–30). The same image is recapitulated, with a disturbing twist, in the Chorus's report of the plot against Henry's life. England, a "little body with a mighty heart" (2.0.17) is found to harbor "A nest of hollow bosoms" (2.0.21) which have been filled by "the gilt of France" (2.0.26). Hollowness, then, is a quality common to Henry's loyal subjects and his treacherous ones. Their bodies are, in the curious phrase coined by Thomas Nashe, "dis-soul-joined" – not dead exactly, but definitely out of joint.[17] While the treacherous bodies are content to harbor French souls (or *sous*), the loyal bodies are bound for France to reclaim their own.

The soldiers who take ship for France are impelled by a kind of nostalgia – the dream of recovering the lost unity of soul and body. But, given the way nostalgia works in *Henry V*, this is an unattainable dream. There is an uncanny logic to the fact that almost as soon as Henry's soldiers set foot on French soil and regain their souls, their bodies begin to wither. By the eve of Agincourt, they have been transformed by this wasting process into "So many horrid ghosts" (4.0.28). While the Chorus perceives them as disembodied souls, Lord Grandpré sees them as soulless bodies: "Yon island carrions" (4.2.39). His compatriot the Constable of France recycles the by now familiar image of British bodies as hollow cases: "Do but behold yon

[17] *The Works of Thomas Nashe*, 2: 241 ("dissoule-joyned").

poor and starvéd band, / And your fair show shall suck away their souls, / Leaving them but the shells and husks of men" (4.2.16–18). But the Constable does not understand what kind of force he is up against; the dis-soul-joining he describes has already taken place, and seems, indeed, to be the army's natural condition. What the French are facing looks disturbingly like an army of the undead – an army that has come to France, as Pistol proclaims, "To suck, to suck, the very blood to suck!" (2.3.47)

Henry's soldiers at Agincourt may be very near to death before the battle even starts – but death itself, as the king explains to the French Herald, would only enhance their power:

> those that leave their valiant bones in France,
> Dying like men, though buried in your dunghills,
> They shall be famed; for there the sun shall greet them
> And draw their honors reeking up to heaven,
> Leaving their earthly parts to choke your clime,
> The smell whereof shall breed a plague in France.
> Mark then abounding valor in our English,
> That being dead, like to the bullet's grazing
> Break out into a second course of mischief,
> Killing in relapse of mortality.   (4.3.99–108)

Here the king makes two points which are central to his understanding of the nation over which he rules. Firstly, the dead are powerful – as or even more powerful than the living. Secondly, there is something about their power that is peculiarly "English." These perceptions are central to Henry's two great orations to his men, at Harfleur and before Agincourt. In these speeches, Henry seeks to command the loyalty of the living by reminding them of the dead and of their own deaths. (A strange way of going about things, one might think – but is not the purpose of addressing the troops, in every age, to "raise their spirits"?)

"Once more unto the breach, dear friends, once more; / Or close the wall up with our English dead" (3.1.1–2). In his first utterance in France, Henry seems – uncharacteristically – to be offering his followers a choice. But the choice is a strange one. I suspect that many readers and auditors mentally supply what seems to be a missing line ("once more, / And either we will overcome Harfleur, / Or..."), making the choice one between glorious victory or equally glorious death. As the text stands, however, closing up the wall with English corpses is not suggested as one possible outcome of storming the breach, but rather as an alternative to it (though not quite the alternative preferred by Pistol and his mates, which is simply to go nowhere near the breach). If the English do not renew the assault on the breach, the bodies of the brave soldiers who have fallen there will be dishonored, used in place of bricks and mortar to seal up the hole in the wall.[18] Henry's men must now choose between continuing the struggle or subjecting those who have already given their lives for England to the ultimate humiliation.

This indeed is precisely what Henry goes on to say, referring now to an earlier generation of national martyrs:

> On, on, you noblest English,
> Whose blood is fet from fathers of war-proof . . .
> Dishonour not your mothers; now attest
> That those whom you called fathers did beget you.   (3.1.16–17, 22–23)

National service – fighting in the English army – turns out to be a service performed on behalf of the dead. Behind Henry's voice in this speech we hear the voices of fathers, mothers, and friends, calling upon the living not to dishonor or betray them. These are the same voices that, two generations earlier, called upon their loved ones for relief from the torments of Purgatory. And they are the same kinds of voices that, more than three centuries later, would cry to the living from their graves in foreign soil:

> Take up our quarrel with the foe:
> To you from failing hands we throw
>   The torch; be yours to hold it high.
>   If ye break faith with us who die
> We shall not sleep, though poppies grow
>   In Flanders fields.[19]

Henry's speech at Harfleur is explicitly a conjuration. Interweaving a spectral discourse with a genealogical one, he commands his followers to "conjure up the blood" (3.1.7). A few lines later comes another conjuration, figured this time as a kind of calisthenics: "Hold hard the breath, and bend up every spirit to his full height" (3.1.16). These "spirits" are on one level physiological substances on a par with "humors," but they are also the spirits of demanding ancestors who have come to inhabit their

---

[18] If "close" is an imperative, then it is the English themselves who will have to repair the wall with the bodies of their comrades, redoubling the shame. But the line is probably better understood as "let the wall close up/be closed up with our English dead."

[19] John McCrae, "In Flanders Fields," in *In Flanders Fields and Other Poems* (New York: Putnam, 1919), p. 3.

descendants' bodies, as Henry's own body is inhabited by Edward III, and many others.[20] Almost as soon as he has conjured these spirits within the circles of his soldier's bodies, Henry contrives to release them into the world:

> the game's afoot;
> Follow your spirit; and upon this charge,
> Cry "God for Harry, England, and Saint George!"   (3.3.32–34)

The spirits, which moments before were inside the soldiers' bodies, are now somewhere ahead of them, and the bodies must race to catch up. The line recalls how Henry's subjects were earlier forced to cross the seas to France to catch up with their missing hearts. "Follow your spirit" may refer as well to the souls of the soldiers who have already fallen at the wall, and are waiting impatiently there for the living to rejoin them. Here time itself is breached; the spirits of the dead come out of the past but they also come from a future that must be caught up with, intersecting the present moment from two directions.[21]

Where most modern texts have Henry exhorting his men to "conjure up the blood," earlier editions prefer another, equally necromantic, verb: "summon." In the Folio text, however, the word is neither of these, but the more puzzling "commune." The appearance of this word in the Folio can be explained as a compositor's error – but if that is what it is, the nameless typesetter had a gift for inspired malapropism to rival that of Hostess Quickly.[22] For Henry's oration, dwelling nostalgically on past glories and calling for their romantic re-enactment, is a conjuration not only of ghosts but of a community. The name of that community is England, the nation. While the aristocrats in Henry's army have noble ancestors to haunt them, the common soldiers – "yeomen / Whose limbs were made in England" (3.1.25–26) – have as their ancestor the nation itself. To "commune up the blood" is to recognize one's membership in and debt of service to a community. It is England whose spirit these yeomen follow to the breach, England

---

[20] The use of the possessive pronoun "his," rather than "its," enhances this reading, though "his" in this era could also be used impersonally. On this passage see Graham Holderness, *Shakespeare: The Histories* (London: Macmillan, 2000), p. 147.

[21] As Derrida asks of the ghost in *Hamlet*, which also demands to be followed: "What does it mean to follow a spirit? And what if this came down to being followed by it, always, persecuted perhaps by the very chase we are leading? Here again what seems to be out front, the future, comes back in advance: from the past, from the back"; *Specters of Marx*, p. 10.

[22] "Walter's emendation, accepted by nearly all recent editors, presupposes an easy minim misreading of *coniure* as *comune*." (Taylor, ed., *Henry V*, note to 3.1.7.)

whose ghost commands that they spend their lives in a king's quarrel on a foreign field. There is much of death in Henry's speech at Harfleur, but there is also a kind of birth: the birth of a nation, a breach birth.[23]

Henry's appeal to the common soldiers – inciting them with neither threats nor promises of gain, but with the spirit of a nation – is a remarkable innovation in Shakespeare's historical world. Like all innovations, it takes a while to catch on. Pistol and his companions are not persuaded of the debt they owe to England's ghost – nor, as Henry discovers on the eve of Agincourt, are the more sober soldiers John Bates, Michael Williams, and Alexander Court. Far from feeling himself to be haunted by any ghost, Williams suspects that the king will be haunted by legions of them, as a consequence of his military adventurism:

> But if the cause be not good, the King himself hath a heavy reckoning to make, when all those legs and arms and heads, chopped off in a battle shall join together at the latter day, and cry all, "We died at such a place" . . . I am afeard there are few die well that die in a battle, for how can they charitably dispose of anything, when blood is their argument? Now, if these men do not die well, it will be a black matter for the King that led them to it . . .   (4.1.128–37)

The fear of dying without the right spiritual preparation – as the Ghost in *Hamlet* puts it, "Unhouseled, disappointed, unaneled" (1.5.77) – was a terrible one. Williams's fear that he will not be able to "dispose of anything" charitably can be taken to mean simply that he will have no chance to prepare his soul for death – but, more specifically, it suggests that he will have no chance to give what little he has for masses to be said in his name, easing his suffering in Purgatory. The king, in short, is guilty of imposing intolerable torments on his men not only on earth but beyond the grave. It is only just in Williams's view that these torments should in turn be imposed on him, by a horde of clamorous and vengeful ghosts.

The disguised Henry's response to Williams is lengthy but all in all rather lame. It consists largely of a string of legalistic assertions: "the king is not bound to answer the particular endings of his soldiers, the father of his son, nor the master of his servant . . . Every subject's duty is the king's, but every subject's soul is his own." Whether or not Henry succeeds logically in

---

[23] Of course, while a monarch like Henry V might for various reasons wish his subjects to feel themselves members of a national community, he would certainly not wish the nation to become a "commune," in the modern sense. As Claire McEachern argues, the communities fostered by the theater and the nation were in need of regulation, for an excess of community (e.g., community of goods) was at least as threatening to the social order as not enough. "The ambiguity which attends a common space, be it of the theater or of the body politic, is rife in the unions which *Henry V* imagines" (*Poetics of English Nationhood, 1590–1612*), p. 107.

countering the charges, he utterly fails on a rhetorical level, offering only bloodless parables and maxims in response to Williams's vivid images of butchered bodies and shrieking heads. Fortunately for his cause, the king has all night to think of a better answer.

When Henry kneels alone to pray to his God, he apparently cannot rid his mind of the awful images implanted there by Williams. He has been forced to remember a certain ghost – perhaps the most terrifying of all the ghosts in the play, the one the king has been most anxious not to see. Henry's prayer is a desperate attempt to forestall or defer this ghost's just demand for retribution: "Not today, O Lord, / O not today, think not upon the fault / My father made in compassing the crown" (4.1.274–76). Henry proceeds to list the steps he has taken to appease the spirit of Richard II. He has given the corpse new burial in Westminster Abbey, and bestowed "contrite tears" upon it. He has endowed almshouses. Finally, he has had recourse to the most effective (and expensive) method of silencing a ghost, which is to pray it into heaven: "I have built / Two chantries, where the sad and solemn priests / Still sing for Richard's soul" (4.1.288–90). In spite of this impressive portfolio of spiritual investments, the king remains fearful of the ghost, convinced that "all that I can do is nothing worth..." If this is not simply more of Henry's false modesty, it may represent a proto-Protestant skepticism about the efficacy of prayer for the dead. But whether or not Shakespeare's king has covert Lollard sympathies, what is clear is that, in the moments before he goes forth to meet his men, his mind is running on Purgatory and the forms of solidarity that have grown up around it. This train of thought is reflected in the famous "Saint Crispin's day" oration, Henry's second and better answer to Michael Williams.

Whereas at Harfleur the king reminded his men of their debt to the dead, at Agincourt he speaks to them of their own deaths. To die in battle, he declares, is not a thing to be feared, but an honor. Honor is a kind of currency to be shared out equally among the combatants, so that the fewer there are, the more each shall receive. Any soldier who does not wish to receive a share, therefore, is offered a passport and money with which to depart: "We would not die in that man's company / That fears his fellowship to die with us" (4.3.49). What "fellowship" connotes in this instance is something much more specific than general comradeship. It is another name for a religious fraternity, or gild.[24]

---

[24] Taylor glosses fellowship as follows: "'right and duty as our companion.' OED gives no exact parallel; this use apparently derives from the sense 'guild, corporation, company' (sb. 7) – fraternal organizations which conferred obligations as well as privileges" (Henry V, note to 4.3.39).

Henry is telling his soldiers that they are members of the same kind of society that, up to 1547, expressed the solidarity of the living with the dead. A man who "fears his fellowship," then, is one who refuses the duty of gild membership because he doubts the power of its solidarity, fearing the gild will do nothing for him after his death. But, it transpires, there is no such man in Henry's army. The theme of "fellowship" is Henry's real answer to the two problems that arose in his debate with Williams: the gaping class division between kings and common soldiers, and the fear of the soul's fate after death. Abandoning the class-consciousness that marked his speech at Harfleur, Henry now offers all his men equal membership in the fraternity: "We few, we happy few, we band of brothers / For he today that sheds his blood with me will be my brother."[25] Nor is death to be feared, for those who die can trust in their place in the annual general obit: "Crispin Crispian shall ne'er go by, / From this day to the ending of the world, / But we in it shall be remembered." Those who read the roll in days to come will not, of course, have earned their membership in this fraternity – the gild of St. Crispian – on the battlefield. Rather, they will have inherited it as patrimony, as part of what it means to be English – or, more properly given the saints in question, British.

Who were Crispin and Crispianus? According to most martyrologies, they were a pair of Roman shoemakers. However, Shakespeare's source for these saint's names, Thomas Deloney's *The Gentle Craft* (1597), tells a different story. In Deloney's version, Crispin and Crispianus are two third-century British princes who withstand and triumph over Roman persecution.[26] Crispin secretly marries the Roman emperor's daughter, thereby restoring the British bloodline to rule over Britain (rather as Owain Tudur would do twelve centuries later, by secretly marrying Henry V's widow). Still more heroically, Crispianus turns soldier and wins a miraculous victory in France. Both genealogically and militarily, then, Crispin and Crispianus come before Henry V (and, like specters, also lie ahead of him). Any commemoration of the putatively "English" victory at Agincourt, "Fought on the day of Crispin Crispian" (4.7.83) is inevitably also a

---

[25] Not all gilds, of course, were equally inclusive. Henry later acknowledges that the French too have a national fraternity, but one which – like the great city gilds – restricts its membership to the elite: "Here was a royal fellowship of death!" (4.8.95).

[26] See *The Works of Thomas Deloney*, ed. F. O. Mann (Oxford, 1912, repr. 1967), pp. 99–102. Shakespeare's use of Deloney's spelling (Crispianus rather than the more usual Crispinian) is pointed out by the Arden editor T.W. Craik (*Henry V* [London, 1995] note to l. 4.3.40). See also Alison A. Chapman, "Whose Saint Crispin's Day Is It? Shoemaking, Holiday Making, and the Politics of Memory in Early Modern England," *Renaissance Quarterly* 54 (2001), 1467–1494.

commemoration of an originary British victory. The national fellowship which Henry sees stretching forward "From this day to the ending of the world" stretches backward beyond the origins of Englishness itself.

"FLAT UNRAISED SPIRITS": SHAKESPEARE'S HAUNTED STAGE

With Crispin's name in their mouths, the members of this English "fellowship" go forth and win the day. Their victory over next-to-impossible odds seems nothing short of miraculous – a perception Henry is quick to exploit after the battle with his sentence of death on any man who fails to attribute the outcome to God alone. If God has indeed worked a miracle on the field of Agincourt, he has presumably done so in answer to Henry's prayer on the eve of the battle, a prayer not simply for victory, but for something more specific, and more peculiar:

> O God of battles, steel my soldiers' hearts,
> Possess them not with fear. Take from them now
> The sense of reck'ning, ere th'opposèd numbers
> Pluck their hearts from them. (4.1.271–74)

Henry here harps on his favorite spectral themes: possession, and the plucking (or stealing) of hearts.[27] But his prayer is really less concerned with the numinous than with numeracy; he is effectively asking God to massage the figures in his favor. The miracle with which God responds is indeed a miracle of mystical "reck'ning." The English win at Agincourt because there are more of them than there are.

This apparent paradox holds true on several levels. It describes, first of all, the superior physical force of the English when their spirits are drawn up to full height. When his men were fresh, says Henry, "I thought upon one pair of English legs / Did march three Frenchmen" (3.6.148–9). It also means that there are many more Englishmen on the field than just Henry's living soldiers – Edward III and his son are there, and all the ghostly ancestors whose names are enrolled in the general obit of the fellowship. Finally, it is to say that each Englishman represents in himself all other Englishmen at Agincourt. The advantage the English have over the French

---

[27] Those listening to rather than reading Henry's prayer – which is to say, both God and the theatrical audience – must inevitably hear the first line as "steal my soldiers' hearts." Henry thus seems to be asking God not to fortify the men's hearts but to remove them before the enemy has the opportunity of doing so.

is cohesive military discipline, a discipline they experience as a kind of spiritual communion, or (to revert to the language of the Folio) "communing up." There are more Englishmen than there are, and at the same time there is only one.

The semi-mystical doctrine of many-in-one and one-in-many had long been associated with the English army, at least by Shakespeare. In *1 Henry VI*, the great English warrior Talbot is briefly captured by the Countess of Auvergne. When she expresses mock astonishment at his puny body, Talbot explains that what she has captured is really only "Talbot's shadow" (2.3.47).

> I am but a shadow of myself.
> You are deceiv'd, my substance is not here;
> For what you see is but the smallest part
> And least proportion of humanity.
> I tell you, madam, were the whole frame here
> It is of such a spacious lofty pitch,
> Your roof were not sufficient to contain't.   (2.3.50–56)

To prove his point, Talbot winds his horn and the English army marches in, introduced by their commander as "his substance, sinews, arms and strength".

There is, for Shakespeare, something peculiarly "English" about this ability to incorporate many bodies in one. The action of "communing up" is at once the special magic of the English and the experience by which the national community is brought into being. This is yet another case in which Englishness takes on a distinctly British hue; for what was the longed-for unification of Great Britain but the incorporation of many national bodies within one? In a different sense, the practice of "communing up" can be recognized as constitutive not of Englishness or Britishness alone, but of nationhood itself. As Benedict Anderson observes, "the members of even the smallest nation will never know most of their fellow-members, meet them, or even hear of them, yet in the minds of each lives the image of their communion."[28] The essence of belonging to a nation is to know – by an act of faith that can never be verified through firsthand knowledge – that there are more of you than are there.

Even when every available actor and stagehand donned a breastplate and rushed on stage to represent Talbot's sinews in the scene with the Countess, they could hardly have been mistaken for an actual army. For the audience to share in the wonder of this moment, they must understand that just as

---

[28] Anderson, *Imagined Communities*, p. 6.

Talbot in his puny body is but a shadow of himself, so the actors on stage are but shadows of a far greater substance. The secret of the English army, that there are more of them than there are, is also the secret of the theater, and it is up to the spectators to create for themselves a miracle of "reck'ning." In *Henry V,* the Chorus explains how this may be done:

> Can this cockpit hold
> The vasty fields of France? Or may we cram
> Within this wooden O the very casques
> That did affright the air at Agincourt?
> O pardon: since a crookèd figure may
> Attest in little place a million,
> So let us, ciphers to this great account,
> On your imaginary forces work....
> Piece out our imperfections with your thoughts:
> Into a thousand parts divide one man,
> And make imaginary puissance.   (Prologue, 11–25)

A crooked figure can attest a million; it can conjure an army, or a nation. Is this math, or is it magic? It seems to be both. A modern reader might mistake the mathematical metaphor for a rationalist denial that there is anything supernatural about the theater, were it not that in the Chorus the "crookèd figure" goes hand in hand with the language of conjuring.[29]

> But pardon, gentles all,
> The flat unraisèd spirits that hath dared
> On this unworthy scaffold to bring forth
> So great an object.   (8–11)

The spirits that are flat and unraised in the opening moments of the play – before the historical characters have appeared on stage – do not long remain so. What is required to raise them is an act of necromantic magic, and the Chorus goes on to tell the spectators how to work the spell. From the beginning, then, it is clear both that the business of the theater is the raising of spirits, and that those who have the power to perform the necessary magic are not the actors, much less the playwright, but rather the audience.[30]

---

[29] Perhaps we today are slower than Shakespeare's original audience to grasp the uncanniness of numbers, the way in which mathematical "figures," like the figures of figural prophecy, can be at once real in themselves and shadows of another reality. Significantly, it is not in the manifest spectacle of his victory at Agincourt but in figures, bodiless and curiously exact, that Henry detects the agency of the supernatural: "But five-and-twenty. O God, thy arm was here" (4.8.104).

[30] On the equation of theater with necromancy in this passage, see Greenblatt, *Hamlet in Purgatory,* p. 258; Rackin, *Stages of History,* pp. 114–15, and Holderness, *Shakespeare: The Histories,* p. 137.

In the Chorus's second speech, the audience is soothed with the promise that it simply has to sit back and enjoy the ride through time and space provided by the players: "to France shall we convey you safe, / And bring you back, charming the narrow seas / To give you gentle pass" (2.0.37–39). But in his next appearance, immediately before Henry's raising of spirits in the breach at Harfleur, the Chorus reveals that the real source of theatrical energy is the audience, who must conjure up the dead by a powerful exertion of communal will. "Follow, follow!" (3.0.17) the Chorus demands, anticipating Henry's exhortation to "Follow your spirit." "Grapple your minds ... Work, work your thoughts, and therein see a siege" (3.0.18–25). The striking similarity between the harangues of the Chorus and the King – both marked by long strings of imperatives, by exhortatory repetitions ("Work, work," "On, on"), by appeals to a past which must be iterated in the present, and by the endorsement of alarums and chambers going off – emphasizes that they are working the same kind of (necromantic) magic.[31]

The conjuring of the spirits of the dead and the mathematical magic of the many-in-one are the devices by which the play brings "the vasty fields of France" within the "wooden O" of the Globe Theatre. And they are also the devices by which the English in the play achieve their victory. Even as the Chorus proclaims the abject insufficiency of the theater to represent Agincourt, the play demonstrates that what happened at Agincourt was really no different from what happens on the stage. The very qualities which seemed to disable the theater as a space in which Agincourt could happen again turn out to ensure that it *does* happen again. What the play delivers is not an inadequate representation but, in the fullest sense of the word, a *performance* of national history.

In the performance of *Henry V,* pedagogical and performative temporalities intersect.[32] The lesson ("this is what we as a people have been") coincides perfectly with the performative enactment ("this is what we, the people, are"). What might seem to be the danger of this intersection – the implication that a nation of warriors has degenerated into a nation of players – is circumvented by the sheer radicalism of the play's nostalgia. The same terms – "player," "spirit" – that are applied to the performers of the play apply as well to Henry V at Agincourt, who seems to recognize himself as both a ghost and an actor, and even to Edward III, who

---

[31] The language of the two speeches is compared by Michael Goldman, *The Energies of Drama* (Princeton: Princeton University Press, 1972), pp. 62–65.

[32] The split in national time created by the competing temporalities of pedagogy and performance is described by Bhabha, *The Location of Culture,* p. 145.

"haunted" the French and "played a tragedy" at Crécy.[33] The intersection of temporalities could be described as seamless – but it is closer to the truth to say it is pure seam. Rather than sealing up the crack in the present moment from which ghosts issue, the play opens it up to make it as wide as the present, and as expansive as the Globe Theater. In a sense, the theater *is* "the breach." While the drama lasts, actors and audience together are enfolded in "Arthur's bosom."[34]

"How it would have joyed brave Talbot (the terror of the French) to thinke that after he had lyne two hundred yeares in his Tombe, hee should triumphe againe on the Stage, and have his bones newe embalmed with the teares of ten thousand spectators at least . . . "[35] Thomas Nashe, who may have collaborated with Shakespeare on *1 Henry VI*, understood the nature of what happens in history plays, and the nature of their appeal. Shakespeare's histories cater simultaneously to two desires, one of them ancient, the other – in his day – comparatively new. Historical drama fulfills the wish of the living to see the dead again, to serve them somehow (with the permissible suffrages of tears and applause), and finally to let them go in a psychologically easeful way (note that Talbot's resurrection ends with his being embalmed a second time).[36] At the same time, this drama simultaneously invents and fulfills the audience's wish to experience imagined community, to participate in the magic of the one-in-many and many-in-one. Both of these powerful experiences are on offer in Shakespeare's theater – and both of them, for the Elizabethan audience, are available nowhere else but in the theater.

---

[33] As Christopher Pye remarks of Henry, "he speaks of himself as one whose time and voice are at once still to come and long since past. Mocking itself across the expanse of time . . . the sovereign's voice conjures with peculiar immediacy a spirit which never appeared in its true likeness"; *The Regal Phantasm: Shakespeare and the Politics of Spectacle* (London, 1990), p. 27. Katherine Eggert also discusses Henry's premonition of his own staging in "Nostalgia and the Not Yet Late Queen," 535–37.

[34] As Joel Altman, reading the play in the context of its first performance, suggests, "By means of an embracing ritual gesture, Shakespeare has joined past to present, audience to soldiery, in an honorary fellowship transcending time and space. Indeed, Harry's vile participation would seem to have fathered the audience at the Curtain or, perhaps, the new Globe Theatre. They are the lineal descendants of those 'Whose hearts have left their bodies here in England, / And lie pavilion'd in the fields of France' (1.2.128–29), and they are doing it all over again"; Joel B. Altman, "'Vile Participation': The Amplification of Violence in the Theater of *Henry V*" *Shakespeare Quarterly* 42 (1991), 16. Whereas Altman sees this communion across time as lasting "at least the duration of the performance and probably beyond" (16), I argue that the national community forged in *Henry V* is strictly confined to the inside of the theater and the duration of the play.

[35] *The Works of Thomas Nashe*, 1: 212.

[36] As Stephen Greenblatt notes of the epilogue to *The Tempest*, the player's plea – "Let your indulgence set me free" – echoes the pleas of souls tormented in Purgatory. "[I]n place of prayers, we offer the actor's ticket to bliss: applause." *Hamlet in Purgatory*, p. 261.

Of course, *Henry V* does refer to contemporary events outside the theater, and with an explicitness unparalleled elsewhere in the works of Shakespeare. Describing Henry's triumphant return to London, the Chorus invokes not only the precedent of Caesar's entry into Rome but the future return of the Earl of Essex from Ireland:

> As by a lower but high-loving likelihood
> Were now the general of our gracious Empress –
> As in good time he may – from Ireland coming
> Bringing rebellion broachèd on his sword,
> How many would the peaceful city quit
> To welcome him! Much more, and much more cause,
> Did they this Harry.

These lines have been read as testifying to Shakespeare's patriotic enthusiasm for Essex and the Irish campaign – as conclusive proof, in other words, that Shakespeare was a full-blooded nationalist.[37] Yet, as others have noted, the comparison is not overly complimentary to the Earl or his expedition: in a few lines, the Chorus manages to belittle Essex in relation to his predecessors, cast doubt (presciently) on the likelihood of his returning victorious, associate him with a threat to London's peace, and declare that any crowds that turned out to welcome him would not only be smaller but would have less cause than those that welcomed Henry.[38] More to the point, whatever Shakespeare's views on the Irish campaign may have been, it is transparently clear that the Chorus does not invoke Agincourt to whip up enthusiasm for Essex, but the reverse. The Earl's explicit function in this passage is that of a minor ingredient in a magic spell (eye of newt, wool of bat), thrown in to assist the audience in the task of "communing up" the image of Henry's entry into London. Essex, in other words, is one of the "ghosts" who hover about Shakespeare's player-king. The Chorus takes from him the image of his triumph, but gives nothing in return.

---

[37] "*Henry V*, so apposite in theme and spirit, as I and many others discovered, to the dispatch of a great expeditionary force in 1914, was actually written for a similar occasion in 1599"; John Dover Wilson, Introduction, *King Henry V* (Cambridge, 1947), p. x.

[38] Gary Taylor remarks of this passage that "the sting in its tail ('much more, *and much more cause, | Did they this Harry*') deserves more attention than it seems to have attracted" (Introduction, *Henry V*, p. 7). Moreover, as Jeffrey Knapp notes, the Chorus "states only that London's citizens *would* welcome Essex, not that they *should* welcome him"; *Shakespeare's Tribe: Church, Nation, and Theater in Renaissance England* (Chicago: University of Chicago Press, 2002), p. 226 n. 60. Yet Willy Maley argues that "the deliberate, strategic diminution of the Irish conquest" is in fact an example of "British mythology at its most powerful" (*Nation, State and Empire*, pp. 25, 24).

I have suggested previously that "nationalism" in the modern sense of the term was in Shakespeare's time primarily a cult of the "literary" class. I have suggested as well that many of those writers who explored nationalist themes were drawn to them more by the prospect of figurative plenitude than out of a precocious political commitment. Both of these points hold true in *Henry V* – the celebration of the nation is on every level a celebration of theater. The play further seems to insist that the experience of nationalism, or "communing up," is possible *only* in the theater. Shakespeare, in what is generally regarded as his most fervently nationalist play, is also at his most introspectively literary. Given the intrinsically theatrical nature of national communion, it is hard to imagine how the nation summoned up in *Henry V* could retain any actuality or meaning outside the Globe. As one of Shakespeare's wizards explains, as he conjures a spirit in a circle: "fear not. Whom we raise / We will make fast within a hallowed verge" (*2 Henry VI*, 1.4.20–21). The ghosts of a nation raised in *Henry V* are just as firmly confined to a circle or, as the Chorus puts it, a "wooden O."

The performance history of *Henry V* testifies to the cultural chasm that has opened up between Shakespeare and ourselves. The play was not revived until 1738 – around the time, that is, when a mass national community such as the play describes was taking actual shape in Britain *for the first time.* Since that initial revival, the play has repeatedly been produced as a patriotic exercise in times of war or rumors of war.[39] Twentieth-century critics and editors such as John Dover Wilson have endorsed the play's place at the heart of a martial English identity.[40] Still more recently, in both the First and Second Gulf Wars – conflicts whose skewed casualty counts recall Agincourt on a sickeningly grand scale – British and American commanders roused their troops with versions of Henry V's battlefield orations.[41] They did not do so in order to suggest that members of the allied forces were in some sense actors or ghosts, but

---

[39] Taylor, Introduction, *Henry V*, p. 11; Emma Smith, *King Henry V* (Shakespeare in Production) (Cambridge: Cambridge University Press, 2002).

[40] "If History never repeats itself, the human spirit often does: Henry's words before Agincourt, and Churchill's after the Battle of Britain, come from the same national mint"; Dover Wilson, Introduction, *King Henry V*, p. xxxi.

[41] Before bombardment commenced in the 1991 Gulf War, Air Commodore Ian Macfadyen quoted from the play; on the eve of the 2003 conflict, Lt. Tim Collins's address to his troops, including such phrases as "your deeds will follow you down history" was widely compared in the British and American press to Shakespeare's play. *Henry V* was also quoted directly by Maj. Gen. Ricardo Sanchez, commander of the US ground forces in Iraq, and thousands of copies of the play were distributed to American soldiers in a Pentagon-approved program.

because they believed Shakespeare's play was relevant to what they were doing – perhaps even that in some vague way it provided a warrant for it. Shakespeare, sadly for him and for us, has proved to be an imperfect conjuror. The spirit he raised within a circle has moved beyond its bounds.

CHAPTER 6

"Is this the promised end?"
James I, King Lear, *and the strange death of*
Tudor Britain

From the dawn of the Tudor era, the fortunes of British nationalism had been closely bound up with those of the ruling dynasty. Yet the initial response of many British nationalists to the death of the last Tudor monarch in 1603 was one of euphoria. The succession of the Scottish king James VI to the English throne meant that for the first time in more than a millennium – by some accounts, since the era of Brutus himself – the whole island would be united under a single ruler. Proclaiming his desire to see a perfect union between his kingdoms under "the true and ancient name which God and time have imposed upon this isle, extant and received in histories . . . and other records of great antiquitie," James adopted the royal style of "King of Great Britain."[1] The most hallowed aims of British nationalism seemed on the point of being achieved. Yet within a few years, that distinctively Tudor form of nationalism rooted in the desire to recapture British antiquity would have been almost completely expelled from English politics and literature. An early sign of this rapid decline would be the unanticipated apostasy of the leading nationalist playwright, William Shakespeare.

FIGURES OF UNION

Many of the poets who celebrated James's accession or lauded him in the first years of his reign were keen to associate the new monarch with the triumph of British nationalism. As Samuel Daniel trumpeted in 1603:

> Shake hands with Union, O thou mighty State
> Now thou art all Great-Britain and no more,

---

[1] Cited in Jenny Wormald, "James VI, James I and the Identity of Britain," in *The British Problem, c. 1534–1707: State Formation in the Atlantic Archipelago*, ed. Brendan Bradshaw and John Morrill (London: Macmillan, 1996), p. 152. See also S. T. Bindoff, "The Stuarts and their Style," *EHR* 60 (1945), 192–216.

> No Scot, no English now, nor no debate;
> No borders but the Ocean and the shore.[2]

Taking their cue from Daniel and his generation, a number of younger poets took up the British theme. In *A Prophesie of Cadwallader, Last King of the Britaines* (1604), William Harbert of Glamorgan rejoiced that James had fulfilled to perfection the angel's ancient promise to Cadwaladr: "A present salve hath cured a pensive sore,/Britaine is now, what Britaine was of yore."[3] Whereas the Tudors had restored British rule, James Stuart could be said to have restored Britain itself. He was not merely, like his predecessors, an heir of Cadwaladr, but – as more than one writer effused – a "second Brute."[4]

In the first years of his reign, James was determined to push a legislative program for the full union of the kingdoms through the (increasingly recalcitrant) parliaments of England and Scotland. The unionist campaign was pursued in the courts and the debating chamber, but also in print and on public and private stages. The years 1603–1606 saw the production of numerous tracts, poems, genealogies, pageants, plays, and miscellaneous pieces in support of the king's British policy.[5] A chief resource for the unionist writers were the pamphlets produced in support of the "Rough Wooing" almost sixty years earlier. Just as Protector Somerset had urged the Scots to "take the indifferent old name of Britaynes again," so Jacobean pamphleteers insisted that the terms "Scottish" and "English" should be forgotten – if the peoples were to be distinguished at all, it must be as "North Britons" and "South Britons." In *The Joiefull and Blessed Reuniting the two mighty and famous kingdomes, England & Scotland into their ancient name of great Brittaine* (1605), John Thornborough denounced the very name of England as a "Badge of slaverie," recalling as it did the Britons' temporary submission to foreign invaders.[6] As the Welsh epigrammatist John Owen rejoiced, pithily and prematurely:

[2] Samuel Daniel, "A Panegyrike Congratulatorie to the Kings most excellent Majestie," in *Complete Works in Verse and Prose of Samuel Daniel*, ed. A. B. Grosart (London, 1885), vol. 1, 143.
[3] *The Poems of William Harbert, of Glamorgan*, in *Miscellanies of the Fuller Worthies Library*, ed. A. B. Grosart (Blackburn, 1870), vol. 1, 88.
[4] Harbert, *Poems*, 88; Anthony Munday, *The Triumphes of Re-United Britannia*, in *Pageants and Entertainments of Anthony Munday*, ed. David M. Bergeron (New York: Garland, 1985), p. 9
[5] The literature on union is discussed by Bruce Galloway, *The Union of England and Scotland, 1603–1608* (Edinburgh: J. Donald, 1986), 33–55; and D. R. Woolf, *The Idea of History in Early Stuart England* (Toronto: University of Toronto Press, 1990), 55–64. See also Brian P. Levack, *The Formation of the British State: England, Scotland, and the Union, 1603–1707* (Oxford: Clarendon Press, 1987).
[6] John Thornborough, *The Joiefull and Blessed Reuniting* (Oxford, 1605), 45.

Tecum participant in nomine Scotus & Anglus,
Iam tu non solus, Walle, Britannus eris.[7]

Britishness, of course, was always more than a matter of nomenclature. It was, as I have argued in previous chapters, a matter of blood, and of ghosts, and of nostalgia giving rise to visions of beauty. Inevitably, the figures that had been developed over the course of the Tudor period to forge a link between the present and the ancient past were mobilized – occasionally with great facility, more often mechanically and repetitively – to serve the cause of Jacobean unionism. The theme of union as a restoration of Britain's ancient condition is especially prominent in the poetic, dramatic, and popular contributions to the union campaign, more so than in the tracts and treatises addressed to the two parliaments by the likes of Sir Francis Bacon and Sir Thomas Craig (neither of whom had much use for Brutus or his brethren). But it is one task to persuade a parliament to enact various commercial and legal reforms, and quite another to persuade ordinary people to start thinking and identifying as Britons. For those writers pursuing the latter goal, only one argument in favor of union really mattered: that the accession of James I heralded the restoration of British antiquity.[8]

John Thornborough, bishop of Bristol, brought deeper learning and a vaster stock of Latin phrases to his work than did most of his fellow propagandists, but he shared fully in their figurative propensities. The classic British tropes spill forth in super-abundance from every page of *The Joiefull and Blessed Reuniting*, offering a copious introduction to the Jacobean unionist lexicon. Thornborough seems genuinely incapable of thinking about Britain without thinking metaphorically, allegorically, or

---

[7] John Owen, *Epigrammatum Libri Tres* (London, 1606), 64. The epigram was translated by Robert Hayman in 1626 as "Wales, Scotland, England, now are joynd in one:/Henceforth Wales is not Brittany alone" (Robert Hayman, *Quodlibets* [London, 1628], p. 18.] The alteration in sense is slight but significant, with the English suggesting appropriation (of Britishness) rather than vindication (of Wales).

[8] If, by the first decade of the seventeenth century, most scholars and statesmen were eager to forget that they had ever placed their faith in the discredited Geoffrey of Monmouth, popular belief in the British History was as yet undiminished. The shows staged in favor of union in fact depend on fairly detailed popular knowledge of Geoffrey's tales; see Richard Dutton, "King Lear, The Triumphs of Reunited Britannia, and the 'Matter of Britain,'" *Literature and History* 12 (1986), 137–151. On the survival of Geoffrey's tales (especially those involving giants and the founding of cities) in the popular imagination, even into the eighteenth century, see D. R. Woolf, *The Social Circulation of the Past: English Historical Culture, 1500–1730* (Oxford: Oxford University Press, 2003), pp. 311, 315–16, 325–31.

analogically. Moreover, he seems incapable of thinking about Britain without thinking about, or through, William Shakespeare.

How joyful it is for us to acknowledge one another Britaines, as it was for them brethren in the Comedy, which after so long time came to knowledge one of another . . . yet may both English and Scottish rejoice, because . . . all of their legitimate children are all now of one name, and one bloud, become, and born again Britaines, as it were by a Pithagorical Palingenesia, even twice Brittaines . . .

Thus we say, and thus we sing, *Redeunt Saturnia Regna*, even the golden age of Brittaines Monarchy is come againe . . . [I]f any drop of our ancestors blood live in us . . . wee cannot, but readily imbrace each other, as the ancient Romans reconciled after long civil war . . . or it may be said to us Brittaines descended from Brutus, as sometimes to another Brutus, in another sense, not here intended: *Dormis Brute, & non es Brutus.*[9]

The immediate reference points in this passage are Plautus and Plutarch, not the plays (*A Comedy of Errors* and *Julius Caesar*) Shakespeare had derived from them in the 1590s. Yet if Thornborough repeatedly reaches for plots, phrases, and motifs still warm from Shakespeare's handling, this is a measure of his dependence on a stock of tropes derived from his Tudor predecessors. All the standard items are here: bloodlines, kinship, nostalgia, rebirth, awakening from sleep. Strangely, and perhaps fatally, the Jacobean propagandists failed to find new ways of thinking and writing about Britain, in spite of drastically altered political circumstances. If anything distinguishes Thornborough from his sixteenth-century forerunners, it is his determination to leave nothing out, so that the somewhat incompatible figures of blood-descent and miraculous rebirth are, "by a Pithagorical Palingenesia," collapsed into one. To the objection that the English have no blood relationship with the ancient Britons, Thornborough's answer seems to be, "they do now."

Although the suggestion that the English, Scots, and Welsh were united by "one bloud" remained problematic, they could at least be said to be united by the blood of their one ruler.[10] Admirers of James I and his unionist program made regular and adoring reference to the new

---

[9] Thornborough, *The Joiefull and Blessed Reuniting*, pp. 42–43.

[10] For some who could not swallow the theory of "Pithagorical Palingenesia," the creation of a British people united by blood remained a consummation devoutly to be wished. As John Davies of Hereford has the English tell the Scots (in a poem addressed to the Prince of Wales on behalf of the Welsh people), "Give us your Daughters, and take ours in marage,/That, Blouds so mixte, may make one flesh, and bloud. John Davies, "Microcosmos," in *The Complete Works of John Davies of Hereford*, ed. A. B. Grosart, (Edinburgh: Printed For Private Circulation, 1878), vol. I, p. II (separately paginated).

monarch's British blood (inherited through his Tudor ancestors, but also through the Scottish Banquo's son Fleance, who had produced an heir with a Welsh princess). Almost as soon as the new king came to throne, the Welsh parson George Owen Harry drew up his (royally sanctioned) *Genealogy of the High and Mighty Monarch, James, by the grace of God, King of great Brittayne, &c. with his lineall descent from Noah, by divers direct lynes to Brutus, first Inhabiter of this Ile of Brittayne; and from him to Cadwalader, the last King of the Brittish bloud; and from thence, sundry wayes to his Majesty.*[11] Drawing as he did on old Welsh sources, Harry's conception of blood was much the same as Dafydd Llwyd's or Lewys Glyn Cothi's. The "Brittish bloud" not only furnishes James with a claim to the throne, but provides the nation with a connection to the ancient British past, mediated through the body of the monarch. This understanding was shared by Harry's fellow Welshman William Harbert, who in *A Prophesie of Cadwallader* described James's ancestor Henry Tudor as "England's Trajane sprung from Trojane race."[12] The line, a fine example of English *cynghanedd*, could have been translated from a *cywydd brud* of 1485.

Beauty, too, has a prominent role to play in Jacobean British propaganda. It was a fundamental tenet of the unionist position that unity is innately preferable to disunity, in part because it is more aesthetically appealing. The union of England and Scotland could therefore be seen as a project of national beautification. The "vile phrase" that so irritated Polonius crops up regularly in unionist effusions. Robert Pricket went to the heart of the matter, urging the Scots and English to "Joyne in on[e] truth, with blessed unitie,/Great Britaines fame adorn and beautifie."[13] In Anthony Munday's 1605 pageant for the Merchant Tailors, *The Triumphes of Re-United Britannia*, Brutus teaches Britain "how to reign as an Imperial lady, building his Troya nova by the river Thamesis, and beautifieng his land with other Citties beside."[14] A few years later, after the close of the unionist campaign proper, we encounter a somewhat sinister echo of Munday's phrase in *A Direction for the Plantation in Ulster* (1610) by Thomas Blenerhasset (the one-time author of *The Second Part of the Mirror for Magistrates*). Describing Ulster as a province "belonging to great Brittaines Imperial Crowne," Blenerhasset calls on the English to

---

[11] George Owen Harry, *The Genealogy of the High and Mighty Monarch, James* (London, 1604), p. 6.
[12] Harbert, *Poems*, p. 81. Significantly, Harbert shared with Llwyd the tendency to describe English / Yorkist blood in far different and more visceral terms, as something to be shed in abundance: "Leicestrian dales their crimson gore did fill,/A scarlet streame frome Richard did distill" (p. 81).
[13] Robert Pricket, *Times Anotomie* (London, 1606), sig. D3ᵛ.
[14] Munday, *Triumphes of Re-United Britannia*, pp. 6–7.

"beautifie her desolation" and concludes with the hope that "the successors of high renowned Lud, will there reedifie a new Troy."[15]

True to his ghost-writing roots, Blenerhasset depicts "depopulated Ulster" as herself a kind of specter, reminiscent of Spenser's Verlame: "Dispoyled, she presents her-self (as it were) in a ragged sad sabled Robe, ragged (indeed) there remayneth nothing but ruynes & desolation."[16] By coincidence, in the same year that saw the publication of his *Direction*, Blenerhasset's thirty-two-year-old *Second Part* was reissued as part of Richard Niccols's mammoth edition of the *Mirror*. Commencing with the legend of King Arthur and concluding with "England's Eliza," the Jacobean *Mirror* was even more overtly nationalistic, and more British in tone than its late Elizabethan precursors.[17] Renewed interest in the *Mirror* had perhaps been sparked by the unionist campaign, in which specters of Britain figured very prominently.

Geists in tune with the *zeitgeist*, Jacobean ghosts of the nation are less given to lamenting their downfalls than to celebrating their miraculous resurrection. As John Thornborough, striving as ever for figurative *copia*, congratulated Britain, "Thou wert lost, and art found, bond, and art free, eclipst, and art glorious, dead, and art alive."[18] In Munday's *Triumphes of Re-United Britannia*, Brutus himself appears, fresh from the grave:

> See, after so long slumbering in our tombs
> Such multitudes of years, rich poesy
> That does revive us to fill up these room
> And tell our former ages history
> (The better to record Brute's memory)
> > Turns now our accents to another key,
> > To tell old Britain's new-born happy day.[19]

There are two separate resurrections heralded here: that of Brutus and his kin, who are awakened from death to appear in Munday's pageant, and that of Britain itself. Technically, it is only the first of these that is attributable to the power of "rich poesy," but the inevitable suggestion is the Britain's rebirth springs from the same cause, indeed from the very "telling" that takes place in the pageant. Munday's implicit boast here is

---

[15] Thomas Blenerhasset, *A Direction for the Plantation in Ulster* (1610), sigs. A2^r, D2^r, D3^r. With a fine disregard for titular technicalities, Blenerhasset dedicates his book to "Henry, Prince of great Brittaine" (sig. A2^r).

[16] Blenerhasset, *Direction*, sigs. A2^r, D1^v.

[17] See Budra, "*The Mirror for Magistrates* and the Politics of Readership."

[18] Thornborough, *Joiefull and Blessed Reuniting*, p. 39.

[19] Munday, *Triumphes of Re-United Britannia*, p. 9.

that poetry can do what royal proclamations and parliamentary wrangling have so far been unable to achieve, that is, bring ancient Britain back to life. As British nationalists had long known, it is language rather than legislation that must forge the links between the present and the ancient past.

The most memorable ghost to be conjured in the unionist campaign is one I have already introduced, the wailing spirit of Britain in William Harbert's "The Lamentation of Britaine" (1606). Much like a ghost in the *Mirror*, Britain complains of her unfortunate fall (likening it to that of such miserable sisters as Rome). Eventually, her lament evolves into an explicit argument for absolute union, "of three warlike Nations to empile / One Monarchy."

> Oh where is Britaine? Britaine where is shee?
> What? smothered in forgetful sepulcher?
> Exilde from mans reviving memorie?
> Oh no, let England like a childe prefer
> That well knowne title of her ancester:
> I know the neighbour sisters of this Ile
> Will greatly glory in so good a stile.[20]

Like a ghost from Purgatory pleading for its promised suffrages, like Old Hamlet haunting his son, the ghost of Britain has returned to remind a child of an unpaid debt.

The story of Brutus and his three sons was invoked time and time again by contributors to the unionist campaign. Harbert simply transposes the tale from a dynastic to a topographical register, making it the story of Britain and her three daughters.[21] The new conceit is obvious enough, and no doubt did not cost him much in the way of contemplation. Yet, if one takes time to think them through, the implications of this twist on the tale are remarkable and disturbing. If England is not already an incorporated part of Britain's body, but rather a child born out of that body, then how can she and her sisters conceivably pay their debt to the importunate ghost? What can it mean for "three warlike nations to empile one monarchy" if not for these daughters to be consumed back into the body of their mother? Britain seems to have forgotten "how great and small, how all must die,"

---

[20] Harbert, *Englands Sorrowe*, sig. G3^r.
[21] There is some precedent for this twist in Munday's *Triumphes of Re-United Britannia*, in which Brutus is described as wedded to the "imperial lady" Britain, and his three sons are accompanied by female representations of England, Scotland, and Wales. These nymphs are not, however, specified to be Britain's daughters – no doubt because Munday was aware of the unsettling implications of incest and cannibalism this would raise.

and to be bent on reversing the natural succession of generations. The plaintive ghost reveals herself at last as a predatory ghoul, breaking forth from her sepulcher to devour the living. This, surely, was no part of Harbert's intention – yet it seems fitting enough that the volume is entitled *Englands Sorrowe.*

"THOU'LT NEVER COME AGAIN": REFUSING RESTORATION IN
KING LEAR

> The barbarous Scythian,
> Or he that makes his generation messes
> To gorge his appetite, shall to my bosom
> Be as well neighboured, pitied, and relieved,
> As thou . . .   (1.1.116–120)[22]

If England were given a chance in Harbert's poem to respond to her mother Britain's regressive and cannibalistic fantasies, she might choose words like these. In *King Lear*, however, these lines are not given to an imperiled daughter addressing a predatory parent, but are instead hurled by a parent (who is king of Britain) at his "sometime daughter" (on whom he had intended to devolve the realm of England). Lear's words to Cordelia inevitably rebound on himself, revealing him as an unnatural parent bent on consuming his daughter's dowry – her topographical substance – back into the body from which it came. (A moment later, however, he instructs his two sons-in-law to "digest" [1.1.126] Cordelia's portion.) The author of *King Lear* (1605–6) may or may not have been able to consult *Englands Sorrowe* (1606), but it is not in Harbert's work alone that the British question becomes tied up with generational themes and intimations of cannibalism – witness James's own troubling description of England and Scotland as "two twins bred in one belly."[23] Lear's terrible words, then, may well be read as reflecting not only on familial relations, but on "the division of the kingdom" (1.1.3–4). If so, they are but one reflection of the play's deeply troubled relation to British nationalism.

That the Jacobean debate over British union bears some relation to *King Lear* is beyond question, and Shakespeare's play has often been regarded as

[22] Except where otherwise noted, all references are to *The Tragedy of King Lear* (i.e., the Folio text) in *The Norton Shakespeare*. Significant divergences between Folio and Quarto texts will be noted where relevant.

[23] Michael J. Enright, "King James and His Island: An Archaic Kingship Belief?" *Scottish Historical Review* 55 (1976), 34.

a contribution – albeit a wary and pessimistic one – to the unionist campaign.[24] Nothing less could have been expected by any well-informed observer when the play was performed at court in December 1606; indeed, the convergence of theme, occasion, and artist would have seemed to promise a masterpiece of British nationalism. The theme was drawn from British antiquity, which had attained even greater political relevance under James than it had possessed in Tudor times. The occasion was a court performance in the midst of the unionist campaign, when writers of all stripes and talents, from bishops to hacks, were bubbling over with prince-pleasing effusions in favor of a reunited Britain. The artist was of course Shakespeare, the most reliably nationalist playwright of the previous decade, who had broken new ground in developing and exploiting the nation's literary potential. Shakespeare surely knew what was called for – the awakening of desire for the restoration of the lost national past. And Shakespeare surely knew better than any how such effects were achieved. Yet, as I shall argue, the play defeats all such reasonable expectation, and does so in a highly conscious and chillingly calculated manner.

The enduring habit of reading *King Lear* as a unionist work rests above all on the evident parallel between Lear's division of Britain between his three daughters and Brutus' division of the island between his three sons. What was, according to British nationalists, a mistake for Brutus, and later for his successor Gorboduc, must surely also have been a mistake for Lear. Yet nowhere in the play is the division of the kingdoms identified as the cause of the tragedy.[25] Lear's great political error, as the Fool and others see it, has not been to divvy up his realm among his children, but to do so while he was still alive, and to suppose that he could retain his royal title and paternal prerogatives afterwards. Lear's stubbornness on the point of his title recalls Britain's ghoulish hankering after her "well knowne title" in Harbert's poem; and, indeed, the royal "name" (1.1.134) Lear insists on retaining is presumably the very title revived by James I, "King of Great Britain." Whilst none of Lear's heirs will ever succeed to this title, neither can they, while it is borne by Lear, regard themselves as governors of distinct and integral nations. Lear's retention of the "name" of Britain

---

[24] See, e.g., Christopher Wortham, "Shakespeare, James I and the Matter of Britain," *English: The Journal of the English Association* 45 (1996), 97–122.

[25] Early audiences would, of course, have been primed by both literary precedents (from *Gorboduc* to *Leir*) and the political climate to anticipate an anti-division moral. This expectation is neither rewarded nor explicitly defeated in Shakespeare's play; it is, for the most part, simply ignored. Many spectators, in common with some later critics, may nevertheless have been content to take the anti-division message as read.

seems designed to keep the daughter-kingdoms in cannibalistic confine-
ment, incorporated and digested within the paternal body. No wonder
their feelings for him are less than filial. Lear's mistake, in other words, may
not lie in the letting go, but in the holding on; not too much devolution,
but not enough.

King Lear, then, can be read as anti-unionist drama, subversively celebrating the division of Britain into England, Scotland, and Wales as a
natural, inevitable, and irreversible historical process. This is not, of course,
the only reading of the play's politics, nor the most obvious one. If it were,
the King's Men would surely not have dared to bring the play to court. The
point I wish to emphasize, however, is not that *Lear* is anti-union, but that
the play is so cagey and ambiguous on the union question that it admits of
flatly contradictory readings – something that could hardly be said of
contemporary works like *A Prophesie of Cadwallader* or *The Triumphes of
Re-United Britannia*. What is most significant and surprising in *Lear*, in
other words, is not what it has to say about Britain, but what it stubbornly
fails to say. Rather than exploiting the cherished tropes of British nationalism, for either loyal or subversive purposes, the play methodically empties
them out and discards them. Having witnessed how these tropes figured in
the unionist campaign, let us now see how they figure – or fail to figure – in
Shakespeare's play.

The word "British" occurs only three times in the Quarto text of *King
Lear* (and just twice in the Folio), and the word "Britain" is never uttered at
all. (By contrast, forms of these words occur more than twenty times in
both the anonymous Elizabethan *King Leir*, and in Shakespeare's own
Cymbeline). Of the three instances of "British," two refer to the forces led
by Edmund and Albany against Cordelia and Lear (4.3.21, and Q scene
20.238 [F has "English" at 4.5.242]). The other occurs in a snatch of old
song recited by Edgar as Poor Tom: "Fie, foh, and fum, / I smell the blood
of a British man" (3.4.164–65). All three references are rather troubling for
British nationalism, those involving Edmund and the army because they
seem to associate Britishness with illegitimacy, treachery, and parricide,
and Edgar's song because it comes across as an awkwardly self-conscious
and perhaps self-consciously awkward substitution of the traditional
"English" for the more politically correct "British."[26] In spite of this,
Edgar does succeed in declaring what Tudor British nationalists had almost

---

[26] In early performances, the line may have invited a joke on Jacobean political correctness; on the
verge of saying "English," Edgar catches himself and pronounces the new approved term with
audible irony.

always been reluctant to say: that Britishness is a matter of blood. Unfortunately, the blood of the hapless Briton in the song provides him with an identity only inasmuch as it exposes him as prey.

The anonymous Briton's experience is one that Edgar, along with many characters in this play, comes to appreciate all too well as he discovers that the ties of blood exist only to be spurned, denied, manipulated or betrayed. Wherever "blood" is invoked in the play to signify the bond between generations, it signals the breaking of that bond. Banishing his youngest daughter, Lear declares: "Here I disclaim all my paternal care,/Propinquity and property of blood" (1.1.111–12). Later, cursing his eldest, he complains "thou art my flesh, my blood, my daughter – / Or rather ... A plague-sore or embossèd carbuncle, / In my corrupted blood" (2.2.386–390). Gloucester, in a similar vein, will declare, "I had a son, / Now outlawed from my blood" (3.4.149–50) and inform Lear that "Our flesh and blood, my lord, is grown so vile / That it doth hate what gets it" (3.4.128–29). The only character in the play who acknowledges feeling the tug of blood is Edmund, who piously insists that "the conflict be sore between [my loyalty] and my blood" (3.5.19–20), even as he works his father's ruin. There is in fact no bond of blood in the play that is not broken by either a parent or a child. Far from forming a chain across time, blood in *King Lear* seems incapable of sustaining a link even between two generations.

The utter failure of blood to provide a bridge between the present and the past is witnessed in the extinction of the royal bloodline at the close of the play. The king is dead, as are all of his daughters, none of whom have left children. With Lear's dynasty extinct, the kingdom seems fated to pass into the hands of the minor nobility.[27] The first audiences would doubtless have been astonished as well as dismayed by the death of Cordelia, which runs against all of Shakespeare's sources. Still, her demise in the play, however senselessly tragic, is genealogically insignificant, for the chronicles reported that she died by her own hand and childless a few years later. Far more disturbing for those who had bothered to peruse their monarch's ancestry would have been the death without issue of Regan and Cornwall. According to Harry's 1604 *Genealogy*, "Ragan" and Henwyn, Duke of Cornwall, were James Stuart's direct ancestors.[28] Indeed, their union was

---

[27] See Andrew Gurr, "Headgear as a Paralinguistic Signifier in *King Lear*," *Shakespeare Survey* 55 (2002), 43–52.

[28] See Harry, *The Genealogy of the High and Mighty Monarch, James* (1604), sig. (b)2r. A compliment to James has been seen in the elevation of the Duke of Albany – a title associated with the Stuarts – to shared governance of the realm at the end of the play. But the compliment is at best only partial compensation for the gratuitous extinction of James's ancestors.

of more than average significance, for it was through them that the bloodlines of Locrine, first king of England, and Camber, first ruler of Wales,
were reunited. It is not only James's descent from Brutus but the presumption that the England and Wales should have a common ruler that is called
into question by the untimely deaths of Cornwall and Regan.

Few members of early audiences, perhaps not even James himself, would
have been so well-versed in genealogical lore as to recognize the full
implications of these particular deaths. But what no one could have missed
is that the utter extinction of the royal house makes nonsense of the
prophecy that the blood of Brutus would one day return to the throne.
There will be no fresh conflagration from a spark long hidden on Anglesey;
at the end of *King Lear*, that fire is well and truly out. This is to say that the
play's withering contempt for every effort to draw connections between the
present and the past extends not only to genealogy, but also to a discourse
even more central to British nationalism, prophecy.

While there is naturally no mention in the play of the angel's prophecy
to Cadwaladr, there is, in the Folio at any rate, a prophecy of Merlin,
recited by the Fool alone on the storm-racked heath:

> I'll speak a prophecy ere I go:
>> When priests are more in word than matter;   (80)
>> When brewers mar their malt with water;
>> When nobles are their tailors' tutors;
>> No heretics burn'd, but wenches' suitors;
>> When every case in law is right;
>> No squire in debt, nor no poor knight;   (85)
>> When slanders do not live in tongues;
>> Nor cutpurses come not to throngs;
>> When usurers tell their gold i' the field;
>> And bawds and whores do churches build;
>> Then shall the realm of Albion   (90)
>> Come to great confusion:
>> Then comes the time, who lives to see't,
>> That going shall be used with feet.
> This prophecy Merlin shall make; for I live before his time.   (3.2.79–94)

The Fool's prophecy has long challenged the ingenuity of critics (or at least
of those who will consent to attribute it to Shakespeare). The conditions
enumerated here are a curious mixture of the already fulfilled (80–83) and
the unfulfillable (84–89), while the conclusion contrives to mingle the
apocalyptic ("great confusion") with the utterly banal ("going shall be
used with feet"). Certain predictions, notably that involving the burning or

otherwise of heretics, have attracted debate as to which phase of James's religious policy they might reflect.[29] Like modern scholars, the play's first audiences would have been inclined to probe the prophecy for specifically Jacobean applications. There is an inevitable narcissism attached to the condition of living in the present, a narcissism expressed in the assumption that when people in the past looked to the future, they were looking forward to "us." For various reasons, this historical narcissism was especially pronounced in Shakespeare's era. Just as Protestant exegetes found the fulfillment of scriptural figures in the events of their own times, so the theater was in the habit of flattering its audiences by confirming that they were the object of national history. Where prophecies of future national bliss occur in history plays, as in *The Misfortunes of Arthur* or *Henry VIII*, they invariably refer to the Elizabethan or Jacobean present. Near the midpoint of the play, when Lear's and Britain's fortunes appear to be at their nadir, and the question of redemption hangs heavy in the air, the natural assumption is that the Fool's prophecy will refer forward to the (Jacobean) restoration of Britain.

However, the Fool is not making a prophecy about the redemption of Britain, nor even about the state of Britain in the early seventeenth century. He is prophesying about sixth-century Britain, about Merlin. The last line *is* the prophecy, and, in a sense, the whole of the prophecy. Rather than predicting anything about brewers, heretics, or the fate of Albion, the Fool is simply predicting that some twelve centuries after his own era, Merlin will make this series of predictions.[30] Whereas the "normal" relationship between prophecy's two temporalities is one of satisfying reciprocity – as the prophecy points forward to its fulfillment, so the event by which it is fulfilled points back to the original prophesy in confirmation – the Fool's prophecy points forward only to another forward-pointing arrow. In the future, there will be prophecy. There is a deep joke here, but not the joke that is usually perceived, that is, a bald parody of Merlinic vaticination. The joke is that the Jacobean audience is forced, almost ineluctably, to reveal itself as both credulous and narcissistic. As soon as the Fool begins to list future contingencies in rhyming couplets, the audience is seduced into making two false assumptions: first, that this is the prophecy which the

---

[29] See John Kerrigan, "Revision, Adaptation, and the Fool in *King Lear*," in *The Division of the Kingdoms: Shakespeare's Two Versions of King Lear*, ed. Gary Taylor and Michael Warren (Oxford: Oxford University Press, 1983), pp. 221–27; and Gary Taylor, "*King Lear*: The Date and Authorship of the Folio Version," in the same volume, pp. 382–85.

[30] An editor could make this point clear by setting lines 81–94, that is, the whole of the rhyming section, within quotation marks.

Fool has just promised to recite, and second, that it applies to their present. (The fact that brewers in every age have been known to dilute their product is no bar to the presumption, verging on a certainty, that it is the scandalous corruption of the contemporary brewing industry that is meant.) Even when the later couplets turn towards the apparently unfulfilled and unfulfillable, the temptation to wrest them to a contemporary application remains strong. (There is, no doubt, some sense in which every case in law is right; slander might be said to live in the ear rather than the tongue; and bawds have been known to build churches . . .) The whole passage is, in other words, a trap designed to expose the egotism of the living in general, and the fatuity of the Jacobean union project in particular. It is not only faith in prophecy that is undercut by the Fool's joke, but something deeper and still more fundamental to nationalism: the assumption that one's own era is the object and the end of history.

Perhaps because its author played such a key role in developing them, *King Lear* is remarkably thorough in its dismantling of the figurative technologies of British nationalism. There is no means left open by which the past can reach forward to touch the present, either through bloodlines or by prophecy. Even the possibility that the past might persist in spectral form, haunting the present, is disallowed. There are no ghosts in the world of *King Lear*, and no second comings. "Speaking to the dead" in this play means precisely that, speaking to those who never do and never can reply. The simplest and hardest truth in the play is spoken by a dying man to a dead woman: "Thou'lt come no more. / Never, never, never, never, never" (5.3.282–3).

It is not simply that there happen to be no ghosts in this play – though that itself distinguishes *Lear* from a good many of the major tragedies. The world of *Lear* is not only ghostless, it is exorcised. True, the specter of spectrality, the possibility of encountering and speaking with the dead, is raised several times in the play. Lear and others repeatedly mistake the living for the dead, and the dead for the living.[31] Yet just as the invocation of blood invariably signals the breaking of familial bonds, so the identification of ghosts in the play is inevitably an error, arising out of an inability or unwillingness to grasp the forms that life can take. Fleeing from the cave in which he has encountered the hideous "Poor Tom," the terrified Fool believes he has seen "a spirit" (3.4.38, 41). Lear himself, awakening from his

---

[31] Here I draw upon Greenblatt's discussion of ghosts in *Lear* in *Hamlet in Purgatory*.

madness to a meeting he has both dreamt of and dreaded, imagines both he and his daughter are dead:

LEAR   You do me wrong to take me out o'th' grave
    Thou art a soul in bliss, but I am bound
    Upon a wheel of fire, that mine own tears
    Do scald like molten lead.

CORDELIA   Sir, do you know me?

LEAR   You are a spirit, I know. Where did you die?   (4.7.43–47)

While Lear is wrong in supposing that he must be in Hell or Purgatory, his words convey a terrible truth: that the torments suffered by some who are still among the living are as great as anything we can imagine of the punishments to come. It is a truth recognized by Kent at the end of the play, as Edgar desperately imitates Lear's own error in attempting to revive a dead body.

    Vex not his ghost. O, let him pass. He hates him
    That would upon the rack of this tough world
    Stretch him out longer.   (5.3.288–89)

Generations of medieval and early modern theologians had debated whether or not ghosts might return to the world of the living, and, if so, whence and in what form. With devastating simplicity, Kent overturns the most fundamental assumption behind these debates. The questions of whether ghosts can or cannot return is moot. Knowing what they do of life, the dead would not want to come back.

At the end of the play, the world of *King Lear* is a world lost beyond any hope or possibility of recovery – even if such a recovery were to be desired. In the course of the drama, Shakespeare runs through all the methods that Tudor writers – not least himself – had developed to forge a link between the present and the past, and systematically disables or explodes each one. But the play goes beyond simply denying the practical possibility of recovering the past. With unforgiving stringency, it highlights the point-lessness and folly of even desiring such a restoration. It stands opposed, in other words, not only to the naïve politics of recovery that typified the Jacobean unionist campaign, but also to the more sophisticated politics of nostalgia that characterized British nationalists like John Bale.

The play ends with a man gazing with ineffable longing at a beautiful dead body. This can be regarded as the master image of both British nationalism and Petrarchan aesthetics, and as the point of their conjunction. "If she could only reply to my words!" "Cordelia, Cordelia: stay a little. Ha? / What is't thou sayst?" (5.3.245–6) An audience doubly primed by the testimony of chronicles and nationalist aesthetics (with both of which Shakespeare takes such tragic liberties) would have every reason to expect even at this late moment that the corpse of Cordelia would arise and speak. When were history and poesy so clearly united in their demands? Lear himself, in his last moments, seems to imagine that his gaze and his desire have succeeded in recreating Pygmalion's miracle. "Look on her. Look, her lips. / Look there, look there." (5.3.309–10) Yet there is no resurrection of the dead. Nor does Lear's longing gaze produce the aesthetic transformation we have come to expect. There will be no forging of beauty in the crucible of nostalgic desire. The longing for reunion with the dead will be fulfilled only through more death.

Full of the bitterness of loss, the play is almost devoid of the bittersweetness of nostalgia. Though conscious that they have lost everything, none of the characters in the play possess vivid or extensive memories of former happiness. Even in his wild regret, Lear does not refer back to the halcyon days before his betrayal of and by his daughters. His memory seems incapable of reaching beyond the first scene of the play, with its string of disastrous errors. "I gave you all" (2.2.415); "I did her wrong" (1.5.22). If nostalgia enters at all into the play, it is only in the final couplet, spoken by Edgar (or Albany, in the Quarto): "The oldest hath borne most. We that are young/Shall never see so much, nor live so long" (5.3.300–301). There is something weirdly inappropriate about this closing sentiment, conveying as it does a grotesque whiff of envy. Edgar (or Albany) seems to be groping towards some way of remembering the time when an octogenarian king underwent suffering beyond the limits of human endurance as a version of the "good old days." Is the speaker, who seems to have become the nation's leader, hoping to use nostalgia for the lost British past to reforge the shattered national community? Perhaps so – but no words in the play ring so hollow as these with which it closes.[32]

---

[32] In Richard Halpern's memorable phrase, "*King Lear* is ... no more nostalgic for what is lost than someone watching a waterfall is nostalgic for the lake above"; *The Poetics of Primitive Accumulation: English Renaissance Culture and the Genealogy of Capital* (Ithaca: Cornell University Press, 1991), p. 269. My reading of the play also accords with that of John Turner, who doubts Shakespeare's enthusiasm for the unionist campaign and argues that *King Lear* depicts "a civilization lost with anguish for all time"; "The Tragic Romances of Feudalism," in Graham Holderness, Nick Potter, and John Turner, eds., *Shakespeare: The Play of History* (Iowa City: University of Iowa Press, 1987), p. 98.

"Nothing will come of nothing" (1.1.88), Lear tells Cordelia in the first scene of the play; later, when the Fool asks him, "can you make no use of nothing, nuncle?" the answer comes again, "Nothing can be made out of nothing" (1.4.116–18). Through the hindsight of this Jacobean tragedy, the great nationalist project of the Tudor era is revealed in a new and unforgiving light, as little more than a bid to get something for nothing. Was not John Bale's ultimate goal in the simplest sense to forge something (a national community) out of an absence (a lost bibliographical heritage)? In *Henry V,* Shakespeare himself had pursued similar aims with the aid of his theatrical nothings, "ciphers to this great accompt." However brave or brilliant these efforts to conjure presence out absence, they wither before the cold calculus of *King Lear.*

So far, I have been discussing *King Lear* almost entirely in terms of its denials, undoings, and evacuations. This cannot, clearly, be the whole story – only a Dadaist would construct an aesthetic object solely on the basis of refusals. Yet what I shall term *King Lear*'s negative program, its rebuttal of British nationalism through the systematic dismantling of its cherished tropes of survival and revival, runs to the very heart of the tragedy. In the plotting and writing of the play, Shakespeare omitted no opportunity to cut the strands between the present and past. This applies even to the earliest choice he must have made, that, in defiance of every source, Lear and Cordelia would die. It was the logic of the negative program, in other words, that required the play to be a tragedy, not the logic of tragedy that necessitated the negative program. (After all, many tragedies – *Hamlet, Macbeth, Julius Caesar* – insist on precisely those links between the present and the past that Lear denies.)

If Shakespeare's program in *King Lear* was a negative one, it was also a potentially disabling one. The unique achievement of Shakespeare's mature history plays lay in conjuring communities, making the audience participate in something larger and more lasting than themselves – even if this "national" community was confined to the circle of the theater. The Jacobean authors of pro-union propaganda were indebted to Shakespeare (as well as to Spenser) for many of the nationalist tropes which came ready-made to their hands. In disowning and dismantling these same tropes, like a conjuror abjuring his art, Shakespeare was committing himself to writing a very different kind of historical drama than that for which he was known. In view of this, it is easy to imagine *King Lear* taking the form of a purely antiquarian (in the modern sense) exercise – a worthy and dull representation of a past world utterly divorced from present concerns and sensibilities. Shakespeare could have made it boring. Instead, he made it unbearable.

The paradox is that while *Lear* allows for no connection between the living and the dead, it offers a deeper and more shattering experience of communion than any previous history play. This at least has been the verdict of centuries of audiences and (especially) readers. "While we read it," wrote Charles Lamb, "we see not Lear, but we are Lear, – we are in his mind."[33] More recent critics have described the play's disturbingly intimate engagement with the mind of the reader or audience member in terms of "presence," of "grasping contact," and even of literal communion, a dramatic "sacrament" in which we "participate."[34] We are sundered from the world of *Lear* by an unbridgeable gap, yet we also experience that world as uncannily close – much, much too close for comfort.

What makes *King Lear* such a drastically different play from *Henry V* is not the absence of communion so much as the absence of community. This is a play without memories and without children, without a meaningful past or an imaginable future. We cannot relate *to* the world of *Lear* because there is no vantage point for us to relate *from*. The communion *Lear* can offer us is thus not a relationship transcending time, a clasping of hands across the gulf between present and past, but only a participation in the play's own irrecoverable and anguished "now." As Stanley Cavell perceives, such joining can take place only through the acceptance – rather than the defiance – of disjunction.

We are not in, and cannot put ourselves in, the presence of the characters; but we are in, or can put ourselves in, their present. It is in making their present ours, their moments as they occur, that we complete our acknowledgment of them. But this requires making their present *theirs*.[35]

What is happening "now" in *King Lear* is almost always, from the first act to the last, loss. Loss arrives in a crushing multitude of forms: rejection, severance, denial, blindness, madness, death. But the special terror of loss in *Lear* arises less from the fact that it is so unremitting than from the fact that it is never final. The lost object is never allowed to recede into the past, where it might become a memory, an object of nostalgia. Rather, loss remains the eternal condition of the present, an experience *Lear* articulates

---

[33] Charles Lamb, "On the Tragedies of Shakspeare, considered with reference to their Fitness for Stage Representation," in *Miscellaneous Prose*, ed. E. V. Lucas (London: Methuen, 1912), p. 124.

[34] Stanley Cavell, "The Avoidance of Love: A Reading of *King Lear*," in *Disowning Knowledge in Six Plays by Shakespeare* (Cambridge: Cambridge University Press, 1987), pp. 39–124; John J. Joughin, "Lear's Afterlife," *Shakespeare Survey* 55 (2002), 67–81; Richard C. McCoy, " 'Look upon me, Sir': Relationships in *King Lear*," *Representations* 81 (2003), 46–60.

[35] Cavell, "The Avoidance of Love," 108.

when he says "now she's gone forever" (5.3.244). The identification of "now" with "forever" is predicated on identifying both with the moment in which "she's [just] gone." "Now" contains an eternity of bereavement, and the time in which the first pangs of bereavement are felt will never cease to be "now." This then is the nature of the transhistorical moment in which *Lear* allows us to participate. The move from *Henry V* to *King Lear* is the move from a community united by longing for what has been lost, to a communion confined within the moment of loss itself.[36]

THE END OF BRITAIN

Performed in the court of the self-styled "King of Great Britain" at the height of the unionist campaign, *King Lear* is remarkable for its refusal to be borne along on the tide of British nationalist propaganda. Structured by its negative program, the play undercuts and annuls the most fundamental assumptions of pro-union works like Thornborough's *Joiefull and Blessed Reuniting* and Munday's *Triumphs of Re-United Britannia*. Yet it would be a mistake to conclude on this basis that the play expresses Shakespeare's fundamental opposition to the union of the kingdoms. There is, notably, no trace of anti-Scottish sentiment in the play. (Albany, the sole presumed Scot, is a virtuous if unglamorous character.) There is no hint of resistance to the naturalization of Scots born after the union, or the dropping of customs barriers, issues actually debated in Parliament in 1606. *Lear* has no quarrel, in short, with the political case for union, as argued by the likes of Bacon and Craig. What the play opposes is the popular / nationalist case for union, founded in the false assumption that the past can be restored. In taking issue with this assumption, the play effectively takes issue with nationalism itself, at least in its dominant sixteenth-century form.

Shakespeare's remarkable turn away from the nationalism he had espoused and exploited in the 1590s would become even more pronounced in his next – and last – play set in ancient Britain. On the face of it, *Cymbeline* is the one play of Shakespeare's which might plausibly be associated with something called "British nationalism." The play depicts the successful resistance to Roman invasion of an ancient and united Britain, and contains a number of powerful patriotic speeches. It also

---

[36] The dramatic and syntactical techniques by which Shakespeare expands the final moment of loss to almost unbearable length are analyzed by Stephen Booth, *King Lear, Macbeth, Indefinition, and Tragedy* (New Haven: Yale University Press, 1983).

includes the overwhelming majority of instances of the words "Britain" and "British" found in Shakespeare's works (some twenty-nine, as opposed to *Lear*'s bare three). Yet whatever name it goes by, and whatever its (ambiguous) boundaries, the insular kingdom ruled by Cymbeline bears precious little resemblance to the familiar object of Tudor nationalist nostalgia – indeed, it can hardly be described as a nation at all.

Revisiting in its distinctive way many of Shakespeare's earlier plays and preoccupations, *Cymbeline* includes a reprise of the nationalist melody familiar from his Elizabethan ("English") history plays.

> Remember, sir, my liege,
> The kings your ancestors, together with
> The natural bravery of your isle, which stands
> As Neptune's park, ribbed and paled in
> With banks unscalable and roaring waters . . .   (3.1.16–120).

This passage echoes and blends together memorable passages from *Henry V* ("Look back into your mighty ancestors . . . Awake remembrance of those valiant dead") and *Richard II* ("England, bound in with the triumphant sea / Whose rocky shore beats back the envious siege / Of wat'ry Neptune"). But the speaker in *Cymbeline* is neither hero-king nor selfless patriot, but the cruel and treacherous Queen. The only character in the play to echo her bombastic tone is her brutal, half-witted son Cloten, who predictably makes a hash of his John of Gaunt: "Britain's a world/By itself, and we will nothing pay / For wearing our own noses" (3.1.12–14). In *Cymbeline*, nationalism is the last refuge of scoundrels. The admirable characters in the play have far more complicated and conflicted loyalties. Both Postumus and Innogen serve for a time (like Cordelia before them) in a foreign army invading Britain, and the play concludes not with a triumphant affirmation of British invincibility, but with a compromise: "Although the victor, we submit to Caesar . . . let / A Roman and a British ensign wave / Friendly together" (5.6.460, 479–81).

Whereas *King Lear* subjects the key figures of British nationalism to systematic evacuation, in *Cymbeline* they are made the matter of often grotesque parody. If on one level the play insists that its theme is union, or rather *re*-union (between parted lovers, parents and children, even estranged nations), on another it mocks the modes by which the present seeks reconnection with the past. As in *Lear*, historical relationships are hopelessly jumbled, defying any attempt to assimilate the characters into a royal genealogy. The admission of the First Gentleman in the first scene regarding Posthumus's lineage – "I cannot delve him to the root" (1.1.28) –

sounds the keynote of a play apparently determined to foil the quest for origins. Unlike *Lear, Cymbeline* does feature ghosts, those of Posthumus's parents and brothers who plead to Jupiter to intercede on his behalf. Jupiter, however, derides these specters as "petty spirits" (5.5.187), sharply rebuking them for concerning themselves with the affairs of the living: "No care of yours it is; you know 'tis ours" (5.5.194). As for that classic Petrarchan expression of the present's longing to recapture the past, the lover gazing on the beautiful corpse of the beloved, this is parodied mercilessly in the scene in which Innogen wakes beside the beheaded body of Cloten, whom she mistakes for her husband.

None of this is to deny that the play comments on contemporary national politics, nor even that it endorses Anglo-Scottish union on some level. *Cymbeline* has been read both as a celebration of Rome's civilizing influence, and of the extension of English sovereignty in the British Isles. "Rome" can be seen to stand for England in its relations with its archipelagic neighbors; alternatively, representatives of Scottishness, Welshness, and Englishness can all be discerned among the play's apparently homogenous "Britons."[37] But while *Cymbeline* does clearly allude, however elusively, to contemporary relations between the nations of Britain, this is very different from making Britain itself the repository of a transhistorical identity – indeed it depends on its not being so. There is no clear connection between British antiquity, conceived here in wildly unhistorical, even mythical terms, and the seventeenth-century present, except perhaps on the level of allegory. Nor does the play's political vision depend on a notion of national communities, constructed either across time, or across space within a single time. *Cymbeline* is not short on British politics, but they are not the politics of nationalism, British or otherwise.

No doubt some members of *Cymbeline*'s first audience would have been offended to hear cherished British sentiments placed in the mouths of fools

[37] For a range of configurations of the archipelagic relationships within the play, see Colin MacCabe, "The Voice of Esau: Stephen in the Library," in *James Joyce: New Perspectives*, ed. Colin MacCabe (Brighton: Harvester, 1982), 111–129; Leah Marcus, *Puzzling Shakespeare: Local Reading and Its Discontents* (Berkeley: University of California Press, 1988); Jodi Mikalachki, *The Legacy of Boadicea: Gender and Nation in Early Modern England* (London: Routledge, 1998); Ronald J. Boling, "Anglo-Welsh Relations in Cymbeline," *Shakespeare Quarterly* 51 (2000), 33–66; Mary Floyd-Wilson, "Delving to the Root: *Cymbeline*, Scotland, and the English Race," in *British Identities*, ed. Baker and Maley, pp. 101–115; Willy Maley, *Nation, State and Empire in English Renaissance Literature: Shakespeare to Milton* (Basingstoke: Palgrave Macmillan, 2003). John Kerrigan has discussed *Cymbeline* in light of a number of other early Jacobean plays set in Roman Britain in a paper on "The Romans in Britain, 1603–1614," delivered at a conference on the year 1603 at the University of Hull, June, 2003.

and villains, while others may well have approved of the playwright's new-found skepticism towards nationalist rhetoric. Quite a few may have been content to hum along to the old patriotic refrain, without worrying unduly about who was now playing the tune. We have little way of knowing which set of feelings predominated among Jacobean theater-goers. What we can say with some certainty about them, however, is that they had little or no desire to see British rhetoric translated into political reality. Londoners may have responded enthusiastically enough to talk of "Neptune's park," and to shows like *The Triumphes of Re-United Britannia*, but they did not rally in support of full legal union with Scotland. Indeed, the fact that James I was eventually forced to shelve his dream in the face of opposition from both the Scottish and English parliaments reveals just how little force nationalist effusions had in the sphere of practical politics.

The failure of the unionist campaign could of course be seen as evidence of the strength of a distinctively *English* nationalism in this period. There is some basis for this view. In the early seventeenth century, the convergence of a number of factors – including the continuing rise of racial conscious-ness, the final collapse of Geoffrey of Monmouth's credibility, and the publication of Richard Verstegan's boldly Teutonophilic *Restitution of Decayed Intelligence* (1605) – encouraged some among the English to regard their Anglo-Saxon ancestors in a newly positive light.[38] The unionist campaign itself enhanced awareness of the distinctive Englishness of insti-tutions such as the common law. In these developments we can perhaps detect the seeds of the fully fledged Saxonism of the eighteenth and nine-teenth centuries. That said, we should not overlook the extent to which English resistance to union with Scotland was based on the desire to preserve specific institutions, traditions, and prerogatives, rather than some amorphous national essence. If Parliament refused to ratify James's change of title, it was not simply out of sentimental attachment to the name of England, but because it was believed that the consequence would be "the utter extinction of all the laws now in force."[39] Members of all ranks also feared that poor Scottish workers and arrogant Scottish noblemen would

---

[38] With the rehabilitation of the Anglo-Saxons would come the possibility of a specifically English brand of nostalgia, focusing on a golden age of freedom before the imposition of the "Norman yoke." See Christopher Hill, "The Norman Yoke," in *Puritanism and Revolution* (London: Secker & Warburg, 1958), pp. 46–111.

[39] David L. Smith, *A History of the Modern British Isles, 1603–1707: The Double Crown* (Oxford: Blackwell, 1998), p. 24. My point can be illustrated by a comparison between English parliamentary resistance to union with Scotland under James, and the resistance of British Conservative politicians to closer integration within the European Union. In the latter case, politicians defend certain institutions and traditions (such as the British currency, or the weighing

come flooding over the border, robbing the English of employment and blocking access to the king's person. Xenophobia was as rife as ever, but no more necessarily linked to nationalism than it had been previously. All in all, it is true to say that nationalist expression in the early seventeenth century tended to be less British and more English in tone than in the Tudor era; but it is also true that there was simply a good deal less nationalist expression of any kind.

By the time *Cymbeline* was performed in 1609 or 1610, the unionist campaign had stuttered to a halt, and patriotic history plays were as firmly out of fashion as Petrarchan sonnets. Nationalism was no longer being promulgated from above, nor was it simmering below. Almost the only vocal exponents of British nationalism left in England were Elizabethan holdovers, men like Michael Drayton and Thomas Blenerhasset still doggedly defending the doctrines of a bygone era. (We may suppose that what readers they had regarded them with a kind of bemused condescension.)[40] Shakespeare was a member of the same Elizabethan generation, and in the 1590s had participated fully in the same literary enthusiasms. Unlike Drayton and Blenerhasset, however, he declined to carry the old Tudor banner into a new century and a new dynastic era. Tellingly, he abandoned the cause not at the point when it was obviously lost (as it was by the date of *Cymbeline*), but earlier, when all still seemed on the verge of being won (the date of *King Lear*).

Why did Shakespeare turn his back on the idea of the nation, and why at such a moment? Neither the plays themselves nor such biographical information as survives can provide us with any insight into the author's motives. What can be said, however, is that under James I, Britain seems to have lost its poetry. Well before the final collapse of British nationalism as a political ideal, it had already been shorn of much of its traditional aesthetic appeal. As we have seen, the aesthetic rewards of nostalgic nationalism – the

of vegetables in pounds and ounces) because they are held to embody or symbolize the essence of the nation. In the former case, by contrast, politicians defended the name of the English nation because it was held to safeguard certain institutions and traditions.

[40] In spite of his sentimental devotion to Geoffrey of Monmouth, it would be an over-simplification to describe Drayton as an unreconstructed British nationalist. Drayton was at least as much a regionalist as a nationalist, and *Poly-Olbion* has been read as being both critical of Jacobean centralism and unenthusiastic about the possibility of a united Britain. See Helgerson, *Forms of Nationhood*, pp. 117–24; Hadfield, *Shakespeare, Spenser, and the Matter of Britain*, pp. 143–150. Nevertheless, the poem presents itself (not least in its frontispiece) as a kind of culmination of Elizabethan British nationalism, and the Jacobean reading public appears to have judged the book by its cover. *Poly-Olbion* did not sell. The booksellers still had so many copies on their hands six years after the publication of the first part in 1612 that they were able to issue them rebound with the second part.

nationalism of John Bale, Richard Davies, and of a play like *Henry V* –
relied fundamentally on the unobtainability of the lost object of desire.
When Britain was in danger of becoming a place on a modern map, rather
than a vision of irretrievable national purity, its aesthetic interest necessarily dwindled. Once national consummation became possible, in other
words, it ceased to appear half so desirable. Indeed, as the case of
Cymbeline suggests, the once-cherished vision could be transformed into
an object of scorn – "Enjoyed no sooner but despised straight," as
Shakespeare wrote in another context (Sonnet 129).[41]

Yet Shakespeare did not turn his back on Britain. Instead, having
abandoned his nationalist investment in ancient Britain, he began to
write about it. The final and perhaps most intriguing paradox of
Shakespeare's approach to national history is the curiously precise divorce
of historical and ideological content. Under Elizabeth, he wrote nine or
more history plays set in medieval England, many of which are suffused
with the language and aesthetic impulses of British nationalism. Under
James he all but abandoned English history, and wrote instead two plays set
in ancient Britain, both devoid of British nationalism. For the playwright,
the end of the old nationalist dream was thus also a new beginning. No
longer an object of nostalgic desire, ancient Britain became a kind of *terra
incognita*, an ideal backdrop for dramas of psychological inquiry, moral
conflict, and highflown invention. With near-total disregard for his
sources, Shakespeare made ancient Britain a place where anything could
happen, where events followed not the logic of history, but that of desire,
dreams, and a callous or beneficent destiny. The past – the British past, at
any rate – had become a foreign country.

---

[41] The same rule clearly does not apply to the experience of many nations, such as Ireland, Israel, and
Croatia, where the realization of national aspirations in the form of an independent state provoked
a renewed outpouring of nationalist energies. In all these cases, however, the state was born into a
climate of ongoing struggle, and the nation could be regarded by its adherents as still imperfectly
realized in crucial respects. There was a national language to be revived (or invented); and
important territories belonging to the imagined nation still lay outside the bounds of the new state.
By contrast, British nationalists after 1603 had trouble knowing what was left to long for. The
revival of Welsh as the national language was obviously out of the question; and if any focus for
irredentism remained after 1603, it could only be in Ireland. As the example of Blenerhasset
suggests, old-fashioned British ideals probably did linger rather longer among settlers in Ireland
than they did on the mainland. Indeed, if a link can be drawn between the British nationalism of
the Tudor era and that of the eighteenth century, it must be routed through Ulster. That question,
however, lies beyond the scope of the current study.

Bibliography

PRIMARY SOURCES

Andre, Bernard. *Historia regis Henrici septimi.* Ed. J. Gairdner. Rolls Series, no. 10. London: Longmans, 1858.

Baldwin, William, et al. *The Mirror for Magistrates.* Ed. Lily B. Campbell. New York: Barnes & Noble, 1938.

Bale, John. *King Johan.* In *Complete Plays of John Bale, Volume 1.* Ed. Peter Happé. Cambridge: D. S. Brewer, 1985.

—. Letter to Matthew Parker, 20 July 1560. In *The Recovery of the Past in Early Elizabethan England: Documents by John Bale and John Joscelyn from the Circle of Matthew Parker.* Ed. Timothy Graham and Andrea G. Watson, 17–53. Cambridge Bibliographical Society Monograph, 13. Cambridge: Cambridge University Library, 1997.

Bale, John, and John Leland. *The Laboryouse Journey and Serche of Johan Leylande, for Englandes Antiquitees.* London, 1549.

Blenerhasset, Thomas. *A Direction for the Plantation in Ulster.* London, 1610.

Brooke, Ralph. *A Discoverie of Certaine Errours Published in Print in the Much Commended Britannia, 1594.* London, 1596.

Buchanan, George. *Buchanan's History of Scotland.* London, 1735.

Burke, Edmund. *Reflections on the Revolution in France.* Ed. A. J. Grieve. London: Dent, 1967.

Chaucer, Geoffrey. *The Riverside Chaucer.* Ed. Larry D. Benson. Third edition. Boston: Houghton Mifflin, 1987.

Churchyard, Thomas. *Churchyard's Challenge.* London, 1593.

—. *The Worthines of Wales.* London, 1587.

Cobbett, William. *A History of the Protestant Reformation.* New edition. London: R. & T. Washbourne, n.d.

Coleridge, Samuel Taylor. *Coleridge's Miscellaneous Criticism.* Ed. Thomas M. Raysor. London: Constable, 1936.

The Complaynt of Scotland . . . with an Appendix of Contemporary English Tracts. Ed. J. A. H. Murray. EETS, extra series, nos. 17, 18. London: 1872–73.

Dafydd Llwyd of Mathafarn. *Gwaith Dafydd Llwyd o Fathafarn.* Ed. W. Leslie Richards. Cardiff: University of Wales Press, 1964.

Daniel, Samuel. "A Panegyrike Congratulatorie to the Kings most excellent Majestie." In *Complete Works in Verse and Prose of Samuel Daniel*. Ed. A. B. Grosart, vol. 1, 143. London, 1885.

—. *Poems and A Defence of Ryme*. Ed. Arthur Colby Sprague. Chicago: University of Chicago Press, 1950.

Davies, John, of Hereford. *The Complete Works of John Davies of Hereford*. Ed. A. B. Grosart. 2 vols. Edinburgh, 1878.

Davies, Richard. Address to the Welsh People. In *Testament Newydd*. London, 1567.

—. "Address to the Welsh People." Trans. Albert Owen Evans. In *A Memorandum Concerning the Legality of the Welsh Bible and the Welsh Version of the Book of Common Prayer*, 83–127. Cardiff: William Lewis, 1925.

Dee, John. "A Supplication to Queen Mary, by John Dee, for the Recovery and Preservation of Ancient Writers and Monuments." In *Chetham Miscellanies, Volume 1*, 46–49. Manchester: Chetham Society, 1851.

Denham, John. *The Poetical Works of Sir John Denham*. Ed. Theodore Banks. Second edition. New Haven: Yale University Press, 1969.

Drayton, Michael. *Works of Michael Drayton*, ed. J. W. Hebel, K. Tillotson, and B. H. Newdigate. 4 vols. Oxford: Basil Blackwell, 1961.

Erasmus, Desiderius. *Christian Humanism and the Reformation: Selected Writings of Erasmus*. Ed. John C. Olin. Third edition. New York: Fordham University Press, 1987.

Fabyan, Robert. *The New Chronicles of England and France*. Ed. Henry Ellis. London, 1811.

Fish, Simon. *A Supplicacyon for the Beggers*. Antwerp?, 1529.

Fisher, Jasper. *Fuimus Troes*. London, 1633.

Foxe, John. *Acts and Monuments*. Ed. S. R. Cattley and G. Townsend. London, 1837–41.

"First Provincial Progress of Henry VII." In *Herefordshire, Worcestershire*. Ed. David N. Klausner. REED. Toronto: Toronto University Press, 1990.

Geoffrey of Monmouth. *The History of the Kings of Britain*. Ed. and trans. Lewis Thorpe. Harmondsworth: Penguin, 1966.

Gerald of Wales. *The Journey Through Wales/The Description of Wales*. Ed. and trans. Lewis Thorpe. Harmondsworth: Penguin, 1978.

Gildas. *The Ruin of Britain and Other Documents*. Ed. and trans. Michael Winterbottom. London: Phillimore, 1978.

Guto'r Glyn. *Gwaith Guto'r Glyn*. Ed. J. Llywelyn Williams and Ifor Williams. Cardiff: University of Wales Press, 1939.

Hakluyt, Richard. *The Principall Navigations, Voiages and Discoveries of the English Nation*. London, 1589.

Harbert, William. *Englands Sorrowe or, A Farewell to Essex*. London, 1606.

—. *The Poems of William Harbert, of Glamorgan*. In *Miscellanies of the Fuller Worthies Library, Vol. 1*. Ed. A. B. Grosart. Blackburn, 1870.

Harry, George Owen. *The Genealogy of the High and Mighty Monarch, James*. London, 1604.

Harvey, Richard. *Philadelphus, or a Defence of Brutes, and the Brutans History.* London, 1593.

Hayman, Robert. *Quodlibets.* London, 1628.

Higgins, John, and Thomas Blenerhasset. *Parts Added to "The Mirror for Magistrates."* Ed. Lily B. Campbell. Cambridge: Cambridge University Press, 1946.

Hill, Aaron. *King Henry the Fifth, or the Conquest of France by the English.* London, 1723.

Holinshed, Raphael, et al. *Holinshed's Chronicles of England, Scotland, and Ireland.* Ed. Henry Ellis. 6 vols. London, 1807–1808.

Kelton, Arthur. *A Chronycle with a Genealogie Declaryng that the Brittons and Welshemen are Lineallye Dyscended from Brute* (London: 1547).

Lamb, Charles. "On the Tragedies of Shakspeare, considered with reference to their Fitness for Stage Representation." In *Miscellaneous Prose.* Ed. E. V. Lucas, 112–36. London: Methuen, 1912.

Lambarde, William. *A Perambulation of Kent.* London, 1570.

Leland, John. *Assertio inclytissimi Arturii Regis Britanniae.* London, 1544.

Letters to Cromwell and Others on the Suppression of the Monasteries. Ed. G. H. Cook. London: John Baker, 1965.

Lewis Glyn Cothi. *Gwaith Lewys Glyn Cothi.* Ed. Dafydd Johnston. Cardiff: University of Wales Press, 1995.

Llwyd, Humphrey. *The Breviary of Britaine.* Trans. Thomas Twyne. London, 1573.

—. *Commentarioli Britannicae Descriptiones Fragmentum.* Colon. Aggripp., 1572.

—. *Cronica Walliae.* Ed. Ieuan M. Williams. Cardiff: University of Wales Press, 2002.

Lydgate, John. *The Tragedies, gathered by Jhon Bochas, of all such Princes as fell from theyr estates.* London, 1558.

McCrae, John. *In Flanders Fields and Other Poems.* New York: Putnam, 1919.

Martin, Roger. "The State of Melford Church and our Ladie's Chappel at the East End, as I did know it." In *The Spoil of Melford Church: The Reformation in a Suffolk Parish.* Ed. David Dymond and Clive Paine, 1–10. Ipswich: Salient Press, 1992.

More, Thomas. *The Supplication of Souls.* In *The Complete Works of St. Thomas More.* Ed. Frank Manley, Germain Marc'hadour, Richard Marius, and Clarence Miller, vol. 7, 107–228. New Haven, Yale University Press, 1990.

Munday, Anthony. *The Pageants and Entertainments of Anthony Munday.* Ed. David M. Bergeron. New York: Garland, 1985.

Nashe, Thomas. *The Works of Thomas Nashe.* Ed. R. B. McKerrow. Revised by F. P. Wilson. 5 volumes. Oxford: Basil Blackwell, 1966.

Owen, George. *The Description of Pembrokeshire.* Ed. Henry Owen. Cymmrodorion Record Series, no. 1. 4 vols. London, 1902–36.

Owen, John. *Epigrammatum Libri Tres.* London, 1606.

Paine, Thomas. *The Rights of Man.* Ed. Arthur Seldon. London: Dent, 1969.

Patten, William. *The Expedicion into Scotlande.* London, 1548.

Pearse, Patrick. *Collected Works of Padraic H. Pearse: Political Writings and Speeches.* Dublin: Maunsel & Roberts, 1922.

Petrarch, Francis. *Letters on Familiar Matters/Rerum familiarum libri XVII–XXIV.* Trans and ed. Aldo S. Bernardo. Baltimore: Johns Hopkins University Press, 1985

—. *Petrarch's Lyric Poems: The* Rime Sparse *and Other Lyrics.* Trans. and ed. Robert M. Durling. Cambridge, MA: Harvard University Press, 1976.

—. *Rerum familiarum libri I–VIII.* Trans. and ed. Aldo S. Bernardo. Albany: State University of New York Press, 1975.

"The Pilgrimage of Grace and Aske's Examination." Ed. Mary Bateson. *English Historical Review* 5 (1890), 330–345, 550–73.

Powel, David. *The Historie of Cambria* (London, 1584).

Pricket, Robert. *Times Anotomie* (London, 1606).

Prise, John. *Historiae Britannicae defensio.* London, 1573.

Rastell, John. *The Pastyme of People & A New Boke of Purgatory.* Ed. J. Geritz. The Renaissance Imagination, 14. New York: Garland, 1985.

Salesbury, William. "Address to the Welsh People." Trans. Albert Owen Evans. In *A Memorandum Concerning the Legality of the Welsh Bible and the Welsh Version of the Book of Common Prayer,* 78–82. Cardiff: William Lewis, 1925.

Shakespeare, William. *The Norton Shakespeare.* Ed. Stephen Greenblatt. New York: W. W. Norton, 1997.

—. *Henry V.* Ed. Gary Taylor. Oxford: Oxford University Press, 1982.

Smith, Thomas. *A Discourse of the Commonweal of This Realm of England.* Ed. Mary Dewar. Charlottesville: The University Press of Virginia, 1969.

Spenser, Edmund. *The Faerie Queene.* Ed. A. C. Hamilton. London: Longman, 1977.

—. *The Poetical Works of Edmund Spenser.* Ed. J. C. Smith and E. De Selincourt. London: Oxford University Press, 1912.

—. *A View of the State of Ireland.* Ed. Andrew Hadfield and Willy Maley. Oxford: Blackwell, 1997.

Stapleton, Thomas. *The History of the Church of England, compiled by Venerable Bede, Englishman.* Antwerp, 1565.

Thornborough, John. *The Joiefull and Blessed Reuniting the two mighty and famous kingdomes, England & Scotland into their ancient name of great Brittaine.* Oxford, 1605.

Vasari, Giorgio. *Lives of the Artists: Volume 1.* Ed. and trans. George Bull. London: Penguin, 1987.

Vergil, Polydore. *The Anglica Historia of Polydore Vergil, A. D. 1485–1537.* Ed. and trans. Denys Hay. Camden Series 3, no. 74. London: Royal Historical Society, 1950.

—. *Polydore Vergil's English History, Vol. 1.* Ed. Sir Henry Ellis. Camden Society, no. 36. London: Camden Society, 1846.

Verstegan, Richard. *Restitution of Decayed Intelligence in Antiquities.* Antwerp, 1605.

Vita Edwardi Secundi/The Life of Edward the Second. Ed. and trans. N. Denholm-Young. London: Thomas Nelson and Sons, 1957.

Wynn, John. *History of the Gwydir Family and Memoirs.* Ed. J. Gwynfor Jones. Llandysul: Gomer Press, 1990.

Yeats, W. B. *The Collected Works of W. B. Yeats.* Ed. Richard J. Finneran. London: Macmillan, 1983.

SECONDARY SOURCES

Allen, Alison. "Yorkist Propaganda: Pedigree, Prophecy and the 'British History' in the Reign of Edward IV." In *Patronage, Pedigree and Power in Late Medieval England.* Ed. Charles Ross, 171–92. Gloucester: Alan Sutton, 1979.

Anderson, Benedict. *Imagined Communities: Reflections on the Origin and Spread of Nationalism.* Revised edition. London: Verso, 1991.

Anglo, Sydney. "The British History in Early Tudor Propaganda." Bulletin of the John Rylands Library (1961), 17–48.

—. *Images of Tudor Kingship.* London: Seaby, 1992.

Armitage, David. *The Ideological Origins of the British Empire.* Cambridge: Cambridge University Press, 2000.

Aston, Margaret. *Lollards and Reformers: Images and Literacy in Late Medieval Religion.* London: Hambledon, 1984.

Bainbridge, Virginia R. *Gilds in the Medieval Countryside: Social and Religious Change in Cambridgeshire, c. 1350–1558.* Woodbridge: Boydell Press, 1996.

Baker, David J. *Between Nations: Shakespeare, Spenser, Marvell, and the Question of Britain.* Stanford: Stanford University Press, 1997.

Baker, David J., and Willy Maley, eds. *British Identities and English Renaissance Literature.* Cambridge: Cambridge University Press, 2002.

Baldo, Jonathan. "Wars of Memory in *Henry V.*" Shakespeare Quarterly 47 (1996), 132–59.

Baxandall, Michael. *Giotto and the Orators: Humanist Observers of Painting in Italy and the Discovery of Pictorial Composition, 1350–1450.* Corrected reprint. Oxford: Clarendon Press, 1986.

Beckingsale, B. W. *Thomas Cromwell: Tudor Minister.* London: Macmillan, 1978.

Berger, Harry, Jr. *Revisionary Play: Studies in the Spenserian Dynamics.* Berkeley: University of California Press, 1988.

Bhabha, Homi K. *The Location of Culture.* London: Routledge, 1994.

Bindoff, S. T. "The Stuarts and their Style." *EHR* 60 (1945), 192–216.

Boling, Ronald J. "Anglo-Welsh Relations in *Cymbeline.*" Shakespeare Quarterly 51 (2000), 33–66.

Booth, Stephen. *King Lear, Macbeth, Indefinition, and Tragedy.* New Haven: Yale University Press, 1983.

Bradshaw, Brendan, and John Morrill, eds. *The British Problem, c. 1534–1707: State Formation in the Atlantic Archipelago.* London: Macmillan, 1996.

Brady, Ciaran. "Comparable Histories? Tudor Reform in Wales and Ireland." In *Conquest and Union: Fashioning a British State, 1485–1725.* Ed. Steven G. Ellis and Sarah Barber, 64–86. London: Longman, 1995.

Brenner, Robert. "The Agrarian Roots of European Capitalism." In *The Brenner Debate: Agrarian Class Structure and Economic Development in Pre-Industrial Europe.* Ed. T. H. Aston and C. H. E. Philpin, 213–327. Cambridge: Cambridge University Press, 1987.

Bruce, Donald Williams. "Spenser's Welsh." *Notes and Queries* 230 (1985), 465–467.

Budra, Paul. "*The Mirror for Magistrates* and the Politics of Readership," *SEL* 32 (1992), 1–13.

—. "*The Mirror for Magistrates* and the Shape of *De Casibus* Tragedy," *English Studies* 69 (1988), 303–12.

Camille, Michael. *The Gothic Idol: Ideology and Image-Making in Medieval Art.* Cambridge: Cambridge University Press, 1989.

Cavell, Stanley. "The Avoidance of Love: A Reading of *King Lear.*" In *Disowning Knowledge in Six Plays by Shakespeare*, 39–124. Cambridge: Cambridge University Press, 1987.

Chedgzoy, Kate. "This Pleasant and Sceptered Isle: Insular Fantasies of National Identity in Anne Dowriche's *The French Historie* and William Shakespeare's *Richard II.*" In *Archipelagic Identities: Literature and Identity in the Early Modern Atlantic Archipelago.* Ed. Philip Schwyzer and Simon Mealor, 25–42. Aldershot: Ashgate, 2004.

Conran, Tony. "Ieuan ap Hywel Swrwal's 'The Hymn to the Virgin.'" *Welsh Writing in English* 1 (1995), 5–22.

Cressy, David. *Birth, Marriage, and Death: Ritual, Religion and the Life-Cycle in Tudor and Stuart England.* Oxford: Oxford University Press, 1997.

Cropper, Elizabeth. "The Place of Beauty in the High Renaissance and its Displacement in the History of Art." In *Place and Displacement in the Renaissance.* Ed. Alvin Vos, 159–205. Medieval & Renaissance Texts & Studies, no. 132. Binghamton, 1995.

Crouch, David J. F. *Piety, Fraternity and Power: Religious Gilds in Late Medieval Yorkshire, 1389–1547.* York: York Medieval Press, 2000.

Curran, John E., Jr.. "The History Never Written: Bards, Druids, and the Problem of Antiquarianism in *Poly Olbion*," *Renaissance Quarterly* 51 (1998), 498–525.

—. *Roman Invasions: The British History, Protestant Anti-Romanism, and the Historical Imagination in England, 1530–1660.* Newark: University of Delaware Press, 2002.

Davidson, Neil. *The Origins of Scottish Nationhood.* London: Pluto Press, 2000.

Davies, C. S. L. "Popular Religion and the Pilgrimage of Grace." In *Order and Disorder in Early Modern England.* Ed. Anthony Fletcher and John Stevenson, 59–91. Cambridge: Cambridge University Press, 1985.

Davies, Ceri. *Latin Writers of the Renaissance.* Writers of Wales series. Cardiff: University of Wales Press, 1981.

Davies, John. *A History of Wales.* London: Penguin, 1994.

Davis, Natalie Zemon. "Ghosts, Kin, and Progeny: Some Features of Family Life in Early Modern France." *Daedalus* 106 (1977), 87–114.

Dawson, Jane E. A. "William Cecil and the British Dimension of Early Elizabethan Foreign Policy." *History* 74 (1989), 196–216.

Dean, C. *Arthur of England: English Attitudes to King Arthur and the Knights of the Round Table in the Middle Ages and Renaissance*. Toronto: University of Toronto Press, 1987.

Derrida, Jacques. *Specters of Marx: The State of the Debt, the Work of Mourning, and the New International*. Trans. Peggy Kamuf. New York: Routledge, 1994.

Dodd, A. H. "'A Commendacion of Welshmen.'" *Bulletin of the Board of Celtic Studies* 19 (1961), 235–49.

Dodds, Madeleine Hope, and Ruth Dodds. *The Pilgrimage of Grace, 1536–1537, and the Exeter Conspiracy, 1538*. 2 vols. London: Frank Cass and Co., 1915.

Duffy, Eamon. *The Stripping of the Altars: Traditional Religion in England, c. 1400–c. 1580*. New Haven: Yale University Press, 1992.

Duncan-Jones, Katherine. "Sidney in Samothea Yet Again." *Review of English Studies* 38 (1987), 226–227.

—. *Sir Philip Sidney: Courtier Poet*. London: Hamish Hamilton, 1991.

Eggert, Katherine. "Nostalgia and the Not Yet Late Queen: Refusing Female Rule in *Henry V*." *ELH* 61 (1994), 523–50.

Ellis, Steven G. *Tudor Frontiers and Noble Power: The Making of the British State*. Oxford: Clarendon Press, 1995.

Enright, Michael J. "King James and His Island: An Archaic Kingship Belief?" *Scottish Historical Review* 55 (1976), 29–40.

Evans, H. T. *Wales and the Wars of the Roses*. Stroud: Alan Sutton, 1995.

Evans, R. Wallis. "Prophetic Poetry." In *A Guide to Welsh Literature, II: 1282–c.1550*. Ed. A. O. H. Jarman and Gwilym Rees Hughes. Revised Dafydd Johnston, 256–74. Cardiff: University of Wales Press, 1997.

Fairfield, Leslie P. *John Bale: Mythmaker for the English Reformation*. West Lafayette: Purdue University Press, 1976.

Ferguson, Margaret W. "'The Afflatus of Ruin': Meditations on Rome by Du Bellay, Spenser and Stevens." In *Roman Images: Selected Papers from the English Institute, 1982*. Ed. Annabel Patterson, 23–50. Baltimore: Johns Hopkins University Press, 1984.

Fichter, Andrew. *Poets Historical: Dynastic Epic in the Renaissance*. New Haven: Yale University Press, 1982.

Flower, Robin. "Richard Davies, William Cecil, and Giraldus Cambrensis." *National Library of Wales Journal* 3 (1943–44), 11–14.

—. "William Salesbury, Richard Davies, and Archbishop Parker." *National Library of Wales Journal* 2 (1941), 7–14.

Floyd-Wilson, Mary. "Delving to the Root: *Cymbeline*, Scotland, and the English Race." In *British Identities*, ed. Baker and Maley, 101–115.

Galloway, Bruce. *The Union of England and Scotland, 1603–1608*. Edinburgh: J. Donald, 1986.

Garber, Marjorie. *Shakespeare's Ghost Writers: Literature as Uncanny Causality.* New York: Routledge, 1987.

Geller, Sherri. "What History Really Teaches: Historical Pyrrhonism in William Baldwin's *A Mirror for Magistrates.*" In *Opening the Borders: Inclusivity in Early Modern Studies.* Ed. Peter C. Herman, 150–84. Newark: University of Delaware Press, 1999.

Gellner, Ernest. *Nations and Nationalism.* Ithaca: Cornell University Press, 1983.

Goldberg, Jonathan. *James I and the Politics of Literature.* Baltimore: Johns Hopkins University Press, 1983.

Goldman, Michael. *The Energies of Drama.* Princeton: Princeton University Press, 1972.

Gordon, Bruce. "Malevolent Ghosts and Ministering Angels: Apparitions and Pastoral Care in the Swiss Reformation." In *The Place of the Dead: Death and Remembrance in Late Medieval and Early Modern Europe.* Ed. Bruce Gordon and Peter Marshall, 87–109. Cambridge: Cambridge University Press, 2000.

Green, Lawrence D. "Modes of Perception in the *Mirror for Magistrates.*" *Huntington Library Quarterly* 44 (1981), 117–33.

Greenblatt, Stephen. *Hamlet in Purgatory.* Princeton: Princeton University Press, 2001.

—. *Renaissance Self-Fashioning: From More to Shakespeare.* Chicago: University of Chicago Press, 1980.

—. *Shakespearean Negotiations: The Circulation of Social Energy in Renaissance England.* Berkeley: University of California Press, 1988.

Greene, Thomas. *The Light in Troy: Imitation and Discovery in Renaissance Poetry.* New Haven: Yale University Press, 1982.

Greenfeld, Liah. *Nationalism: Five Roads to Modernity.* Cambridge, MA: Harvard University Press, 1992.

Greenlaw, Edwin. *Studies in Spenser's Historical Allegory.* Baltimore: Johns Hopkins University Press, 1932.

Griffiths, Huw. "Translated Geographies: Edmund Spenser's 'The Ruines of Time.'" *Early Modern Literary Studies* 4.2/Special Issue 3 (September 1998) [journal on-line]. Available from http://purl.oclc.org/emls/04-2/griftran.htm. Internet.

Gruffydd, R. G. "The Renaissance and Welsh Literature." In *The Celts and the Renaissance: Tradition and Innovation.* Ed. Glanmor Williams and Robert Owen Jones, 17–39. Cardiff: University of Wales Press, 1990.

Gurr, Andrew. "Headgear as a Paralinguistic Signifier in *King Lear.*" *Shakespeare Survey* 55 (2002), 43–52.

Hadfield, Andrew. "Briton and Scythian: Tudor Representations of Irish Origins." *Irish Historical Studies* 28 (1993), 390–408.

—. *Literature, Politics and National Identity: Reformation to Renaissance.* Cambridge: Cambridge University Press, 1994.

—. *Shakespeare, Spenser, and the Matter of Britain.* Basingstoke: Palgrave, 2003.

Halpern, Richard. "'Pining their Maws': Female Readers and the Erotic Ontology of the Text in Shakespeare's *Venus and Adonis*." In *Venus and Adonis: Critical Essays.* Ed. Philip C. Kolin, 377–88. New York: Garland, 1997.

—. *The Poetics of Primitive Accumulation: English Renaissance Culture and the Genealogy of Capital.* Ithaca: Cornell University Press, 1991.

Hay, Denys. *Polydore Vergil: Renaissance Historian and Man of Letters.* Oxford: Clarendon Press, 1952.

Heal, Felicity, and Clive Holmes. *The Gentry in England and Wales, 1500–1700.* London: Macmillan, 1994.

Healy, Thomas. "Remembering with Advantages: Nation and Ideology in *Henry V*." In *Shakespeare in the New Europe.* Ed. Michael Hattaway, Boika Saklova, and Derek Roper, 174–93. Sheffield: Sheffield Academic Press, 1994.

Helgerson, Richard. *Forms of Nationhood: The Elizabethan Writing of England.* Chicago: University of Chicago Press, 1992.

Henken, Elissa R. *National Redeemer: Owain Glyndwr in Welsh Tradition.* Cardiff: University of Wales Press, 1996.

Henry, Bruce Ward. "John Dee, Humphrey Llwyd, and the Name 'British Empire.'" *Huntington Library Quarterly* 35 (1971–72), 189–90.

Highley, Christopher. *Shakespeare, Spenser, and the Crisis in Ireland.* Cambridge: Cambridge University Press, 1997.

Hill, Christopher. "The Norman Yoke." In *Puritanism and Revolution,* 46–111. London: Secker & Warburg, 1958.

Hillman, Richard. *Intertextuality and Romance in Renaissance Drama: The Staging of Nostalgia.* London: Macmillan, 1992.

Hills, Catherine. *Origins of the English.* London: Duckworth, 2003.

Hobsbawm, Eric. *Nations and Nationalism since 1780: Programme, Myth, Reality.* Second edition. Cambridge: Cambridge University Press, 1992.

Holderness, Graham. *Shakespeare: The Histories.* London: Macmillan, 2000.

Holderness, Graham, Nick Potter, and John Turner. *Shakespeare: The Play of History.* Iowa City: University of Iowa Press, 1987.

Honan, Park. *Shakespeare: A Life.* Oxford: Oxford University Press, 1998.

Howells, Brian E. "The Lower Orders of Society." In *Class, Community and Culture in Tudor Wales.* Ed. J. Gwynfor Jones, 237–59. Cardiff: University of Wales Press, 1989.

Hoyle, R. W. *The Pilgrimage of Grace and the Politics of the 1530s.* Oxford: Oxford University Press, 2001.

Hudson, Anne. "*Visio Baleii*: An Early Literary Historian." In *The Long Fifteenth Century.* Ed. Helen Cooper and Sally Mapstone, 313–29. Oxford: Clarendon Press, 1997.

Hulse, Clark. *The Rule of Art: Literature and Painting in the Renaissance.* Chicago: University of Chicago Press, 1990.

Hutton, Patrick H. *History as an Art of Memory.* Hanover, NH: University Press of New England, 1993.

Ivic, Christopher. "Spenser and the Bounds of Race." *Genre* 32 (1999), 141–73.

Janowitz, Anne. *England's Ruins: Poetic Purpose and the National Landscape.* Oxford: Basil Blackwell, 1990.

Jarman, A. O. H. "Cerdd Ysgolan." *Ysgrifau Beirniadol* 10 (1977), 51–78.

——. "The Later Cynfeirdd." In *A Guide to Welsh Literature, Vol. 1.* Ed. A. O. H. Jarman and Gwilym Rees Hughes, 90–122. Revised edition. Cardiff: University of Wales Press, 1992.

Jones, Edwin. *The English Nation: The Great Myth.* Stroud: Sutton, 1998.

Jones, J. Gwynfor. *Concepts of Order and Gentility in Wales, 1540–1640.* Llandysul: Gomer, 1992.

Jones, W. Garmon. "Welsh Nationalism and Henry Tudor." *THSC* (1917–18), 1–59.

Joughin, John J. "Lear's Afterlife." *Shakespeare Survey* 55 (2002), 67–81.

Kemper, Steven. *The Presence of the Past: Chronicles, Politics and Culture in Sinhala Life.* Ithaca: Cornell University Press, 1991.

Kendrick, T. D. *British Antiquity.* London: Methuen, 1950.

Ker, N. R. "Sir John Prise." *The Library,* 5th series, 10 (1955), 1–21.

Kerrigan, John. "Revision, Adaptation, and the Fool in *King Lear.*" In *The Division of the Kingdoms: Shakespeare's Two Versions of King Lear.* Ed. Gary Taylor and Michael Warren, 221–27. Oxford: Oxford University Press, 1983.

Kidd, Colin. *British Identities Before Nationalism: Ethnicity and Nationhood in the Atlantic World, 1600–1800.* Cambridge: Cambridge University Press, 1999.

King, John N. *English Reformation Literature: The Tudor Origins of the Protestant Tradition.* Princeton: Princeton University Press, 1982.

Knapp, Jeffrey. *An Empire Nowhere: England, America, and Literature from Utopia to The Tempest.* Berkeley: University of California Press, 1992.

——. *Shakespeare's Tribe: Church, Nation, and Theater in Renaissance England.* Chicago: University of Chicago Press, 2002.

Knowles, Dom David. *The Religious Orders in England, volume 3: The Tudor Age.* Cambridge: Cambridge University Press, 1959.

Koebner, Richard. "'The Imperial Crown of this Realm': Henry VIII, Constantine the Great, and Polydore Vergil." *BIHR* 26 (1953), 29–52.

Kreider, Alan. *English Chantries: The Road to Dissolution.* Cambridge, MA: Harvard University Press, 1979.

Lapsley, Gaillard Thomas. *The County Palatine of Durham: A Study in Constitutional History.* New York: Longmans, 1900.

Le Goff, Jacques. *The Birth of Purgatory.* Trans. Arthur Goldhammer. London: Scolar Press, 1984.

Levack, Brian P. *The Formation of the British State: England, Scotland, and the Union, 1603–1707.* Oxford: Clarendon Press, 1987.

Levy, F. J. *Tudor Historical Thought.* San Marino: Huntington Library, 1967.

Lloyd-Morgan, Ceridwen. "The Celtic Tradition." In *The Arthur of the English: The Arthurian Legend in Medieval English Life and Literature.* Ed. W. R. J. Barron, 1–9. Cardiff: University of Wales Press, 1999.

—. "Prophecy and Welsh Nationhood in the Fifteenth Century." *THSC* (1985), 9–26.

Low, Anthony. "*Hamlet* and the Ghost of Purgatory: Intimations of Killing the Father." *English Literary Renaissance* 29 (1999), 443–467.

Lowenthal, David. "Nostalgia Tells It Like It Wasn't." In *The Imagined Past: History and Nostalgia*. Ed. Christopher Shaw and Malcolm Chase, 18–32. Manchester: Manchester University Press, 1989.

Macaulay, Rose. *The Pleasure of Ruins*. London: Weidenfeld and Nicolson, 1953.

MacCabe, Colin. "The Voice of Esau: Stephen in the Library." In *James Joyce: New Perspectives*. Ed. Colin MacCabe, 111–129. Brighton: Harvester, 1982.

McCoy, Richard C. "'Look upon me, Sir': Relationships in *King Lear*." *Representations* 81 (2003), 46–60.

McEachern, Claire. *The Poetics of English Nationhood*. Cambridge: Cambridge University Press, 1996.

McKisack, May. *Medieval History in the Tudor Age*. Oxford: Clarendon Press, 1971.

McRae, Andrew. *God Speed the Plough: The Representation of Agrarian England, 1500–1660*. Cambridge: Cambridge University Press, 1996.

—. "Husbandry Manuals and the Language of Agrarian Improvement." In *Culture and Cultivation in Early Modern England: Writing and the Land*. Ed. Michael Leslie and Timothy Raylor, 35–62. Leicester: Leicester University Press, 1992.

Maley, Willy. *Nation, State and Empire in English Renaissance Literature: Shakespeare to Milton*. Basingstoke: Palgrave Macmillan, 2003.

Marcus, Leah. *Puzzling Shakespeare: Local Reading and Its Discontents*. Berkeley: University of California Press, 1988.

Marshall, Peter. "'The Map of God's Word': Geographies of the Afterlife in Tudor and Early Stuart England." In *The Place of the Dead: Death and Remembrance in Late Medieval and Early Modern Europe*. Ed. Bruce Gordon and Peter Marshall, 110–130. Cambridge: Cambridge University Press, 2000.

Marx, Karl. *The Eighteenth Brumaire of Louis Bonaparte*. In *Surveys From Exile: Political Writings, Volume 2*. Ed. David Fernbach. Trans. Ben Fowkes, 143–249. London: Penguin, 1992.

Mason, Roger A. "The Scottish Reformation and the Origins of Anglo-British Imperialism." In *Scots and Britons: Scottish Political Thought and the Union of 1603*. Ed. Roger A. Mason, 161–86. Cambridge: Cambridge University Press, 1994.

Mazzotta, Giuseppe. "Antiquity and the New Arts in Petrarch." In *The New Medievalism*. Ed. Marina S. Brownlee, Kevin Brownlee, and Stephen G. Nicholls, 46–69. Baltimore: Johns Hopkins University Press, 1991.

Meagher, John C. "The First Progress of Henry VII." *Renaissance Drama*, n.s. 1 (1968), 45–73.

Michaels, Walter Benn. "'You who never was there': Slavery and the New Historicism, Deconstruction and the Holocaust," *Narrative* 4 (1996), 1–16.

Mikalachki, Jodi. *The Legacy of Boadicea: Gender and Nation in Early Modern England*. London: Routledge, 1998.

Millican, Charles Bowie. *Spenser and the Table Round*. London: Frank Cass and Co., 1967.

Morgan, Hiram. "British Policies Before the British State." In *The British Problem, c. 1534–1707: State Formation in the Atlantic Archipelago*. Ed. Brendan Bradshaw and John Morrill, 66–88. London: Macmillan, 1996.

Muir, Kenneth. *Life and Letters of Sir Thomas Wyatt*. Liverpool: Liverpool University Press, 1963.

O'Brien, Conor Cruise. *Ancestral Voices: Religion and Nationalism in Ireland*. Chicago: University of Chicago Press, 1995.

Osborn, James M. *Young Philip Sidney*. New Haven: Yale University Press, 1972.

Otter, Monika. "'New Werke': *St. Erkenwald*, St. Albans, and the Medieval Sense of the Past." *Journal of Medieval and Renaissance Studies* 24 (1994), 387–414.

Padel, O. J. "Some South-Western Sites with Arthurian Associations." In *The Arthur of the Welsh: The Arthurian Legend in Medieval Welsh Literature*. Ed. Rachel Bromwich, A. O. H. Jarman, and Brynley F. Roberts, 229–48. Cardiff: University of Wales Press, 1991.

Panofsky, Erwin. *Renaissance and Renascences in Western Art*. New York: Harper & Row, 1972.

Phillips, John. *The Reformation of Images: Destruction of Art in England, 1535–1660*. Berkeley: University of California Press, 1973.

Pye, Christopher. *The Regal Phantasm: Shakespeare and the Politics of Spectacle*. London: Routledge, 1990.

Quint, David. "'Alexander the Pig': Shakespeare on History and Poetry." *Boundary* 2 10 (1982), 49–68.

Rackin, Phyllis. *Stages of Histoy: Shakespeare's English Chronicles*. Ithaca: Cornell University Press, 1990.

Rees, David. *The Son of Prophecy: Henry Tudor's Road to Bosworth*. Ruthin: John Jones, 1997.

Reynolds, Susan. "What Do We Mean by 'Anglo-Saxon' and 'Anglo-Saxons'?" *Journal of British Studies* 24 (1985), 395–414.

Roberts, Peter. "Tudor Wales, National Identity and the British Inheritance." In *British Consciousness and Identity: the Making of Britain, 1533–1707*. Ed. Brendon Bradshaw and Peter Roberts, 8–42. Cambridge: Cambridge University Press, 1998.

Ross, Trevor. "Dissolution and the Making of the English Literary Canon: The Catalogues of Leland and Bale." *Renaissance and Reformation* 15 (1991), 57–80.

Scarisbrick, J. J. *The Reformation and the English People*. Oxford: Basil Blackwell, 1984.

Scarry, Elaine. *On Beauty and Being Just*. Princeton: Princeton University Press, 1999.

Schmitt, Jean-Claude. *Ghosts in the Middle Ages: The Living and the Dead in Medieval Society.* Trans. Teresa Lavender Fagan. Chicago: University of Chicago Press, 1998.

Schwyzer, Philip. "British History and 'The British History': The Same Old Story?" In *British Identities and English Renaissance Literature.* Ed. David Baker and Willy Maley, 11–23. Cambridge: Cambridge University Press, 2002.

—. "A Map of Greater Cambria" in *Literature, Mapping, and the Politics of Space in Early Modern Britain.* Ed. Andrew Gordon and Bernhard Klein. Cambridge: Cambridge University Press, 2001.

—. "Purity and Danger of the West Bank of the Severn: The Cultural Geography of *A Masque Presented at Ludlow Castle, 1634.*" Representations 60 (1997), 22–48.

Shagan, Ethan H. *Popular Politics and the English Reformation.* Cambridge: Cambridge University Press, 2003.

Sherman, William. *John Dee: The Politics of Reading and Writing in the English Renaissance.* Amherst: University of Massachusetts, 1995.

Shuger, Debora Kuller. *The Renaissance Bible: Scholarship, Sacrifice, and Subjectivity.* Berkeley: University of California Press, 1994.

Simpson, James. "Ageism: Leland, Bale, and the Laborious Start of English Literary History." In *New Medieval Literatures, Volume 1.* Ed. Wendy Scase, Rita Copeland, and David Lawton, 213–36. Oxford: Clarendon Press, 1997.

Smith, Anthony D. *Myths and Memories of the Nation.* Oxford: Oxford University Press, 1999.

—. *National Identity.* London: Penguin, 1991.

Smith, David L. *A History of the Modern British Isles, 1603–1707: The Double Crown.* Oxford: Blackwell, 1998.

Smith, Emma. *King Henry V.* Shakespeare in Production. Cambridge: Cambridge University Press, 2002.

Smith, R. B. *Land and Politics in the England of Henry VIII: The West Riding of Yorkshire, 1530–46.* Oxford: Oxford University Press, 1970.

Sorensen, Janet. "Writing Historically, Speaking Nostalgically: The Competing Languages of Nation in Scott's *The Bride of Lammermoor.*" In *Narratives of Nostalgia, Gender and Nationalism.* Ed. Jean Pickering and Suzanne Kehde, 30–51. New York: New York University Press, 1997.

Starobinski, Jean. "The Idea of Nostalgia." *Diogenes* 54 (1966), 84–103.

Stewart, Susan. *On Longing: Narratives of the Miniature, the Gigantic, the Souvenir, the Collection.* Durham, NC: Duke University Press, 1996.

Sullivan, Garrett A., Jr. *The Drama of Landscape: Land, Property, and Social Relations on the Early Modern Stage.* Stanford: Stanford University Press, 1998.

Summit, Jennifer. "Monuments and Ruins: Spenser and the Problem of the English Library," *ELH* 70 (2003), 1–34.

Taussig, Michael. *The Magic of the State.* New York: Routledge, 1997.

Taylor, Gary. "*King Lear:* The Date and Authorship of the Folio Version." In *The Division of the Kingdoms: Shakespeare's Two Versions of King Lear.* Ed. Gary Taylor and Michael Warren, 382–85. Oxford: Oxford University Press, 1983.

Thirsk, Joan. "Making a Fresh Start: Sixteenth-Century Agriculture and the Classical Inspiration." In *Culture and Cultivation in Early Modern England: Writing and the Land.* Ed. Michael Leslie and Timothy Raylor, 15–34. Leicester: Leicester University Press, 1992.

Thomas, Hugh, ed. *Cyfnod y Tuduriaid.* Cardiff: University of Wales Press, 1973.

Thorpe, Nick. "Romanians Gamble with their Future." BBC News: From Our Own Correspondent, Sunday 3 December, 2000 [on-line]. Available from http://news.bbc.co.uk/hi/english/world/from_our_own_correspondent/newsid_1052000/1052551.stm. Internet.

Tromly, Frederic B. "'Accordinge to Sounde Religion': the Elizabethan Controversy over the Funeral Sermon." *Journal of Medieval and Renaissance Studies* 13 (1983), 293–312.

Turville-Petre, Thorlac. *England the Nation: Language, Literature, and National Identity, 1290–1340.* Oxford: Clarendon Press, 1996.

Van Dorsten, J. A. *Poets, Patrons and Professors : Sir Philip Sidney, Daniel Rogers and the Leiden Humanists.* Leiden: Leiden University Press, 1962.

van Es, Bart. *Spenser's Forms of History.* Oxford: Oxford University Press, 2002.

Voekel, Swen. "'Upon the Suddaine View': State, Civil Society and Surveillance in Early Modern England." *Early Modern Literary Studies* 4.2/Special Issue 3 (September 1998) [journal online]. Available from http://purl.oclc.org/emls/04-2/voekupon.htm. Internet.

Williams, Glanmor. "Prophecy, Poetry and Politics in Medieval Wales." In *British Government and Administration.* Ed. H. Hearder and H. R. Loyn, 104–16. Cardiff: University of Wales Press, 1974.

—. *Renewal and Reformation: Wales, c. 1415–1642.* Oxford: Oxford University Press, 1993.

—. "Some Protestant Views of Early Church History." In *Welsh Reformation Essays,* 207–219. Cardiff: University of Wales Press, 1967.

—. *Wales and the Reformation.* Cardiff: University of Wales Press, 1997.

Williams, Gruffydd Aled. "The Bardic Road to Bosworth: A Welsh View of Henry Tudor." *THSC* (1985), 7–31.

Williams, Gwyn A. *Madoc: The Making of a Myth.* Oxford: Oxford University Press, 1987.

Wilson, John Dover. "Introduction." In *King Henry V.* Cambridge: Cambridge University Press, 1947.

Woolf, D. R. *The Idea of History in Early Stuart England.* Toronto: University of Toronto Press, 1990.

—. *The Social Circulation of the Past: English Historical Culture, 1500–1730.* Oxford: Oxford University Press, 2003.

Wortham, Christopher. "Shakespeare, James I and the Matter of Britain." *English: The Journal of the English Association* 45 (1996), 97–122.

Wright, C. E. "The Dispersal of the Libraries in the Sixteenth Century." In *The English Library Before 1700*. Ed. Francis Wormald and C. E. Wright, 148–75. London: Athlone Press, 1958.

Yates, Frances. *The Art of Memory*. Chicago: University of Chicago Press, 1966.

Youings, Joyce. *The Dissolution of the Monasteries*. London: George Allen and Unwin, Ltd., 1971.

Index